The European Community

ECONOMICS TODAY
Edited by Andrew Leake

The *Economics Today* series surveys contemporary headline topics in applied economics. Each book in the series is written by an expert in the field in a style that is fluently readable. It serves the student of introductory economic principles while also making the subject accessible to a more general reader. The series embraces the problem-solving skills of the new generation of students and stresses the importance of real-world issues and the significance of economic ideas.

Published

Andrew Leake: **The Economic Question**
Jean-Louis Barsoux and Peter Lawrence: **The Challenge of British Management**
Andy Beharrell: **Unemployment and Job Creation**
Frank Burchill: **Labour Relations**
Kenneth Durham: **The New City**
S. F. Goodman: **The European Community**
Jenny Wales: **Investigating Social Issues**
John Wigley and Carol Lipman: **The Enterprise Economy**
Margaret Wilkinson: **Taxation**

Series Standing Order

If you would like to receive future titles in this series as they are published, you can make use of our standing order facility. To place a standing order please contact your bookseller or, in case of difficulty, write to us at the address below with your name and address and the name of the series. Please state with which title you wish to begin your standing order. (If you live outside the UK we may not have the rights for your area, in which case we will forward your order to the publisher concerned.)

Standing Order Service, Macmillan Distribution Ltd, Houndmills, Basingstoke, Hampshire, RG21 2XS, England.

THE EUROPEAN COMMUNITY

Second Edition

S. F. Goodman

MACMILLAN

First published 1990 by
THE MACMILLAN PRESS LTD
Houndmills, Basingstoke, Hampshire RG21 2XS
and London
Companies and representatives
throughout the world

ISBN 0–333–58356–6 (hardcover)
ISBN 0–333–58357–4 (paperback)

A catalogue record for this book is available
from the British Library.

Printed in Hong Kong

Reprinted 1991, 1992
Second edition 1993
Reprinted 1993

For Helen

Contents

List of Tables and Figures

Tables

Preface

The European Community has an exceptionally good statistical office (Eurostat). Its publications are available in all good reference libraries. Eurostat has recently broken new ground with an excellent sixty-page illustrated booklet called '*Europe in Figures*', first published in 1988 and revised every two years. This is an ideal publication for the general reader who wants an easily assimilated and comprehensive coverage of the Community in statistical terms. It is superbly presented and is something that the United Kingdom Statistical Office could profitably emulate.

The Community also has a first-class information service. The Information Office of the Commission of the European Communities at 8 Storey's Gate, London SW1P 3AT, provides a wide range of free material as well as subscription matter. Some is in the form of Background Reports and some are periodicals in the *European Documentation* series. These periodicals, of which there are a large number, cover specific topics in great detail. They are an excellent starting point from which to begin the study of a given subject. The European Parliament has its own information service at 2 Queen Anne's Gate, London SW1H 9AA. Their material too is up to date and well-presented. Its monthly newspaper *European Parliament News* is rather an odd mixture of news and opinion but is worth reading for the breadth, if not the depth, of its coverage. Its coverage has improved over the last year but it is a pity that it cannot be doubled in size.

Since these largely free sources of up-to-date information about the Community are readily available, I have tried in this book to concentrate on ideas, trends and developments rather than upon creating a factual reference book. By far the best single-volume reference book about the European Communities is the annually revised *The European Community: A Practical Guide for Business, Media and Government* by Morris, Boehm and Geller (Macmillan). It contains excellent flow charts of all the main institutions and policies and an explanatory dictionary of all the main terms and bodies connected with the Community. It also lists all the legislation applicable to different areas of Community activity. The reader who wants a much more detailed analysis of the economic theory underlying the Community should read Edward Nevin's *The Economics of Europe* (Macmillan 1990). You will also find there a detailed explanation of the Common Fisheries Policy, an area of great importance but of immense complexity and one which is, I regret, barely touched on in this work. The other area only lightly touched on here is the science and research field. Again the detail is extremely complex and constantly changing and reveals the Community at its best, or worst, in creating acronyms. The reader who wants to know more about 'Sprint', 'Esprit 2', 'Ted', 'Diane', 'Delta', 'Drive', 'Aim', 'Impact', 'Race', all of which have an impact on our lives, should read the *European Documentation Periodical* 2/1988 on *Research and Technological Development*, and Morris, Boehm and Geller.

I have tried to stimulate deeper thought about the Community and the ordinary citizen's place within it. This edition, although using many United Kingdom examples, is aimed at a broader European perspective and assumes that some of the conflicts of the past have been superseded by new issues. This is not, as will be apparent to the reader, a neutral book. It is written from the viewpoint that, although it has its faults, the Community has major achievements to its credit and that the United Kingdom would benefit from a more wholehearted commitment to it. The Community would be better for such a commitment. Although some people would interpret the recent events in Central and Eastern Europe differently I would argue that the age of the nation state is on the wane; the future lies in cooperation and pooled sovereignty.

This edition includes discussions of the Treaty of Union agreed at Maastricht in December 1991 and signed in February 1992 and the creation of the European Economic Area from 1993. The process of ratification required referendums in Ireland and Denmark and made one a possible option in France. The whole future of the treaty was placed in doubt by the Danish referendum in early June 1992 when a small majority rejected the proposed changes. The rejection was due to the disappointment of left-wing parties with the democratic and social provisions of the Treaty and to the right-wing parties' concern over the issues of sovereignty and centralisation of power in the Community. The other eleven members stated their intention of refusing to renegotiate the Treaty and of continuing with their own ratification procedures. In the immediate aftermath of the shock of the rejection President Mitterrand announced that France would, after all, hold its own referendum on the Treaty in September (51 per cent voted 'yes'). In the United Kingdom the committee stage of the Bill to implement the Maastricht agreement was suspended. The Irish referendum on 18 June assumed a greater significance in the light of the these events and was itself influenced by the internal row on the right of Irish women to travel freely to other countries to have abortions. It produced a 69% 'Yes' vote. The Danish 'No' vote also encouraged the growing opposition to the Treaty in Germany and revived the despondent 'Eurosceptics' in the United Kingdom. The sections in this edition on the Treaty on Union need to be read in the light of this uncertainty.

This edition also considers the creation of the European Economic Area from 1 January 1993 from the two groupings of the Twelve in the European Community and the Seven in the European Free Trade Association. The Community is embarking on a period of unprecedented change, with the single market beginning in January 1993, and the process of economic and monetary union evolving into a single currency and greater economic cohesion by the year 2000. Developments in these areas, and in social policy, together with the enlargement of the Community will make the Europe of the twenty first century very different from that of the late 1950s when the European Economic Community was conceived

Jean Monnet, the 'father of the Community' said 'we are not forming coalitions between states, but union among people'. In other words, European integration is aimed at the hearts and minds of ordinary people. He concluded his memoirs by saying 'and the Community itself is only a stage on the way to the organised world of tomorrow'.

This great vision of Monnet, who was an extremely practical man, can only be fully appreciated against a historical background. This is why this book has a section evaluating the historical context of the progress of the Community. The Anglo-Saxon experience of modern history has been markedly different from that of the continental European. In this difference lies the explanation of our alternative views of the Community, its institutions and its future.

S. F. GOODMAN

Contemporary Issues 1

The European Community has been at a major crossroads in its development in the late 1980s but recent decisions, culminating in those made at the Maastricht Council of Europe in December 1991 and the Union Treaty to be ratified in 1992, will dictate what sort of institution will evolve in the next decade. The way ahead is obscured by the 'No' vote in the Danish referendum to ratify the Treaty and by the confusion of events in Central and Eastern Europe, but there is a definite movement towards greater and deeper integration of the existing twelve members, together with certain expansion through the admission of new members, and a widening to include the European Free Trade Association (EFTA) countries. We shall have to adjust to talking about the 'European Economic Area' (EEA) when referring to the nineteen nations of the Community and EFTA, and to the European Community as the 'Union' or 'Economic Union'.

Some still fear that a 'fortress Europe' will emerge, devoted to economic and political self-interest and impervious to the needs of the rest of the world. Others, mainly European socialists or social democrats, fear that a Europe fit only for capitalists will emerge, although the Social Chapter protocol of the Union Treaty makes this very unlikely. Some others are frightened of the prospect of the development of an interventionist bureaucracy trying to foist its ideas of a social market on to unwilling victims. There is an anxiety about loss of national sovereignty in key areas of decision-making. In contrast, others extol the virtues of the pooling of sovereignty. The few visionaries who, in the 1980s, foresaw the creation of a federal state of Europe with federal institutions such as a single

1

currency, a central bank, a European police force and eventually a European defence and foreign policy are being joined by many others who have accepted the inexorable logic of the creation of a single market. They argue that a genuine, unified market, creates an imperative for a more coordinated and centralised system of decision-making and that this is best achieved by an approach from first principles. Some see themselves in the same position as the fathers of the constitution of the United States, in a place of destiny shaping the world of the future. Others, perhaps more practically, see a slow but inexorable pressure building up towards the establishment of more institutions in common. They expect to see greater uniformity of policies and the setting up of joint facilities and cooperation procedures, such as common defence and foreign policies, alongside, but not initially completely replacing, existing national policies. They are willing to wait to allow the economic and political pressures involved in the realisation of a single European market to show the logical inevitability of their ideas.

Not all European political parties or governments are entirely happy about the deepening of the Community, especially into defence, foreign affairs and social policy, although some governments are very keen on such trends. Enthusiasm tends to vary in inverse proportion to the perceived adverse effects. Germany's government, for example, has been in the forefront of the moves to a single European currency, but the closer it gets to realisation, the greater the opposition of the German public. Within the United Kingdom, the government under Mrs Thatcher's personal direction began a policy that contributed to her downfall in 1990, of waging an active campaign against any extension of Community powers into the social, political and economic spheres beyond those strictly necessary to implement the achievement of the single internal market. The same basic policy has been pursued by the government formed under Mr Major and resulted in a special opt-out protocol on monetary union's third stage for the United Kingdom in the Union Treaty and on the extraordinary device of the other eleven members opting out with their own protocol on the Social Chapter. In contrast, the Labour Party in the United Kingdom has begun to reverse its traditional antagonism to the Community and has discovered new delights in the European proposals for a social market. They hope to derive all sorts of benefits from Europe that they have failed to obtain within the United Kingdom.

To some extent the success of deepening will depend on the outcome of the efforts to create 'cohesion' within the Community, that is, greater uniformity of prosperity throughout the membership and the reduction of regional disparities in the quality of life. Some members have only supported some of the changes in the Union Treaty in return for greater financial assistance and the creation of a 'Cohesion Fund'. Regional policies will assume much greater importance over the next twenty years, especially if the Community's membership is broadened. It is, in any case, essential to achieve greater cohesion if the introduction of a single currency is not to create economic chaos.

The Single European Act

The catalyst for change has been the Single European Act. This is referred to throughout this book and its likely effects on the Community are discussed fully in Chapter 10. In brief, the Act is an attempt to realise the original objective of the creation of the European Economic Community under the Treaty of Rome in 1957. The intention then was to have a single market without barriers of any kind between the six countries that made up the original Community. As the Community enlarged to twelve members it became increasingly clear that many physical and technical barriers remained to prevent the free movement of goods, services and people. Internal customs barriers had gone but Europe was not a single market. As a result, in 1985, the heads of government of the Twelve agreed to complete the single internal market progressively by 31 December 1992. The Single European Act which implemented their agreement was signed in February 1986 and came into force on 1 July 1987. The establishment of the truly frontierless single market has involved the passing of 282 measures. By early 1992 about 80 per cent of them had already been approved. The remainder were mainly on schedule although areas of dispute remained and there were great differences in the rate at which the members had transposed the Community legislation into their national laws. The last areas under discussion were direct taxation, financial services, transport and company law and the detail of some schemes such as the systems of collecting VAT which remained to be settled in the future. Social measures were a source of dispute, although strictly speaking they are not a direct part of the single market programme, but the Commission of the Community is keen to press ahead and cater for what they call the 'social dimension' of the single market. As President Mitterrand of France has said, 'Europe will be for workers as well as for bankers.'

Decision-Making in the Community

Before discussing these areas of controversy, it will help if an outline is drawn of the Community's institutions and the process of decision-making. Details of these are discussed in subsequent chapters, especially in Chapters 4 and 9.

The Community has four main institutions: the Commission, the Council, the European Parliament, and the European Court of Justice.

The Commission

This consists of seventeen members who are appointed for four years. It proposes policy and legislation. The Council discusses the proposals and the Commission will then amend or adopt them. The Commission also executes the Council's decisions and supervises the daily running of the Community. Finally the Commission acts as the guardian of the treaties and can take legal action against members who do not comply with Community rules. After 1995 the term of office will be five years and the number of Commissioners may be reduced to twelve as a result of discussion arising from the Union Treaty.

The Council

This body makes the decisions for the Community. The Council sometimes comprises meetings of ministers for a subject (Council of Ministers) or Council Working Groups who are officials from member states. The term Council also includes the Committee of Permanent Representatives of the members (COREPER). The meetings of ministers are held each April, June and October with extra meetings as required. At least twice a year the heads of government meet in what is called the European Council. Some decisions can be made under a qualified majority vote (QMV) of the Council but many still have to be unanimous (see Chapters 4 and 9).

The European Parliament

It consists of 518 members directly elected for five years. There were elections in June 1989 so the next are due in 1994. Under the 'cooperation procedures' adopted by the Single European Act its opinion is required on many of the Commission's proposals before the Council can adopt them. It is not a legislative body in the usual sense of the word in that it does not directly initiate legislation. The Parliament's activities are based in three locations. It meets in Strasbourg, but its committee meetings are in Brussels and its secretariat operates in Luxembourg. It is making a brave, and so far fruitless, attempt to locate all its activities in Brussels. The Maastricht agreement and the Union Treaty contain several changes in the role and powers of the European Parliament, particularly a 'negative assent' procedure. Its power over the budget remains that of advice, attempts at amendment with Council and Commission approval, and rejection. The changes arising from the new treaty will probably increase its importance and effectiveness. They are discussed in detail in Chapter 9.

The Court of Justice

This court has thirteen judges and six advocates-general. It includes, since 1988, a Court of First Instance. It rules on the interpretation and application of Community law and its judgments are binding in member states (see Chapter 9).

There are in addition to these four institutions, a Court of Auditors to audit the revenue and expenditure of the Community, an Economic and Social Committee with 189 members to advise on proposals relating to economic and social matters, and a European Investment Bank. The Economic and Social Committee has a membership of representatives of employers, trade unions and consumers. The Union Treaty will establish another large advisory committee of 189 members for European Regions. The treaty will also eventually produce a European Monetary Institute (EMI), a European System of Central Banks (ESCB) and a European Central

Bank (ECB). Fortunately, if all goes as planned, one set of the initials that plague the student of the Community will disappear when the EMI is superseded by the ECB in the late 1990s (see Chapter 7).

Community Legislation

It will also be helpful to see in what forms the Community achieves its will. The Council and Commission may make regulations, issue directives, take decisions, make recommendations or deliver opinions.

Regulations

These are applicable to all member states and do not need to be approved by national parliaments. The regulation takes legal precedence if there is any conflict with national law (see Chapter 9).

Directives

These state the result that must be achieved within a stated period and it is up to each member to introduce or amend laws to bring about the desired effect. If the member fails to implement the directive the Commission may refer the matter to the Court of Justice if other approaches fail. Some parts of the directive may come into direct effect even if the member has not embodied the required changes into its national law.

Decisions

These are addressed to member states, companies or individuals and are completely binding on them. If they impose financial obligations they are enforceable in the member's courts.

Recommendations and opinions

These simply state the views of the institution that issues them and are not binding.

Although the legislative power of the Community lies in the Council it delegates some of its power to the Commission. This delegation is usually of routine and technical matters and is subject to the advice and assistance of committees composed of people from each member state.

Until the Single European Act decisions of the Council had to be unanimous. As a result the Community began to suffer from what was called 'Eurosclerosis', that is, it crawled along at the pace of the most reluctant or intransigent. Since its passage decisions in some areas of policy still have to be unanimous. But one of the most significant changes to the principles of the Community has been to end an individual country's power of veto in areas where the qualified majority vote (QMV) applies. Thus in areas directly associated with the creation of the single market it is possible to proceed with a qualified majority of 54 votes out of a total of 76. The United Kingdom, France, Germany and Italy have 10 votes each; Spain has 8; Belgium, Greece, the Netherlands and Portugal 5 each; Denmark and Ireland 3 each and Luxembourg 2. For qualified majority decisions that do not require a Commission proposal the 54 votes needed must be cast by at least eight of the members.

The process of decision-making under the cooperation procedure adopted in the Single European Act is very complex and creates a great range of opportunities for pressure groups and lobbyists. Figure 1.1 is a summary of that legislative process. The bottom right-hand section shows the additions made by the SEA. A more complex version will need to be drawn up when the Union Treaty proposals for 'negative assent' on some areas of legislation come into effect in 1993.

There is another simplified version of this flow chart in Chapter 4 where unanimity and national sovereignty are discussed. Suffice it to say, however, that such flow charts do not reveal where the power of decision actually lies. In the Community the location of final decision-making may be the Council but those decisions are based upon a long series of discussions, meetings and lobbying in Brussels and Strasbourg and in members' own corridors of power. Some commentators attribute most power to the permanent officials of the Commission, to COREPER and to those Commissioners who are active and well-versed in Community power-broking. In the background there is always a tension between the national representatives working in Europe who tend to develop a wider European vision, and their departments back home who tend to have a more constricted view. The truth is that the power of decision-making is shared and

FIGURE 1.1
Community Legislative Process – New Cooperation Procedure (After Single European Act until 1993 when the Union Treaty comes into force)

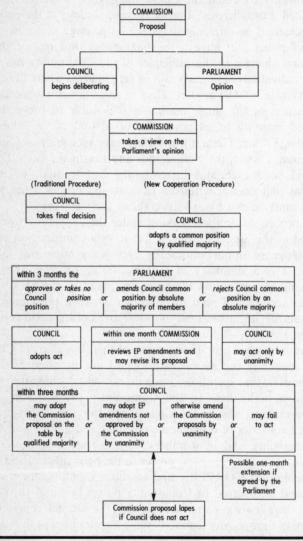

SOURCE   *The Single Market – the Facts* (London: DTI, COI).

also shifts between and within groups according to personalities, subject matter and national perceptions of their self-interest. There is not yet the same degree of interest shown by political scientists writing in English in the Community's power structures as there has been in national structures such as those of the United States or Britain. It is worth bearing in mind, however, the question of the process of decision-making when we return to considering the issues currently arising in the Community.

What Sort of Community is Emerging?

A 'fortress Europe'

This may evolve as a result of the changes in progress for establishing the single internal market although this is definitely not the stated intention of the heads of government or Community officials. The phrase 'fortress Europe' has several interpretations and it is used, essentially, as a term of abuse. It means, in principle, that the Community will be setting up a unified market of 345 million relatively affluent people which will be able to fix an external tariff barrier to protect itself against competition from Japan, the Far East and the United States. The establishment of the EEA in January 1993 when the Community and EFTA combine will expand the population to 380 million, and will bolster the economic bargaining strength of Western Europe against the individual nations of the world to obtain raw materials, primary products and energy at low cost. It will be able to use its establishment, or harmonisation, of standards to place external suppliers at a disadvantage (see the sections on trade theory in Chapter 3). In negotiations under the General Agreement on Tariffs and Trade (GATT) it could, if it chose, act in a selfish and self-centred manner. Some observers argue that it has been acting like this in the Uruguay round of GATT talks that broke down in December 1990, staggered into life through 1991, and resumed in 1992. It already speaks with a unified voice at GATT talks but there are still some national divisions of interest and emphasis in the discussions that establish a common bargaining position. Divisions are particularly obvious on agricultural policy.

It is also possible, if the 'fortress Europe' approach came to be adopted, that the banking, monetary and financial systems might be used to discriminate against non-members. This will, of course, be easier when the Community adopts a single currency and forms a European central bank, either after 1996, or certainly after 1999. Such discrimination would presumably not find favour with all members, especially those most heavily dependent on foreign trade. When the European Community does establish a single currency, especially if it includes sterling, it would be the most important financial unit in world markets. (See Chapter 7 for an elaboration of this discussion.)

Another aspect of the potential 'fortress Europe' which worries some observers is that the Community might become less accessible or even inaccessible to some groups of outsiders. Within the members' boundaries there should emerge, by 1993, complete freedom of movement of citizens to work, live and set up enterprises. One of the debates at the Maastricht summit concerned immigration and the fear that the rules and regulations used to establish the mobility of Community citizens will be constructed in such a way as to exclude non-Community nationals. There is no doubt, on the one hand, that entry for tourism by non-Community nationals will be easier with only a single visa required for travel in all twelve states. On the other hand, however, there is great concern about the fate of those seeking asylum. The twelve ministers responsible for immigration agreed, in 1989, to the principle that a refugee will be able to apply once to enter the Community. If one country rejects him they all will. Once accepted by one country he will be accepted by all. They will also work out harmonisation procedures to deal with those seeking asylum. The ministers reaffirmed their support for the United Nations Convention on Refugees. This means that they will not return refugees to a country in which they have a well-founded expectation of persecution. The Community will, therefore, become a single entity for the purpose of seeking asylum. This, in itself, may not be cause for too much concern though a great deal depends on the detail of the harmonisation regulations. It also necessitates intergovernmental agreements on policing of the system.

The Maastricht agreement provides for unanimous agreement until 1996 on a list of nations whose citizens will require a visa to enter the Community. After 1 January 1996 the list can be agreed by qualified majority. There is also a provision to deal with unforeseen emergencies such as a sudden potential inflow of refugees. Germany is particularly concerned about the possible influx of economic refugees from the Central and Eastern European states as they adjust to free market mechanisms or dissolve into political chaos. The United Kingdom has the potential flood of refugees from Hong Kong at the forefront of its desire for a strong exclusion policy. The various agencies which deal with refugees have expressed grave concern about the proposed new system. They are probably right to be concerned because the new system is almost bound to cause entry requirements of each country to be geared up towards the toughest. The country which admits the refugee will take responsibility for him under the proposals. The new system will, however, put an end to asylum seekers 'country hopping' in order to find one that will accept them. It is, of course, often very hard to tell the difference between genuine asylum seekers and those who simply want a better economic environment. There will be a common system for short-term visas of six months' duration and a tightening up of regulations on family members who are allowed to join the relatives already legally settled within the Community. The United Kingdom expressed great concern on both issues because it fears short-term refugees will stay permanently.

There have been various responses to the threat of the creation of 'fortress Europe'. One response has been from the Japanese who have increased the rate at which they have been investing in new manufacturing plants in Europe. A high proportion, about 40 per cent, of their total European investment has been in the United Kingdom but, despite some large additional investments in vehicle plants, the proportion began to decline during 1991. The United Kingdom has been attractive to the Japanese because of the government's commitment to free trade, the relatively cheap labour force, the favourable tax system, improving labour relations, the absence of foreign exchange controls and the English language. There was also the very important factor of the favourable experience of the large number of already established Japanese firms. The existence of plenty of good golf courses may also be a consideration!

There were indications in 1991 to 1992 that the Japanese were beginning to shift the concentration of their expansion towards Germany to take advantage of the potential markets of Central and Eastern Europe, and of the higher degree of training of the German workers. The nature of this latest wave of investment seems to be different from the predominantly 'screwdriver' plants established in Britain to take advantage of a cheap, docile labour force. It seems to contain more advanced processes that rely on skill and organisational talents. The attempt of the United Kingdom government at the Maastricht summit to keep the United Kingdom in the ranks of cheap-labour countries by its refusal to accept the Social Chapter proposals will probably prove fruitless because in the long run there is a strong likelihood that more investment from both outside and within the Community will find its way to the cheaper-labour regions such as Portugal until such time as they raise their living standards, that is until 'cohesion' comes about. In early 1992 a study by the Japanese Export–Import Bank said that the basic aim of Japanese companies investing in Europe, to protect local production capacity against potential import restrictions, was largely completed. One-fifth of Japanese overseas investments were in Europe in the period from 1986 to the end of 1991.

Investment from the United States is also tending to increase and much of it in the 1980s was concentrated in the United Kingdom but the recession of the early 1990s and the trends in Eastern Europe are again shifting the balance. Large American multinationals are already established throughout Europe but the attractions of the United Kingdom will continue to include the language. It is apparent that both American and Japanese businesses were rather sceptical of the claims that there will not be a 'fortress Europe' or tougher barriers to surmount after 1992 but the practical details of the single market as it is being established have probably begun to reassure them. The same anxieties have been expressed by businesses in other European countries that are not in the Community, for example Switzerland and Sweden. Companies from both nations are busy getting inside the Community by take-overs and new investment. Nestlé's purchase of Rowntree was an example. This process is likely to continue even when the EEA is established. Indeed Sweden has been so concerned that it has applied for full membership of the Community and is expected to join in 1995. In May 1992 Switzerland also announced its application for membership.

One aspect of the threatened 'fortress' is the effect it might have on Third World countries. The Community has an assortment of programmes to help such countries and is, on the whole, generous. Through the four Lomé Conventions it has allocated large sums to helping African, Caribbean and Pacific (ACP) countries. The Fourth Lomé Convention will run from 1990 to 2000 and in the first five years to 1995 the Community will provide 12 billion ECU in aid in the form of grants, soft loans and subsidies on interest rates, a 20 per cent increase in real terms compared with Lomé 3. This money is paid through the European Development Fund. The details of this and other schemes are discussed in Chapter 6. The ACP countries in the Lomé Convention have free access to the Community for most of their agricultural and manufactured goods. There is a special system called Stabex to help stabilise their export earnings, and another called Sysmin to stabilise earnings from mining products. The fear is that Third World countries that are not favoured by the Lomé Conventions or by bilateral agreements will suffer from Community competition in world markets. They may also be deprived of fair competition for their goods within Europe. Some experts allege that the Community has already damaged less developed countries by subsidising exports of food and by undercutting their embryo manufacturing industries. The Lomé Convention is undoubtedly an excellent and generous scheme but, like all such schemes, it is not perfect. It gives aid in what seems to be a relevant, specific and well-balanced manner aimed at self-sufficiency and independence. The main concern is for those nations who are not signatories, especially Asian countries.

A free market for capitalists

There has been a stark contrast between the attitude of the United Kingdom Conservative governments and most of the other governments of the Community over the type of Community they wanted. The United Kingdom government was an enthusiastic supporter of the Single European Act and used its House of Commons majority, with a three-line whip and procedural guillotine, to ensure its swift ratification. It seems to have been somewhat carried away by its own propaganda about its own success in sweeping away regulations, controls and bureaucracy in creating the British 'economic miracle'. It seems to have deluded itself that its simple acceptance of an updated version of Adam Smith's idea of free market forces was also intended by the other eleven members. It is, of course, possible to debate the existence and reality of the alleged British 'economic miracle' of the mid-1980s and of the real nature of cause and effect of change. The extent, for example, of the reduction of controls and bureaucracy in the United Kingdom was usually exaggerated. The concept of an 'economic miracle' leads to what are essentially semantic arguments. The stated growth rates of the United Kingdom economy depended upon the criteria for growth that were adopted and the base years chosen.

The other eleven members, and particularly the original six, were in favour of the single market because they saw it as a logical necessity if further economic growth and the reduction of unemployment were to be achieved. A detailed analysis of the costs of a 'non-Europe' showed that all members would benefit from extra growth, a lower rate of inflation and rising employment. They realised that the new breeze of competition would carry with it some degree of social consequence in terms of the restructuring of industry, commerce and employment. They supported the proposed controls on agricultural spending in order to leave more money available for the Social and Regional Funds of the Community. These motives led them to expect and support proposals to add new social provisions to the Community alongside the economic changes required to create the single market.

The Single European Act permitted qualified majority decisions on measures to implement the single internal market. These included transport and environmental matters but excluded items relating to taxation, the free movement of persons and the interests of employees. It came as a shock to some British politicians, and even apparently to some members of the government, that the Community was producing binding regulations which affected everyday life in the United Kingdom to a marked extent. Many of these applied to the environment in areas such as the decision to enforce catalytic converters on vehicles to control exhaust emissions, or to control the quality of public water supplies. Mrs Thatcher, in early 1989, decided that her ministers were giving too much away in some areas. She appeared to regard this as a threat to national sovereignty and as bureaucratic control and, therefore, took personal charge of supervising the outcome of departmental discussions in the Community, hoping thereby to withstand the tide of change. Inevitably she was likened to King Canute, although we all know that King Canute was an exceptionally able king who was teaching his sycophantic courtiers a lesson by proving that he could not stem the tide as they had suggested. The outcome has been much the same. The powers were assigned by the Single European Act and it was already too late to be squawking about them. There are regular reports of changes that will be imposed against the British government's wishes – transport regulations, speed limiters for heavy goods vehicles, tobacco advertising controls, for example.

The real fear of the pro-free marketeers has been that the single market will turn out to be overregulated, bureaucratic and protectionist. Mrs Thatcher made this plain in her famous Bruges speech in 1988. Her views were restated by Mr Lawson, at that time Chancellor of the Exchequer, in 1989. He had a vision of 'a deregulated, free market, open Europe, driven by consumer choice...by transferring power not to Brussels but to the people'. These views have been a potent force in the formation of British policy in the negotiations for the Union Treaty of 1992.

The United Kingdom's opposition to proposals for the single market have been strongest in the field of monetary union, sterling's membership of the Exchange Rate Mechanism (although it did join the ERM in October 1990), merger and competition policy, the Social Charter, and the relaxation of border controls. In all these areas the United Kingdom Conservative governments argued that too much regulation, harmonisation and loss of sovereignty were involved. The details are discussed in Chapters 4 and 7.

A two-speed Europe

There is a very real danger that a two-speed Europe will develop in the 1990s with the United Kingdom relegated to the sidelines of European decision-making. There was some expectation among some Conservative politicians that the fall of Mrs Thatcher, largely over the strident tone of her anti-monetary union approach as well as the poll tax fiasco, would create a significant shift of attitude in the party leadership. Indeed the new leader talked about being at the 'heart of Europe' but this sentiment was not borne out by the negotiating position adopted at Maastricht. On many issues, the United Kingdom stood alone. On others, it alienated opinion by its doctrinaire intransigence. Its opposition has been ineffective where majority decision-making applies although the qualified majority system has rarely been invoked. Moreover the other members have found ways of circumventing British opposition in areas where a majority is required. In 1990 for example, Germany, France and the Benelux countries, later joined by Italy, made their own 'Schengen Group' agreement on removing border controls on the basis of an earlier 1985 scheme.

The British government also excluded itself, by choice, from some areas of scientific research, from the Lingua programme to teach further foreign languages in schools, and from proposals to cut cardio vascular disease by discouraging smoking. It was also against a Community-wide pensioners' identity card to give them access to cheaper fares and facilities. It proved particularly obdurate over attempts under the Social Charter to improve working conditions for the low-paid, women and the young.

This tendency to isolationism is disliked by many in Britain and is resented by other member states. Nor is it an attitude supported by British public opinion if the results of regular 'Eurobarometer' surveys are to be believed. The main issues came to a head during the intergovernmental conferences on economic and monetary union and on political union which led up to the Maastricht summit in December 1991 and the Union Treaty of 1992. The demand for an opt-out clause from the application of Stage 3 of monetary union, on the implausible grounds that the United Kingdom Parliament would have to be *consulted*, rather than *managed* as has been the tradition, was granted as a recognition of the internal political difficulties of the British Conservative Party. The United Kingdom's early Victorian attitude to social affairs led to the other eleven members creating their own opt-out protocol under which they will manage social policy with qualified majority voting using Community institutions (see Chapter 8).

Thus the United Kingdom was left completely isolated as the other nations who might have shown some support accepted the give and take of Community debate. Their 'take' was money in the form of the Cohesion Fund! The differences also boiled up during the discussions on the reform of the Common Agricultural Policy and the Uruguay round of the General Agreement on Tariffs and Trade (GATT) talks in 1990 and 1991.

The possibility exists of the United Kingdom, although it itself will probably meet the criteria, forming a focus for those nations who are unable by 1996 to meet the convergence criteria required for movement to Stage 3 of monetary union when a single currency and central bank will be formed. If the Cohesion Fund and regional policies fail to work to raise living standards in countries such as Greece, Portugal, and Ireland, Britain could find itself leading the 'second division' nations in an inferior economic league. Spain may, by then, be in the 'first division'.

Federalism and Subsidiarity

Federalism is discussed in Chapters 2 and 4 but it will be helpful to explain the principle of 'subsidiarity' here because its adoption prevents the centralising tendency that many people, especially in the United Kingdom, associate with what they call federal government. The Union Treaty agreed at Maastricht starts with the following phrases:

> By this Treaty, the High Contracting Parties establish among themselves a European Union. This Treaty marks a new stage in the process creating an ever closer Union among the peoples of Europe, where decisions are taken as closely as possible to the citizens.

The words 'ever closer Union' replaced the original draft phrase of 'Union with a federal goal' which created such a furore among certain anti-Community elements in Britain. The treaty went on, in Article 3b, to define the principle of subsidiarity for the first time although Jacques Delors, President of the Commission, defined it in a speech to the French bishops at Lourdes in 1989. He said,

> Finally, the fourth principle is subsidiarity. I would say that, solely from the view of political effectiveness (I could quote de Tocqueville and others here), it is important not to concentrate too much power at the top, to be able to combine decision-making from the top and from the bottom and, wherever possible, to leave responsibility for solving a problem at the level closest to that problem.

The treaty says:

> The Community shall act within the limits of the powers conferred upon it by this Treaty and of the objectives assigned to it therein. In the areas which do not fall within its exclusive jurisdiction, the Community shall take action in accordance with the principle of subsidiarity, only if and insofar as the objectives of the proposed action cannot be sufficiently achieved by the member states and can therefore, by reason of the scale or effects of proposed action, be better achieved by the Community. Any action by the

Community shall not go beyond what is necessary to achieve the objectives of the Treaty.

Conclusion

There will probably not be a 'fortress Europe' unless there is a major international recession. Nor will there be a 'market for bankers and not workers'. The possible failure of the GATT talks in 1992 leaves an ominous cloud on the horizon, as does the trend towards bilateral trade agreements. The likelihood is that there will be a free single internal market, sensibly regulated and with a strong 'Social Charter' to maintain the rights of workers and consumers, pensioners, women and minorities. The European Parliament will probably be more effective and there will be greater democratic participation. This view is supported by the fact that the Danish referendum's rejection of the Maastricht Treaty was partly on the grounds of the inadequacy of the democratic elements contained in it. The growing unpopularity of the Treaty in Germany was also partly caused by the failure of the Treaty to reduce the 'democratic deficit'; although fears about the future of the German currency was a stronger element in creating opposition. People will come to regard national sovereignty as pooled rather than sacrificed. The addition of members such as Sweden, Austria and Finland will tilt the balance even further in favour of a social market rather than a market for capitalists. Their advent may, however, accentuate the Europe of two divisions if economic and monetary union are not accompanied by greater cohesion.

Ideas into Institutions – How the European Community Began

Many of those who witnessed the appalling slaughter and destruction of the First World War realised that only some form of unification of the states of Europe could prevent further conflict. The Great Powers' struggle of the nineteenth century, the competition for empire and the arms race had culminated in a great cataclysm. Yet the nineteenth century had shown, in the case of the unification of Germany and Italy, that wars could be reduced by political and economic union. Further afield, the success of the American federal system, despite the supreme test of the Civil War, gave hope to the European democrat. The immediate aftermath of the First World War saw the creation of several new nation states and the resurrection of old states as the Austro-Hungarian empire collapsed and the Baltic states achieved temporary independence, since regained. Many boundaries were redrawn or established and we know, with the benefit of hindsight, that the Treaty of Versailles in 1919 contained the seeds of the Second World War. Perceptive critics of the time recognised that fact. The years 1919–39 can be regarded as an extended armistice.

It was against this background that the League of Nations was formed. It is fashionable to scoff cynically at the naïvety of those who thought that the League would ensure that the Great War would be 'the war to end all wars'. Admittedly, the League got off to a very bad start when the American President, Woodrow Wilson, one of its chief architects, failed to get the endorsement of the American people for his policies at Versailles and for the League. Yet millions saw in it a great hope for the future. The League did have some achievements.

Disarmament agreements were reached. Naval building programmes were curtailed. Millions joined the Peace Pledge Union or its equivalent in other countries. The fact that these people's hopes were destroyed by the demonic forces of national socialism and deranged nationalism is for the whole of mankind to regret.

It was within this context of post-First World War reconstruction that a Pan-European Movement was launched in the 1920s. It called, in 1923, for a United States of Europe based mainly on the model of the United States of America. A few years later, in 1929, the League of Nations' Assembly in Geneva was the forum for an attempt to form a European Union within the context of the League of Nations. This was proposed by the French and German foreign ministers. The objective was very limited. It was to leave the separate states fully sovereign but would promote closer cooperation. The great depression in industry, commerce and finance which followed prevented this scheme from being adopted. The slump also created a breeding-ground for the extension of versions of fascism from Italy to Germany and the Far East. Hopes for European unity were lost until after the Second World War.

The United Kingdom and Early Ideas for European Unity

The United Kingdom and the Commonwealth had suffered a great loss of life during the First World War. The United Kingdom also lost its economic preeminence in several fields to the United States and new producers had sprung up, especially in the Far East. Despite this, Britain had not suffered the extensive physical war damage of France, Belgium, northern Italy, and parts of Germany. There was not the same imperative for the British to seek European unity. Britain could still find comfort in the Victorian and Edwardian visions of Empire. Although the war had enabled the independent dominions to reach maturity, the emotional ties of imperial grandeur lingered. They persisted until it became blatantly obvious, with the independence of India, Pakistan, and Ceylon and then the flight from colonialisation in Africa after 1957, that Britain's future no longer lay outside, but within, Europe. The transition from imperial power to becoming a partner in a European Community was to prove slow, painful, and erratic. Some would say that it has not yet been achieved in the hearts of many British people.

The New Ideas after 1945

As the tide of war turned in the Allies' favour after 1943 they began to plan for the peace. Many lessons had been learned from the aftermath of the First World War. The need to have carefully worked-out schemes to deal with the inevitable postwar chaos was fully understood. There was also a strong determination to try to avoid the perceived causes of the Second World War – namely, cyclical unemployment, protectionism, poverty and deprivation. These, and other similar factors, were seen as a breeding-ground for fascism. There was also a fear in some quarters that postwar dislocation of society would enable communism to flourish. In Britain, this planning for the postwar years included the Beveridge Report, *Full Employment in a Free Society*. This was published in November 1944 but several parts of it had received a public airing beforehand and the government had issued its White Paper on Full Employment before Beveridge's work itself was formally published. Another great factor in postwar social change was the so-called Butler Education Act of 1944 which extended secondary education to all and opened up the higher education sector to large numbers of less-well-off people. Another was the Barlow Royal Commission Report of 1941 which was reprinted in 1943 and which dealt with industrial location and population trends.

On the international scene there was a great proliferation of new institutions which applied either on a worldwide scale or on a regional basis. The major worldwide schemes, which have had a profound effect on European development, were the International Monetary Fund (IMF) and the International Bank for Reconstruction and Development (IBRD), usually called 'the World Bank'. With modifications these have survived to make a major contribution to international economic stability and cooperation. Another body of great long-term importance has been the Organisation for Economic Cooperation and Development (OECD). This was originally the Organisation for European Economic Cooperation (OEEC). Initially, the defeated powers, Germany and Japan, were excluded but were incorporated once their industrial and political potential was required as a pillar of American anti-communism. West Germany was resurrected into full ally status after NATO was formed as a response to the blockade of Berlin by the USSR. Japan was 'recreated' when its geographical position made it vital as a base for United Nations' operations during the Korean War of 1950–3. Meanwhile, in Eastern Europe, the previously independent nations became communist by fair and foul means and were eventually welded into an economic trading bloc with the formation of Comecon in 1949.

In Western Europe a bewildering variety of organisations was created. Out of some of these eventually emerged the European Economic Community (EEC) or the European Community (EC) as it is now generally known.

The New Organisations

Three broad types of organisation were created. The United States and Canada had been deeply involved in the European war and in reconstruction afterwards. It was natural, therefore, that the first type had North American involvement.

The Organisation for European Economic Cooperation

In 1948, the USA sponsored the formation of the OEEC. This organisation made possible the successful implementation of the Marshall Plan. This plan, named after the American Secretary of State, provided immense amounts of financial aid in return for European cooperation in reconstruction. The sum of $17 billion was spent in the four years of the plan's operation from 1948 to 1952. It was this scheme that enabled West Germany, Italy, France and the Benelux countries to modernise their industry, to provide employment, and to create political stability in the democratic mould. The United Kingdom, which benefited only marginally or indirectly from the Marshall Plan, was left largely to its own devices. The United Kingdom, mainly from its own resources, had to reconstruct war-ravaged capital goods industries, its transport system and its housing. As a matter of what can be regarded as misplaced honour, the government committed itself to repaying its debts to the United States, thus adding a further burden to the nation. As a partial consequence of this, and of the problems of reconstruction, a large additional loan had to be obtained from the USA. As that was spent, the pound had to be devalued in 1949. It is from this period that some of the seeds of Britain's poor postwar economic performance relative to other European nations dates. It can be argued that the United Kingdom concentrated on social reforms, on the creation of educational and health systems, on the redistribution of wealth, and on social justice at the expense of reconstructing its obsolescent industrial structures. In the long run, there has proved to be little truth in the saying that the spoils of war go to the victor.

The OEEC was formed after an attempt in 1947 by France, the USSR and the United Kingdom to reach an agreement on a European recovery plan failed because of Soviet objections to the impairment of national sovereignty. France and the United Kingdom then invited all European countries except Spain (which was still a fascist dictatorship) to a conference. The list of those who accepted and took part is interesting in the light of later developments. They were Austria, Belgium, Denmark, Eire, Greece, Iceland, Italy, Luxembourg, The Netherlands, Norway, Portugal, Sweden, Switzerland, and Turkey. (Czechoslovakia initially accepted but withdrew into the Soviet bloc.) These fourteen countries, plus the United Kingdom and France, signed a convention in 1948. The zones of Germany occupied by the British, the French and the Americans were also signatories, as was the Anglo-American zone of Trieste.

The initial requirement for the OEEC was to solve the problem of Europe's enormous trade deficit with the USA, to promote maximum cooperation among the sixteen nations, to establish internal financial stability and to maximise production. In order to achieve this a Council, a Secretariat, an executive committee and several *ad hoc* committees were established. There was a very great incentive to make the system work because American aid under the Marshall Plan (European Recovery Programme) was contingent upon intra-European cooperation. It is generally agreed that the OEEC was very successful, so much so that an American administrator of Marshall Aid, Hoffman, called on the nations of the organisation to create a Western Union, a permanent free trading area of 270 million people when the European Recovery Programme ended. This has not yet fully materialised because the countries of Europe diverged for a time into different economic groupings, the EEC and EFTA (European Free Trade Association) but the European Economic Area (EEA) agreed in 1991 and due to commence in 1993 is the fulfilment of the idea.

In 1961, the OEEC was transformed by a change of membership and by new objectives. It was renamed the Organisation for Economic Cooperation and Development (OECD). Its membership broadened to include the USA, Canada, Finland, Spain, West Germany, and Japan. The organisation has a Council on which each country is represented, and a secretary-general with a permanent staff. Its fundamental purpose is 'to achieve the highest sustainable economic growth and employment and a rising standard of living in member countries, whilst maintaining financial stability, and thus contribute to the development of the world economy'. The intention was to achieve this by freeing international trade and movements of capital. New ground was broken by the additional aim of coordinating economic aid to less developed countries (LDCs). The organisation is consultative and its decisions are not binding on its members.

The North Atlantic Treaty Organisation

NATO too was sponsored by the USA. It was formed in 1949 to create a counterweight to the military strength of the USSR and its allies. In the first phase NATO was dominated by the USA which provided huge financial and military assistance. West Germany's membership in 1955 began a new phase and the balance of power within NATO shifted more towards Europe. The period until 1967 saw the adoption of nuclear policies and the relative relegation of conventional arms into second place. This was partly a response to manpower problems but was also due to the economic and political cost of any attempt to possess both full-scale conventional and nuclear forces. Since the late 1960s France has withdrawn to the sidelines of NATO. Other countries such as Spain and Greece have reviewed their positions in relation to American bases and there have been major squabbles about the sharing of costs on an equitable basis. There has been a trend towards the USA negotiating directly with the USSR over the heads of her NATO allies and now with Russia and the Commonwealth of Independent States.

In terms of our subject, the European Community, NATO is of importance in several ways. First, its existence should prevent any future European war because the military commands of the nations, their equipment and logistics are so interdependent. Second, the accumulated expenditure, capital investment, and annual expenditure on arms and defence-related research are so enormous that they have a profound effect on industrial and scientific development, location of industry, communications and employment. Although the standardisation of equipment still leaves a lot to be desired, NATO purchasing exerts a great influence. A successful order for NATO equipment enables economies of scale to be achieved in manufacture and reduces costs and prices in the international market. Third, the existence of NATO, with its transatlantic component of the USA and Canada and its non-European Community membership of Norway and Turkey, can be regarded as a major obstacle to the permanent, closer political unity of Europe. Its presence makes a common foreign policy harder to achieve, especially because of different national attitudes to nuclear weapons. Some would disagree and assert that NATO should make political unity easier because it has created a mechanism for systematic cooperation and consultation.

The whole purpose of NATO, and its future, has been under very close scrutiny since the negotiation of the 1987 Treaty on Intermediate Range Nuclear Forces (INF Treaty), and the Strategic Arms Reduction Talks (START Treaty) which began in 1988, continued with interruptions, and resumed in April 1991. It has been called even more into question by the progress of the talks on Conventional Forces in Europe in 1990–91 after the Paris summit agreement in November 1990, and subsequent troop withdrawals. The détente between the USSR and NATO, the end of the cold war, the breakup of the Warsaw Pact in 1990, and the reunification of Germany in 1990, have all put pressure on the Community to develop both a common foreign policy and a new, common, defence policy. NATO appears to have little purpose now there is no longer a Warsaw Pact and there is a powerful body of opinion in the Community which wants to have a common defence policy to replace NATO. The United Kingdom has been extremely reluctant to see any diminution in the role of NATO but the Gulf crisis, in 1990–91, accelerated the trend towards a new Community foreign and defence policy. The details emerged from the Maastricht meeting of the European Council in December 1991. Some countries have seen the revival of the Western European Union as the way forward and the new Franco-German army corps of 40 000 men announced in May 1992 will be placed under the control of the WEU. In June 1992 it was decided that NATO would be prepared to operate outside its members' borders in a peace-keeping role.

The Brussels Pact and Western European Union

At the end of 1947 a Four Power Conference on the future of Germany failed to reach agreement. The division of Germany became inevitable. In early 1948 therefore, the British Foreign Secretary, Ernest Bevin, put forward the idea of a 'Western Union'. The Russian *coup d'état* in Czechoslovakia, overthrowing the democratic government, hastened the signing of the Treaty of Brussels, in March 1948, between the United Kingdom, France, Belgium, The Netherlands, and Luxembourg. These countries agreed to support each other militarily and to cooperate in economic matters. They set up a permanent consultative council in London. In 1949, they set up the Council of Europe which has a ministerial committee that meets in private, and a consultative body that meets in public. Under the Treaty of Brussels a defence establishment was set up at Fontainebleau under the command of Field Marshal Montgomery. He became very frustrated whilst in that job because of the vacillation of the politicians and the rigid nationalist aspirations of the French. He felt that little was achieved in terms of effective military organisation. The formation of NATO in 1949 overshadowed this aspect of the Brussels Pact.

In May 1955, the Brussels Treaty was extended to include West Germany and Italy and create the Western European Union. (Portugal has since joined.) This modification of the treaty took the form of a 50 year Western European Unity Treaty and the formation of the Western European Union. This resulted from an idea, born in 1948 at the Hague Conference, to form a supranational European army. The plan was conceived by the French Prime Minister René Pleven and later put forward to the Council of Europe in 1951 by Robert Schuman, the French foreign minister. It was intended to make German rearmament acceptable. It would also make progress towards a federal Europe easier. This idea of a European Defence Community was supported by the USA but opinion in France, Italy, and Scandinavia was very divided. A preliminary treaty was concluded but gradually East–West tension decreased. De Gaulle was strongly opposed to the plan because he favoured a confederation of sovereign European states with France in the ascendancy. He wanted

Europe to be independent of American dominance. The plan for a European Defence Community failed because the United Kingdom would not cooperate as a result of its commitment to the defence of its remaining empire. There was no further discussion on the political union of Europe until 1961. The British government under Churchill and Eden refused to sacrifice British independence to a European integration of forces. The French Assembly rejected the European Defence Community in 1954 and the United Kingdom proposed a compromise in the form of a high level of cooperation between the national armies. This was to be controlled by the Council of the Brussels Treaty. As a result the Western European Unity Treaty was signed and the Western European Union established. It was under this treaty that West Germany agreed not to attempt any changes to its borders by force, and not to make nuclear, chemical or biological weapons. It also agreed not to make large naval vessels, long-range bombers or long-range missiles.

In practice, as has already been said, the major military coopera-tion in Europe is through NATO, rather than through the Western European Union. Although the cooperation on defence matters has been largely carried out by NATO the WEU has, since 1984, become a vehicle for establishing a stronger European voice in the defence of Europe as against American influence. France, which became a peripheral member of NATO under President de Gaulle, has instigated a revival of the WEU. This has been significant as the USA and USSR took increasingly to direct negotiations with each other on armaments, as in the Geneva Treaty of 1988 and the Conventional Forces in Europe agreements of 1990–1. In October 1991 the USA announced large-scale, unilateral, reductions in its nuclear arsenal, especially of short-range tactical weapons, after only a peremptory discussion with other NATO members. The failure of the anti-Gorbachev coup in the USSR in September 1991, and the break-up of the Soviet federal union followed by its partial replace-ment by the CIS, has given greater emphasis to the Conference on Security and Cooperation in Europe (CSCE) as a peacemaking body. The Yugoslavia crisis in 1991–2 put both the Community and the CSCE to the test.

The Brussels Treaty signed in March 1948 setting up the Western European Union was for 50 years and the issues raised by its renewal will become very important as 1998 approaches. It may be during this period that the role of NATO is most seriously questioned because its functions will overlap those of an improved WEU. The discussions at Maastricht in 1991 were a prelude to what may be a major clash of opinion between the NATO supporters and those of the WEU.

The Council of Europe

European nations differ greatly in the degree to which they are able or willing to sacrifice or subordinate their sovereignty to international or supranational bodies. Sweden and Switzerland have a long history of neutrality. Austria has neutrality forced upon it by the treaty re-establishing it as an independent state. It has also come to value neutrality. Others, such as France and the United Kingdom, are very reluctant to cede sovereignty. There is, therefore, a place for an organisation which enables states to belong without commitment to ideas of political union, federal or confederate. The Council of Europe is just such an organisation. It was established in May 1949 by ten nations (United Kingdom, France, Benelux, Italy, Ireland, Denmark, Norway and Sweden). The number was increased to 21 by the addition of Austria, West Germany, Cyprus, Switzerland, Portugal, Spain, Greece, Turkey, Iceland, Malta and Liechtenstein. The Council of Europe is an important means through which nations cooperate. Superficially, its constitution looks unpromising. Its decisions are made by a Committee of Ministers and they must be unanimous. In practice, therefore, each nation can operate a veto. There is a consultative body called a Parliamentary Assembly. It cannot pass legislation but simply makes recommendations to the Committee of Ministers. After they have agreed a proposal it still has to be ratified by the parliaments of each nation. Despite this inauspicious arrangement the Council of Europe has produced many agreements in legal, social, cultural and economic spheres. Most noteworthy is the European Convention for the Protection of Human Rights and Fundamental Freedoms which was adopted in 1950. This convention set up the European Court of Human Rights and the European Commission for Human Rights.

The Economic Organisations

The day-to-day working of the Organisation of European Economic Cooperation after 1948 in putting the European Recovery Programme (Marshall Plan) into effect forced the nations of Europe into economic and financial cooperation. As the Marshall Plan was scheduled to end in 1952 there was pressure to create a permanent economic organisation. It is from this area that the European Community as we know it came into being. The Community is technically and legally three organisations operating together. These are the European Coal and Steel Community (ECSC), the European Atomic Energy Community (Euratom) and the European Economic Community (EEC).

When these three bodies and their development are studied it is apparent that they have created a unique structure. They have not adopted either of the two major suggestions for a unified Europe that have been put forward over the years – that is, the federal and the confederate solutions. A federal system is one where states form a political unity while remaining independent as to their internal affairs. This sounds a simple concept but the main problem, and area of future dispute, is the degree of decision-making given to the central government. The central government always manages defence and foreign policy but there remain 'grey' areas of disputed jurisdiction which emerge over time. The written constitution of such federal states usually includes a statement about 'residual' powers and who is to possess them. This is frequently the central government. Two classic cases are nuclear energy and air transport regulation in the USA. The founding fathers of the American constitution could not predict either. Such conflicts make the existence of an arbitrating body essential, as in the US Supreme Court. None of the suggestions for a federal state of Europe has made progress despite the relative success of the federal system in West Germany, the USA, Canada and Australia. One of the most interesting speculations about the future of the Community is whether there will be a stronger trend towards a more federal approach, that is a Community foreign policy and defence policy.

Until June 1991, the word 'federal' had not appeared in discussion of the Community's future. It then appeared in the preamble to a draft treaty for political union presented to the Luxembourg meeting of the European Council where mention was made of a 'federal goal'. The word was again used in a replacement version of the treaty which was presented to Community foreign ministers in October 1991. The United Kingdom, which places a different interpretation on the word 'federal' from that used by the other members, objected strongly and the argument affected the timetable for the draft treaty on political union presented to the European Council at Maastricht in December 1991. The basic argument, however, was about the change in the powers and functions of the European Parliament and the Commission, and the adoption of common foreign and defence policies. In the preamble to the final Union Treaty the words were replaced by 'ever closer Union among the peoples of Europe' but no one really thought that the intention had changed.

A confederation is an alliance or league of states who retain their independence and who make decisions by consultation. Although central administration and decision-making bodies have to be set up, the emphasis is on the sovereignty of the separate states. Confederacies tend to be weak and relapse into separatism and acrimony in times of stress. Some of the European organisations already discussed are essentially confederal in nature.

The unique structure of the Community lies in the fact that the twelve members have adopted what is generally called 'integration' as a policy. They have ceded parts of their national sovereignty to the Community and given it some sovereign powers which it can exercise. These powers, in certain circumstances, have the force of national law. The objective is to create a permanent and indissoluble organisation and political entity. It should be remembered that a major motive in the steps towards European unity was the removal of any future possibility of the re-emergence of an expansionist, militarily strong, Germany. The way to prevent this was to bind Germany inextricably into an economic web and into a mutual defence organisation. The USSR, whilst not wholly in favour of a rich, economically powerful West Germany, was happier that no independent West German military power could be envisaged. It is ironic that Germany, whose constitution forbids the use of its armed forces abroad except as part of a NATO defence force, was criticised for not sending forces to the Gulf in 1990. There is now pressure on her to rewrite her constitution to enable the newly united nation to be able to contribute to Community forces if they were sent to places such as Yugoslavia as part of United Nations peace-keeping forces.

The first economic institution – the European Coal and Steel Community

The ECSC was formed by a treaty signed, in April 1951, by Belgium, France, Germany, Italy, Luxembourg and The Netherlands. It came into force in July 1952. It originated in a plan put forward in May 1950 by Robert Schuman, the French foreign minister. He and Jean Monnet proposed that French and German coal and steel production should be put under a joint authority in an organisation which other countries could join. The ECSC Treaty is another 50-year agreement and discussions have already begun in the early 1990s on how to replace it, if at all. Some see this plan as stemming from a typically Churchillian proposal at Zurich in 1946 when he called for a United States of Europe in order to create Franco-German cooperation. Needless to say, he did not see the United Kingdom as a member of such a United States because of Britain's imperial, world status, but merely as a sort of benevolent promoter.

After the formation of the ECSC there followed a period of political manoeuvring to ensure that a rearmed Germany could be contained. German rearmament had become essential for political and manpower reasons after the Berlin blockade by the USSR in 1948–9. NATO had been formed and the Warsaw Pact signed. The so-called Iron Curtain dividing East and West had fully descended and the 'Cold War' had begun in earnest. As mentioned above, one attempt to solve Europe's defence problems was the European Defence Community (treaty 1951) which would have created a supranational European defence force. Britain refused to join in and the French Assembly rejected the plan in 1954. As a result a new way forward had to be found. This took the form of an initiative by the ECSC foreign ministers in 1955. Their experience of working through ECSC indicated that a united Europe could be created. They met at a conference at Messina and set up a committee under Paul Spaak, the Belgian foreign minister, to study possibilities for further integration. The committee reported in 1956. A series of negotiations followed and two treaties were signed in Rome on 25 March 1957. These established the European Economic Community (EEC) and the European Atomic Community (Euratom). They took effect on 1 January 1958.

The British responded by a proposal to set up a European Free Trade Association (which became known as EFTA). This had the great benefit of involving no loss of national sovereignty and was, therefore, more attractive to those members both of the Conservative Party who were in government and of the Labour Party in opposition who were strongly antagonistic towards any transfer of parliamentary powers to a European body.

We have seen the long, involved and uncertain progress of ideas into real organisations from the early 1920s to 1956. To understand the process fully we need to try to see it from the point of view of a continental European trying to prevent yet another devastating power struggle following two world wars. This gives a completely different perspective from that of the Briton who tends to see only loss of sovereignty, budget problems and food surpluses when looking at the European Community. In terms of its political objective of securing peace and cooperation between France and Germany, the Community has been an outstanding success. The problem for the future will be to apply and interpret the new treaty on political union from 1992 in such a manner as to sustain this cooperation in the context of a newly reunited Germany and a new situation in Eastern Europe.

Date Chart

1923–9   Pan-European movement within the League of Nations. It proposed a federal state of Europe. It failed with the onset of the depression.

1948–52   European Recovery Plan (Marshall Plan). This pumped American money into the reconstruction of Europe.

1948   The Organisation for European Economic Cooperation was formed to make the Marshall Plan effective. Sixteen countries joined initially: Austria, Belgium, Denmark, Eire, France, Greece, Iceland, Italy, Luxembourg, The Netherlands, Norway, Portugal, Sweden, Switzerland, Turkey, and the UK. It also included the zones of Germany occupied by Britain, France and the USA. In 1961 it was renamed the Organisation for Economic Cooperation and Development and extended to include the USA, Canada, Finland, Spain, West Germany, and Japan.

1949   The North Atlantic Treaty Organisation (NATO) was instituted in April by twelve nations: the USA, the UK,

Luxembourg, Canada, France, The Netherlands, Belgium, Norway, Italy, Denmark, Portugal and Iceland. West Germany joined in 1955.

1948   The Brussels Treaty was signed in March by the UK, France, Belgium, The Netherlands, Luxembourg, to create military and economic cooperation. It led to:

1949   The Council of Europe (May 1949). This originally consisted of ten nations; the UK, France, Belgium, The Netherlands, Luxembourg, Ireland, Italy, Denmark, Norway, Sweden. (It now consists of 21 nations.)
It, in turn, led to:

1950   The European Convention for the Protection of Human Rights and Fundamental Freedoms which led to the setting up of the Court of Human Rights and the Commission for Human Rights.

1951   European Defence Community Treaty. This failed to set up a supranational European army.

1955   The Western European Union was set up in May by the UK, France, Belgium, The Netherlands and Luxembourg, the signatories of the Brussels Treaty of 1948, plus West Germany and Italy. Portugal has since joined. It was a compromise suggested by the UK after the 1951 European Defence Community Treaty failed in 1954.

1951   The European Coal and Steel Community Treaty was signed in April by Belgium, The Netherlands, Luxembourg, France, Italy and West Germany. It came into force in July 1952.

1957   The Treaties of Rome were signed on 25 March by the 'Six', Belgium, France, West Germany, The Netherlands, Luxembourg, Italy, creating Euratom and the European Economic Community. They came into force on 1 January 1958.

1972   Accession of Denmark, Ireland and the United Kingdom. Signed 2 January 1972. Came into force 1 January 1973.

1979   Accession of Greece. Signed 28 May 1979. Came into force 1 January 1981.

1985   Accession of Portugal and Spain. Signed 12 June 1985. Came into force 1 January 1986.

1986   The Single Act, signed 17 and 28 February 1986. Came into force 1 July 1987. Establishes the single market from 1 January 1993.

1990   The newly unified Germany was incorporated as a single market state in the Community on 3 October 1990. On 1 July 1990 monetary union between the two states of Germany was begun. Full political reunion took place on 3 October 1990.

1991   European Economic Area, EFTA plus EC, formed. Signed October 1991. Due to be ratified early 1992. Comes into force 1 January 1993.

1991   Maastricht agreement on Union Treaty signed. The treaty was initialled in February 1992 and is due to be ratified by national parliaments during 1992. Comes into force in January 1993.

Development and Change

3

The Six

The Six set themselves economic and political targets. People in the United Kingdom and elsewhere viewed these at first with scepticism and then with trepidation as they were achieved or surpassed. Some of the targets had a time-scale attached. The first major objective, without which the others could not be achieved, was to form a customs union. There was a wide diversity of customs tariffs on imports into and between the six countries. They tended to be low into Germany and the Benelux countries and high into Italy and France. The Six aimed at abolishing these differences within twelve years from 1958. They wanted all duties on the movement of goods within the Community abolished. They would then set up a common customs tariff (a CCT) on goods entering the Six from abroad. They achieved this ahead of schedule. In 1968, customs duties within the six states were abolished. They then established a common external tariff on all goods entering the Community from non-member states. As the stages towards the successful accomplishment of this target were completed, those outside the Community became more keenly aware that they would eventually be forced into a very uncompetitive position in their major European markets because their goods would have to overcome the CCT. Meanwhile, the European producers would have the benefits of the greater economies of scale derived from their larger home markets. These would give them lower average costs of production within Europe and in world

35

markets. The benefits obtained from similar reductions in tariffs between EFTA countries were not enough to compensate for this disadvantage.

What are the Economics of the Community as a Customs Union?

The European Community is a classic example of a customs union. The members agree to remove customs or tariff barriers between them and to impose a common external tariff on imports from non-member countries. This external tariff can be used as a protectionist hurdle by being set at a level that places the imports at a cost disadvantage. It can be made more favourable to friendly nations. Such an action has tended to provoke retaliation and bilateral or preferential trading agreements. The General Agreement on Tariffs and Trade (GATT) was set up to reverse the 1930s' trend which had seen the world sink into a desperate round of protection and 'beggar my neighbour' policies. The Community has been an important participant in GATT and in the regular 'rounds' of discussions that try to improve its application and effectiveness. Two major rounds, the Kennedy and Tokyo rounds, and some minor rounds, have been completed and a third, the Uruguay round, was resumed in 1992 after lengthy delays in December 1990 and 1991.

Despite its members being signatories of the GATT agreements, and despite the participation of the Community as a single entity in the successive rounds, the European Community has frequently come into conflict with other nations about its trading policy. The Community has gradually removed its less acceptable practices in relation to the Third World in a series of negotiations ending in the 1975 Lomé Convention. The convention is regularly updated and the Fourth Agreement will run from March 1990 to 2000. The conventions are mainly concerned with aid but also relate to trade. Some critics think that there is a cosmetic element in the conventions to cover up the real harm that they allege stems from Community trading policies, especially the subsidising of exports from the Twelve.

One of the most constructive and promising developments from the Lomé Conventions is a fund called Stabex. This is used to stabilise the earnings of the 69 African, Caribbean and Pacific

(ACP) countries in the agreement. It applies to exports of 48 agricultural commodities. Stabex is an insurance fund financed largely from the European Development Fund and augmented by payments from the ACP countries when their export earnings exceed certain levels. This principle has also been extended to mining products with a fund called Sysmin.

Whilst Third World opposition to the European Community has become muted there has been growing criticism from the United States. Japan too has voiced its concern. The United States has traditionally been a fairly protectionist country, some say excessively so. The nature of the United States Congress means that each Senator and Representative must fight for his own state or district and its industries. As a result the United States has a formidable set of quota and tariff barriers together with a maze of administrative and health regulations. They all tend to restrict imports. In recent years, therefore, it has been inevitable that major clashes should have occurred between the United States and the Community. The main areas of dispute have been steel products, agricultural goods and textiles. Other products have been drawn into the fray as part of retaliatory measures. It is usually the United States that is alleging 'unfair' competition. From its point of view the European Community protects its own markets and sometimes subsidises exports. Most of these disputes are eventually resolved peacefully. Another area of dispute has been the United States' attempts to control the export and re-export of certain high-technology products such as computers and electronic systems to the old Soviet bloc. This is seen by many European companies as a gross interference with their commercial freedoms.

The main theoretical objection to customs unions such as the European Community is expressed in the so-called Law of Comparative Cost Advantage. This theory concludes that free trade maximises the use of the world's resources and that any interference, such as tariffs or quotas, with the free movement of goods and services reduces mankind's economic satisfaction. It states that a country will tend to specialise in, and export, those goods in which it has the greatest comparative cost advantage in production, or in which it has the least comparative cost disadvantage. It should be emphasised that trade benefits both the most and the least favoured nation if their comparative costs of production differ. This applies even if one country is superior, in cost terms, at producing everything. These comparative costs and the terms of trade can explain which goods a country exports and which it imports. Most economics textbooks contain a numerical example to illustrate the principle of comparative cost advantage. The theory is a specific application of Adam Smith's demonstration of the gains to be had from the division of labour and specialisation. The theory tends to rely too heavily on the idea of the factors of production, land, labour and capital, being more mobile within each country than they actually are. It also tends to gloss over problems related to transport costs, economies of scale and different currencies. The simple versions conveniently overlook the growing role of powerful multinational corporations in world trade. Having said that, it is still generally accepted that free trade is an ideal that should be aspired to by all nations. The reader who would like a very detailed theoretical analysis of the economics of the Community as a customs union is advised to read *The Economics of Europe* by Edward Nevin (Macmillan 1990, ISBN 0–333–051632–X), especially Part II.

The European Community's external tariffs are a clear breach of the ideal of free trade and so are the various methods used by individual members to restrict imports. Unfortunately, it is always possible for nations to ignore the economic imperative of the theory of comparative cost advantage and to argue in favour of protectionism for strategic reasons. They also sometimes claim that foreign countries are 'dumping' goods on them. This is a complex field but means that the seller is selling at a price below the average cost of production. This has certainly been done with some Soviet bloc products. It is also alleged that it is done for gains in short-term market share with some Japanese products. Needless to say, it has been alleged by the USA that the European Community has also 'dumped' agricultural products and some types of steel. The GATT is intended to help prevent and stop dumping.

Have the Hopes Been Met?

The statistical problems of determining the economic effects on growth and trade from the creation of the Community are enormous, if not unsurmountable, because of the large number of economic variables involved. It also requires the comparison of what has happened, assuming that that can be agreed or measured, with what might have happened if the European Community had not been formed. There is an additional problem that the operation of the Community has involved large shifts or redistributions of funds among the members. Some of these have been intended and are, therefore, presumably desirable. The conventional measures of economic welfare do not take much account of the non-monetary welfare obtained by, say, the German people from assisting the economic growth of Greece, Portugal or the other relatively poorer members.

If we examine the case of the United Kingdom there is no doubt that those who believed the optimists who predicted enormous gains from trade from joining the Community have been sadly disappointed. The accession of the United Kingdom, Denmark and Ireland in 1973 coincided with the onset of the international recession so the effects of joining are difficult to isolate. The major gains have apparently been to continental firms who have exploited the United Kingdom market. This is not too surprising since they were already obtaining some of the benefits of a larger market. It could be argued also that British industry and commerce were too complacent, too sheltered and too much in the grip of slack management and overpowerful trade unions. Moreover, few could have predicted the powerful expansion of the Japanese into British, European and world markets. They, of course, achieved this success through very thorough planning, marketing skills and a very close partnership between government, civil service, business leaders and trade unions.

Gradually, the United Kingdom has begun to exploit and benefit from the larger European market. Lessons have been learned, firms have become more efficient and competitive. Many large British firms are developing into market leaders in Europe and are assuming a more multinational aspect. It is stated that the removal of barriers to trade by 1992 presents a great challenge to businesses. This is a statement of the obvious. What is less accepted is that it also represents an enormous challenge to government to ensure that the right infrastructure is in place in time. This requires first-class transport and communications systems. There is little sign that this need has been recognised and there is every possibility that British industry will not be able to benefit fully from the greater freedom of the single market and its potential economies of scale. The United

Kingdom may end up as a peripheral backwater economically unless the means of moving goods cheaply, quickly and competitively are provided. The other members of the Community see this as a role for government. They have been proved right in the past. Experience suggests that the United Kingdom government will realise too late and will react with inadequate resources. Its response in the discussions on the Union Treaty at Maastricht in December 1991 seemed restricted to the principle of keeping the United Kingdom as a low-wage economy with poor employment conditions, in order to compete with the Pacific Rim countries. The stated motives for its opting out of the Social Chapter evoked echoes of Victorian debates on restricting child labour or on providing cheap bread in order to keep factory workers' wages down. The lesson that well-paid workers with good working conditions and job security have higher overall productivity than those paid wages close to social security benefit levels and working unrestricted hours in poor conditions seems to have been ignored.

The benefits of membership of the European Community to the United Kingdom need to be seen against the enormous potential advantages conferred by the possession of North Sea oil and gas. It is safe to predict that by the year 2000 there will be many books discussing the vexed question of what happened to the North Sea oil revenues. They could have been used to create an infrastructure suitable for the single European market.

Other members of the Community have benefited in varying ways and to differing degrees from their membership and the passage of time has sometimes changed initial benefits into disadvantages. Countries such as Ireland, Greece, Portugal, and Spain have gained financially from their membership but have had to pay a cost in terms of social adjustment and upheaval. There have also been transfers from sector to sector with the agricultural sector gaining at the expense of others despite the redressing effects of the Regional and Social Funds. The main financial net contributors to the Community, Germany, France and Britain, have gained in terms of the greater political and social stability of Europe and from its increased 'cohesion'. Donne's statement that 'no man is an island unto himself' is frequently quoted but remains true nonetheless, especially in the context of the rich northern states of the Community benefiting from the improved standards of living of the poorer southern states.

Economies of Scale – the Great Sales Pitch?

The concept of economies of scale needs to be understood if the motivation for creating the Community, and for the United Kingdom's desire to join, are to be appreciated. 'Economies of scale' was a phrase very much in vogue in the 1960s and was used to justify many mergers, take-overs and nationalisation schemes. The proponents of such schemes conveniently forgot that there are *diseconomies* of scale, particularly in management, and that a high level of demand needs to exist to enable large plants to produce at their most efficient or lowest cost per unit. For example, a steel plant designed to produce 3 million tonnes of steel per year only has cost advantages derived from large-scale output if it is actually producing its designed output. If it is producing only 1 million tonnes as a result of depressed demand, it may have average costs per tonne which are higher than a smaller plant which *is* producing at *its* designed optimum. Large plants have larger capital costs in terms of interest charges and depreciation. These need to be spread over a greater volume of output. 'Economies of scale' is still a popular phrase despite a great deal of evidence to indicate that 'medium'-sized firms are frequently more efficient and profitable than 'large' firms.

An economy of large-scale production simply means that the average cost of production per unit of output falls as the level of output produced by additional inputs of all factors of production together is increased. The costs may fall because of technical factors derived from the size of plant and equipment. For example, a 200 000-tonne oil tanker does not cost twice as much to build and operate as two 100 000-tonne tankers. A larger internal market, such as the Six, or the present Twelve, obviously increases the potential for obtaining technical economies of scale. There is, however, a risk of diseconomies arising from having inflexible levels of output. This occurred with steel production where too many extremely large plants were built at a time when the demand was dropping. This happened because of recession and the growth of demand for substitutes for steel. These substitutes are mainly plastics and aluminium alloys, or, in the case of office machinery or cash registers, electronic chips.

The other two main types of economy of scale which were most relevant to those viewing the early development of the EEC were those normally called 'commercial' economies and 'marketing' economies. Commercial economies refer to those reductions in costs derived from being able to buy raw materials and components in bulk at cheaper prices per unit. These apply most obviously in the types of large-scale retailing pioneered by Tesco, Sainsbury and Marks & Spencer, and the equivalents such as Aldi, LeClerc and Intermarché in other countries. They also apply to large-scale manufacturers of domestic consumer durable goods such as cars and white goods. 'Marketing economies', which have been used to justify all sorts of mergers between firms producing unconnected products, derive from reductions in costs per unit in the selling, distribution and advertising of products and services. Certain volumes of sales are usually necessary before national advertising, particularly on television, is worthwhile. These economies partly explain the trend towards 'product ranges', company 'logos', company own brands and international firms, or multinationals. Economists and entrepreneurs saw endless scope for these types of economies in scale within the Six, particularly as the growth of incomes and demand was very high.

The pursuit of economies of scale went hand in hand with attempts to spread the risks of enterprise. This partly explains the growth of conglomerates and diversifying mergers since 1970 although the late 1980s saw a contrary trend towards the break-up of some conglomerates. The Community's competition and monopoly control policies have had little impact here.

There are other types of economies of scale in the usual classifications. In one of these, 'financial economies', many people in the United Kingdom felt that they had a great deal to teach the Europeans. This sense of superiority, which has turned out to be largely unfounded, was based upon the different historical experience of the United Kingdom and most European countries in the financial crash of 1931 and the great depression generally. It was also based upon the then dominant international role of the City of London in world financial and capital markets, and sterling in the 'sterling area'. This dominance in the 1950s (except over New York) has disappeared as the relative isolation of markets has vanished with the advent of advanced telecommunications. It has also succumbed to the effects of stronger economic growth in Japan and West Germany. Moreover, the supposed superiority of the United Kingdom banking system over the continental system is now regarded as a source of relative weakness. In the 1930s continental banks suffered very badly because they were directly concerned with the ownership of shares in large, and small, companies. Their fortunes were entwined and, as the depression bit deeply, the companies collapsed and brought down the banks. In the United Kingdom, the system of branch banking and the avoidance of direct investment in company equities enabled United Kingdom banks to survive. They preferred purchases of government stock (gilt-edged investment) and secured loans to industry to the purchase of stock in companies. This tradition has persisted and some people regard it as a major cause of the alleged failure of the City of London to provide risk capital to British entrepreneurs. The continental system encourages a longer-term view of the return on capital than the British which tends towards an extremely short-run view. There is also a different attitude to dividends. United Kingdom firms are reluctant to cut dividends when profits fall because of pressure from financial institutions and because it makes them more vulnerable to takeover bids. They often use reserves to maintain dividends instead of using them for new investment to prepare for the end of the recession.

It was, therefore, the 'holy grail' of economies of scale which acted as a major lure to British business and politicians in the early 1960s as they saw the Six successfully building their customs unions and achieving faster economic growth than the United Kingdom.

The economic case for the United Kingdom joining the EEC was strongly based on the idea that British industry could compete effectively against continental firms in the larger market, especially with the backing of a large overseas market as well. It was also thought, though not as frequently expressed, that the new competition would give British industry a much-needed jolt and force it to adopt a more cost-conscious and consumer-oriented approach. (There were grave doubts about the effects on United Kingdom agriculture. These will be discussed in Chapter 5.) The economic case for entry seemed strong although some prescient folk realised that the United Kingdom might suffer in its internal markets from fierce competition from some already more efficient continental producers. These doubters' fears were borne out in the 1970s and 1980s in the case, for example, of motor vehicle manufacture. Some long-sighted folk worried that the United Kingdom might become a mere periphery of an industrial and commercial economic core centred between France and Germany and spilling over into Belgium and The Netherlands. Improvements in road transport, containerisation, specialised vehicles, refrigerated lorries and higher average speeds and loads, favour the drift to location in larger markets. 'Larger' here means in terms of numbers of people and in terms of average incomes per head.

These references to the United Kingdom case were only partially applicable to the other applicants for entry, Denmark and Ireland. (Norway, which had applied, withdrew after a referendum produced a strong vote against membership. Norwegians took the view that their fishing industry would suffer from membership. They also expected to be independent as a result of their newly developing oil and gas reserves.) Ireland and Denmark both had important agricultural sectors which stood to benefit from membership. Moreover, the Irish economy was so heavily dependent on that of the United Kingdom that it could not stand alone if Britain joined.

The economic case for joining was gradually accepted, although many thought a similar case could be made, in the case of Britain, for staying with the European Free Trade Association (EFTA) and the Commonwealth and the North Atlantic link. There was, however, a major change in British political attitudes in the 1950s and 1960s arising from the decline of the Empire with the granting of independence to colonies. An understanding of this background is useful if the later events leading to the Single European Act in 1986 and to the Union Treaty of 1992 are to be comprehended.

Changing Political Attitudes in the United Kingdom

The emphasis of victory over Germany and Japan in 1945 after six weary years of war disguised for a time the reality of the United Kingdom's position in global politics. Politicians of all complexions were slow to grasp the new conditions of world dominance by the USA and USSR. For a time all efforts were concentrated on the reconstruction of a distorted and investment-starved industrial structure from war production to peaceful applications. Demobilisation and redistribution of labour were at the forefront of everyone's mind. Rationing intensified despite the peace, and a fuel shortage persisted. Power cuts were an accepted winter occurrence until the early 1960s as demand outstripped supply. Efforts were made by all the colonial powers, including the United Kingdom, to restore their prewar colonial possessions. From these efforts, which were only temporarily successful, stemmed the Vietnam War and the Algerian conflicts as the French colonial yoke was resisted. Britain, for its part, faced a succession of colonial struggles, all of which ended in independence for the colony. To many British people, however, the full knowledge of the 'end of empire' only came with the débâcle of the Suez Canal in 1956. This humiliation in late 1956 was a watershed in British political thinking. The Prime Minister Anthony Eden resigned, ostensibly through ill health, and was succeeded in January 1957 by Harold Macmillan.

A Slow Change in the United Kingdom's Political Orientation

A conflict developed in the late 1950s and early 1960s between those who saw Britain's future in the European context and those who saw it in an international, outward-looking role rooted in the Commonwealth and transatlantic special relationship. Some saw the European Economic Community as a narrow, self-seeking, inward-looking customs union. The issue caused splits within the parties. The anti-Common Market faction tended to attract supporters from the left and the right of British politics. They were concerned with parliamentary sovereignty, with the alleged bureaucracy of the Community and with the effects on food prices and agriculture. The impact on the poorer members of the Commonwealth and on New Zealand, which relied heavily on the United Kingdom market for its lamb sales, caused great concern. The issue of the Commonwealth Sugar Agreement loomed large, as did the future of the Commonwealth Preference system which favoured imports from, and exports to, ex-colonies. The pro-Common Market factions extolled the economies of scale available in a larger market. They welcomed what they thought would be a breath of competitive fresh air throughout British industry. They were forerunners of the Thatcherite vision of a free market, except of course, that a more detailed study revealed the Community to be a strongly regulated market with a weak anti-monopoly policy and a powerful interventionist philosophy.

As the United Kingdom shifted its role away from colonialism, France, Belgium and The Netherlands were also involved in disengagement from their colonial past. General de Gaulle returned to power in France in 1958, in the wake of the political chaos caused by the Algerian War. He replaced the Fourth Republic with a new constitution. Against powerful and violent opposition he settled the

North African crisis. An independent Algerian state was recognised in 1962. In 1960, Belgium withdrew from the Congo. This led to a long-drawn-out, and bloody, civil war together with foreign intervention, before the new nations were firmly established. The Netherlands withdrew from most of their overseas possessions in the period 1949–54. France subsequently withdrew from the southern Saharan and West African states, although she has retained a powerful political and military presence in some of the countries. The rise to power of General de Gaulle, with his strongly nationalistic attitudes, was of great significance in delaying the United Kingdom's entry into the Economic Community.

De Gaulle cultivated personal aloofness and obviously believed that 'familiarity breeds contempt'. He carried this personal attitude over into his political life in attempting to restore French pride and self-esteem by an aggressively independent stance. He created a separate French nuclear strike force and withdrew from operational participation in NATO. De Gaulle wanted a restoration of the gold standard for settlement of international debts and pursued a pro-gold between nations international monetary system. He even issued silver coins, most of which quickly disappeared from circulation. In addition he was suspicious of Anglo-American relations and treated the United Kingdom's avowed aspiration to be 'European' with scepticism. There was much reference to 'perfidious Albion'.

In October 1961, the United Kingdom made its first formal application to join the EEC. Negotiations took place which ended in January 1963 when de Gaulle exercised his personal veto, on behalf of France, against Britain's application for membership. His remarks about the United Kingdom not being truly European were a reflection of his intense anger at the Nassau Agreement of December 1962 between Macmillan and President Kennedy. This agreement was for the USA to supply missiles for British nuclear submarines, that is the Polaris system. Ironically Macmillan had been forced into the Nassau Agreement by the failure of a proposed independent British nuclear weapons delivery system. The French veto was a severe blow to Macmillan and it also blocked the applications of Denmark, Norway and Ireland.

Macmillan resigned because of ill health in October 1963 and was succeeded by his Foreign Secretary, the Earl of Home, who renounced his peerage in order to become an MP. Home was a foreign affairs expert and was, self-confessedly, not an economist. His government was narrowly defeated by Labour, under Harold Wilson, in October 1964. Wilson called another election in March 1966 and received a greatly enlarged majority. The whole course of his government was dominated by balance-of-payments problems and the necessity of maintaining the pound at its fixed level. The reader might well ask how this differed from the problems of the early 1990s arising from membership of the Exchange Rate Mechanism with its relatively fixed rates against the German mark and other European currencies. Economic growth was slow and attempts at national planning quickly foundered. Envious eyes were cast on the successful French system of indicative planning and at the higher rates of growth and lower inflation rates of the EEC. Thus despite strong ideological objections from the left wing of the Labour Party, Wilson applied for the United Kingdom to join the Community in 1967. This second application of the United Kingdom, together with those of Denmark, Norway and Ireland, was again rejected by de Gaulle in 1967. The way was blocked until de Gaulle resigned his office in April 1969 after badly misjudging the mood of the French people over a referendum to modify the constitution.

EFTA

There was a nine-month gap between the signing of the Treaties of Rome in March 1957 and their coming into force on 1 January 1958. The United Kingdom used this period to try to establish a different type of organisation, a European Free Trade Association, among the seventeen members of the OEEC. Such a market would be free from tariffs and trade barriers between members but would allow each country to set its own trade conditions with non-members. This would combine the benefits of a partial customs union with the advantage of no loss of sovereignty to the member. It was a 'partial' customs union because it did not have a common external tariff. The system appealed to countries which favoured political neutrality and to the United Kingdom which had obligations to its Commonwealth friends. It did not, however satisfy the basic desire of the six signatories of the Rome treaties because they wanted deeper political involvement and commitment, with a view to obviating any future European war. France was strongly opposed to the British initiative and ended discussions in November 1958. When EFTA was formed by the Stockholm Convention of January 1960, its membership was the United Kingdom, Austria, Denmark, Norway, Portugal, Sweden and Switzerland. Iceland became a full member in March 1970. Finland became an associate member in June 1961 and a full member in 1985. EFTA became operational in May 1960. Over the years its membership has fluctuated as countries joined and/or left to join the EEC instead. The 1992 membership was Austria, Finland, Iceland, Norway, Sweden, Switzerland and Liechtenstein. Close working agreements between the Community and EFTA were developed from 1972 in the form of Free Trade Agreements (FTAs). These required revision as the completion of the single European market, aimed at January 1993, drew closer. The result of the revision was the agreement between the European Community and EFTA in October 1991 to create the European Economic Area (EEA) which is discussed below. See page 57.

Britain quickly realised that EFTA would not satisfy its economic and political needs in a changing world. Its markets were not large enough for sufficient economies of scale to be derived, compared with the EEC markets. More importantly, it did not provide sufficient opportunity for the United Kingdom to exercise its political weight. The United Kingdom was in danger of becoming a politically isolated off-shore island near the continent of Europe. It is ironic that, at the negotiations at Maastricht in 1991 leading to the Union Treaty, the policies of opting out of the Social Chapter and the monetary union sections of the treaty create the risk of producing exactly that isolation which was once feared and avoided. An alternative future was as an undeclared state of the American Union, dependent on the USA economically and politically. The so-called 'special relationship' between the United Kingdom and the United States had never been one of equals but no one wanted it to degenerate into an overtly master–vassal relationship.

EFTA is very different in operation from the European Community. It is run by weekly meetings of officials and meetings of ministers two or three times a year. There are no powers devolved by each country on a central organisation so there is nothing supranational about it. It has been successful in abolishing almost all import duties on industrial goods between members and has generally harmonised its external tariffs with those of the EC. It was expected that the departure of the United Kingdom on joining the EC would see the end of EFTA but that did not happen.

The United Kingdom's Successful Application

Soon after the fall of de Gaulle in April 1969, his successor, President Pompidou, made it clear that his government would not object in principle to the entry of Britain and the other applicants provided that enlargement would strengthen rather than weaken the Community. In December 1969, a summit was held at The Hague. This agreed to major alterations in the way that the Community was to be financed and developed; it also agreed to prepare for negotiations on its enlargement. In May 1970, the Labour government announced that it would restart negotiations as soon as possible. There was a change of government in June 1970 and the Conservative government under Mr Heath began negotiations at the end of June. The continuity of policy irrespective of governing party is shown clearly by the fact that the negotiations were on the lines prepared by the Labour government. Within a year the negotiations were complete except on the issue of fisheries.

There was no United Kingdom referendum on entry to the EEC. In the 1960s and early 1970s the only referendums held were on whether Welsh public houses should open on the Sabbath! Although there was eventually a referendum in June 1975 called by the Labour government on whether the United Kingdom should *remain* in the Community, the original entry was by decision of the House of Commons. In May 1967 the Labour government had announced its decision to apply for membership. There was a three-day debate which ended in a vote in favour of the application of 488 to 62. This majority of 426 is one of the largest ever majorities of the House of Commons in peacetime. This fact has tended to be obscured over the years as more and more politicians have found it expedient to side with the critics of the development of the Community. Those who objected at the time did so on grounds of fear for national or parliamentary sovereignty, of fears for the Commonwealth relationship, or on sectional interest grounds related to agriculture or fishing. They were drawn from both extremes of the political spectrum.

When it was decided to reapply for membership in 1970 a new White Paper, *Britain and the European Communities: An Economic Assessment* (Cmnd 4289), was published in February 1970. This updated the figures of likely costs and benefits of membership, concluding that the economic balance was a fine one and that in the short term there would be some economic disadvantages. The range of figures given for possible balance-of-payments changes, agricultural expenditure changes and alterations in capital movements was very wide. The statisticians had to make many assumptions about such variables as growth rates, patterns of trade and agricultural prices. In general, the conclusion was that it was the long-term economic advantages and, even more, the political advantages, which would prove decisive. In the background was the knowledge that it was impossible to calculate the full economic consequences of *not* entering the European Community: these consequences were in terms both of being excluded from and being in competition with an increasingly integrated European economy, on our doorstep, several times the size of our own and probably faster growing. It was also impossible to quantify the so-called 'dynamic' effects resulting from membership of a much larger and faster-growing market. The sorts of figures which had a powerful persuasive effect were comparative growth figures like those in Tables 3.1 and 3.2.

The figures were presented in a more readily understood form in a nationally distributed booklet, *Britain and Europe*, which explained the government's White Paper *The United Kingdom and the European Communities* (Cmnd 4715) as in Table 3.2.

The Entry Terms

The terms negotiated for entry on almost all major points were published in a White Paper in July 1971. In October 1971, the House of Commons voted by 356 to 244 in favour of joining the EEC on these terms. In January 1972, the Treaty of Accession was signed and the resulting European Communities Act received the royal assent in October 1972, after a fairly stormy passage through Parliament.

The agreement fixed a transitional period of five years from the start of Britain's membership on 1 January 1973 to 31 December 1977. In that period all tariffs between Britain and the Six were to be abolished in five equal stages, so that within three years of entry there would be virtually free access to the European market for British exporters.

Agriculture required very detailed terms involving a gradual increase in market prices so that direct subsidy payment to farmers (in the form of deficiency payments) could be phased out. The

TABLE 3.1
Growth of GNP per Head at 1963 Market Prices, 1958–67

EEC countries	Average annual % increase	EFTA countries	
West Germany	3.7	United Kingdom	2.5
France	3.9	Sweden	3.8
Italy	4.8	Norway	4.0
Belgium	3.8	Denmark	4.2
Luxembourg	n.a.	Austria	3.7
Netherlands	3.7	Switzerland	3.1
		Portugal	5.2
Average all EEC countries	4.0*	Average all EFTA countries	3.0*

* At 1963 exchange rates.

SOURCE *Britain and the European Communities: An Economic Assessment,* Cmnd 4289 (London: HMSO, 1970).

TABLE 3.2
Increase in Average Income per Employed Person in Real Terms, 1958–69

Italy	> > > > > > > > > > > > > > > > >92%
France	> > > > > > > > > > > > > > >77%
Netherlands	> > > > > > > > > > > > > >74%
West Germany	> > > > > > > > > > > > > >72%
Belgium	> > > > > > > > > > >52%
Britain	> > > > > > > > >39%
Average EEC	> > > > > > > > > > > > >76%

government kept the power to help groups such as hill farmers and to retain the marketing boards. It was anticipated that agricultural output would increase by about 8 per cent over the transitional five years as home production was substituted for imports. A special agreement was made so that New Zealand could continue to have access to the British market for at least 75 per cent of its current exports of butter and cheese to Europe beyond the end of the transitional period. Similarly, the United Kingdom retained its obligations under the Commonwealth Sugar Agreement to buy agreed quantities of sugar from existing sources until 1974 and to protect the relationship thereafter. This was to quell well-substantiated fears that Caribbean cane-producing countries would suffer if the United Kingdom were forced to buy European beet sugar.

The question of budget contributions was resolved by fixing the British part of the total budget as a gradually rising percentage from 8.64 per cent in 1973 to 18.92 per cent in 1977.

There were additional agreements on the free movement of labour, regional development, the Coal and Steel Community, and Euratom. In most cases the United Kingdom accepted existing practices without reservation, although Northern Ireland was excluded from free movement of labour for five years. Commonwealth countries in Africa, the Indian Ocean, the Pacific and the Caribbean were offered 'association' with the EEC in order to protect access for their exports to the Community. Australia and Canada were not thought to require any special arrangements.

Renegotiation and the Referendum

A significant number of important persons and groups within the Labour Party were against the United Kingdom's membership of the EEC. This opposition went so far as to prevent any Labour Party representatives going to the European Parliament (until July 1975). As a result of this pressure the party manifesto at the February 1974 general election promised that the electorate should have the opportunity of deciding on whether Britain should stay as a member or not. The new Labour government under Wilson, therefore, began talks in April 1974 for renegotiation of the terms of membership. These were concluded in March 1975 and Parliament endorsed the terms of the agreement on a free vote by 396 votes to 170 in early April.

This was a rather confusing period politically and indicates the extent to which the European Community concept split the parties. Mrs Thatcher became Leader of the Opposition in February 1975 after the fall of Mr Heath who was the great champion of membership and who, according to his critics, was willing to accept any terms, however harsh, for entry. The Prime Minister, Mr Wilson, was having trouble within his party and had to accept the idea of giving his Cabinet colleagues a 'licence to differ' instead of insisting on the traditional doctrine of collective responsibility. As a result, on the free vote in the House of Commons, the 396 votes in favour of remaining in the EEC consisted of 249 Conservatives, 135 Labour and 12 Liberals. The 170 votes against were 144 Labour, 7 Conservative, 11 Scottish Nationalist, 6 Ulster Unionist and 2 Plaid Cymru. No fewer than seven Labour Cabinet ministers voted against together with 30 other ministers.

The Labour Party responded to this Commons vote by calling a special Labour Party Conference at the end of April. This approved a recommendation from the National Executive Committee that Britain should leave the EEC. The party was not happy with the renegotiated terms: the voting was 3 724 000 to 1 986 000. A few days earlier, the TUC had adopted a document opposing the United Kingdom's continued membership, although individual unions were left free to express different opinions.

The solution for the government was to lie in the promised referendum. This took place on 5 June 1975. Voters had to vote 'yes' or 'no' to the question 'Do you think that the United Kingdom should stay in the European Community (the Common Market)?' The overall result was a 64.5 per cent vote of 'yes' but there were significant regional differences as can be seen in Table 3.3.

TABLE 3.3
The Referendum of June 1975

	% Turnout	% 'Yes'
England	64.6	68.7
Wales	66.7	64.8
Scotland	61.7	58.4
Northern Ireland	47.4	52.1
United Kingdom	64.5	67.2

Only the Shetland Isles (56.3% 'No') and the Western Isles (70.5% 'No') voted against.

The resounding and unequivocal 'yes' vote cleared the air and national energies could now be devoted to making Britain's membership work to the nation's greatest benefit. Despite this, membership of the Community was often made a scapegoat for problems which were already deeply ingrained in Britain's industrial and social structures. The early years of transitional membership coincided with rapidly rising unemployment, the swift decline of the manufacturing industry, poor industrial relations, international inflation and recession, and uncertainty in politics. Inevitably, the Common Market was thought by some to exacerbate these problems. The Labour Party, for some years, promised withdrawal from the Community if it were re-elected to government. In 1983, however, it modified this stance and made withdrawal 'an option' rather than a certainty if it should be returned to power. The Conservative Party, for its part, concentrated upon altering the budgetary imbalance and on pursuing an aggressively self-interested national policy. General de Gaulle might very well have admired Mrs Thatcher's approach although there often seemed to be a major discrepancy between what was agreed between the members and what the British public was told had been achieved. In December 1979, Mrs Thatcher, at the Dublin summit meeting, asked for 'Britain's money back'. There was a short-term palliative agreement in 1980 but it was not until the Fontainebleau agreement in June 1984 that there was a full settlement of the United Kingdom's grievance (see Chapter 9). The figures in Table 3.4 support the validity of the sense of injustice.

The Enlargement of the Community

The accession of the United Kingdom, Denmark and Ireland was agreed in January 1972 and took effect on 1 January 1973. The next addition to the Community occurred when Greece acceded in May 1979 with effect from 1 January 1981. There was then a five-year gap involving complex negotiations before Spain and Portugal acceded in June 1985 and began active membership on 1 January 1986. In all three cases one of the factors taken into account by the existing members was the welcome return of the applicant to full democratic forms of government after periods of authoritarian rule. The terms of entry included special provisions for the transition periods as their economies adjusted to the full force of competition from the established members. Topics of particular concern were agriculture, fishing quotas, vegetables, fruit, and wine production.

The accession of these three countries marked a profound change in the nature of the Community although the full effects have not yet

TABLE 3.4
**The Basis for the United Kingdom's Grievance: United Kingdom's
Contributions and Receipts from the Community Budget (£ millions)**

	Gross Contributions	Receipts	Net Contributions
1973	181	79	102
1974	181	150	31
1975	342	398	− 56
1976	463	296	167
1977	737	368	368
1978	1348	544	804
1979	1606	659	947
1980	1767	1061	710
1981	2174	1777	997
1982	2863	2257	606
1983*	3120	2473	647

* Estimates.

SOURCE *The Government Expenditure Plans, 1977–78 to 1982–83*, Cmnd 7439 (London: HMSO, 1984), quoted in Butler, D. E., *British Political Facts, 1980–85*, 6th edn (London: Macmillan, 1986).

been absorbed. Until then, with the exception of southern Italy, the Community had been essentially a Northern European institution of a predominantly industrial character, albeit with a large agricultural sector in certain countries. Its average income per head and standards of living had been high. Well-established democratic forms of government were accompanied by good standards of social provision and effective bureaucracies and financial systems. The three newcomers presented problems of redistribution of income through the budget from North to South, of absorption of higher and more expensive standards of social care and employment conditions, and of low-wage competition. Remarkable progress has been made in overcoming these problems since 1981 although there is much still to be achieved before an acceptable level of 'cohesion' is achieved. The Treaty of Union agreed at Maastricht in 1991 was made possible, in part, by the acceptance by the richer northern members of the need to set up a 'cohesion' fund to finance the raising of standards in the poorer southern members. In other words, they had to receive promises of more money from regional and social funds, as well as from the new cohesion funds required to achieve monetary union, before they would agree to the new treaty on economic and monetary union and to progress on political union. The EFTA countries similarly will have to contribute cohesion funds as part of the price of forming the European Economic Area.

The experience of absorbing the three new members will be extremely useful in the future when countries such as Sweden, Austria, Finland, Switzerland and some of the other members of EFTA join the Community. It was also these experiences which helped to deter the Community from accepting the idea that there should be a 'big bang' increase in membership with all the EFTA members and countries such as Hungary, Czechoslovakia, Poland, and Yugoslavia (before its civil war) joining at once.

The Treaty of Rome says that an application to join the Community from any *European* country must be considered by the Council of Ministers after it has asked the advice of the Commission. There must then be a unanimous vote for the application to succeed and it has been this need for unanimity that has prevented Turkey, which applied for membership in 1987, from joining. Turkey's request presented the Community with a problem in that its average income per head is well below that of the poorest members' least prosperous areas, and it gave rise to an embarrassing debate as to whether Turkey was European. Turkey's application was effectively vetoed by Greece which has a long-standing dispute with Turkey over the invasion and partition of Cyprus. As a result decision on the application has been postponed into the indefinite future, presumably until the resolution of the dispute. In the meantime Turkey's associate status granted in 1962 has been reaffirmed and improved, in 1980, to make its trade with the Community easier. An additional complication in the issue has been Turkey's membership of NATO, and, more recently, its cooperation with the United Nations over the Gulf crisis in the war against Iraq. Both have added weight to its claim for membership of the Community. The main bone of contention, Cyprus, is also intent on joining the Community and was granted entry in 1987 to what will become a full customs union with the Community by the end of the century. Its acceptance as a member depends on the settlement of the dispute between Turkey and Greece. Malta, which was granted an association agreement in 1976, has also indicated that it intends to apply for membership.

The European Economic Area

In January 1989 Jacques Delors, President of the Commission, initiated discussions between the European Community and the European Free Trade Association (EFTA) with a view to greater integration. His motive was mainly to provide an alternative to full membership applications to the Community by the seven members of EFTA. He also aimed at creating a pause whilst the process of deepening and strengthening the institutions of the EC was completed. The formal negotiations began in June 1990 and sufficient progress was made for the optimists to expect an agreement to be initialled in June 1991, but the final problems were not resolved until 22 October 1991. The agreement, and the EFTA–EC Treaty resulting from it, will need to be ratified by national parliaments and the European Parliament. It will come into force in January 1993, at the same time as the single market. The agreement will be reviewed every two years.

The EEA consists of the twelve European Community countries and the seven EFTA members, Austria, Finland, Iceland, Liechtenstein, Norway, Sweden and Switzerland. The EFTA nations will accept about 12 000 pages of Community legislation which is known as the *acquis communautaire*. They will also accept any new Community laws that are relevant and will be consulted in their formulation, although they will not have voting rights or a veto. The EEA is not a customs union like the Community because there will still be controls, though not taxes, at EC borders for goods coming from the EFTA countries.

The EEA will be a tariff-free zone for industrial goods and for some processed agricultural products. Non-tariff and technical barriers to trade will be removed along the same lines as in the single market legislation. The Common Agricultural Policy will not apply to the EFTA countries and they will continue with their own individual policies in respect of trade quotas or tariffs on non-EEA countries' goods. The two groups must agree on a system for classifying which goods are to be regarded as originating within the EEA, a task which is not as easy as it might appear at first glance if experience with the long-drawn-out row over Japanese cars assembled in the United Kingdom is anything to go by. Special arrangements will persist for fish, food, energy and coal and steel.

The Common Fisheries Policy will not apply to the EFTA countries although the agreement includes improved access for

Icelandic cod and haddock into the Community together with a general reduction of 70 per cent in the levy on EFTA fish products entering the Twelve. Norway will allow Spain, Portugal and Ireland, who have been excluded from Norwegian waters, to fish 6000 tonnes of cod from its waters, and will double the present quota allowed to United Kingdom fishermen. Foreign investment in the Norwegian and Icelandic fishing industries will not be allowed, an arrangement that will not be popular in the United Kingdom industry where some UK quotas have been expropriated by Spanish boats being registered in the United Kingdom. The 1988 Merchant Shipping Act that was intended to restrain this practice was declared illegal under Community law by the European Court in July 1991.

One of the most important effects of the agreement will result from the inclusion of services in the free trade category. Beforehand, the agreements between EFTA and the Community covered only goods, and the service sectors were highly protected. Under the new arrangements any national of the EEA countries will be able to provide financial, commercial or professional services throughout the nineteen countries. Many of the restrictions on capital flows will also disappear but some controls will remain on investment in real estate and some direct investment in the EFTA countries.

Flanking Policies

The creation of the EEA has extended the use of Eurojargon. A 'flanking' policy is one which *accompanies* other policies. In the case of the EEA the flanking policies will be a strengthening of cooperation in the areas of the environment, education, training and youth, research and technological development, small and medium-sized enterprises, and statistics. There are indications from the negotiations leading up to the creation of the EEA that the EFTA countries want a stronger approach in some of these areas, particularly the environment. They want to go beyond what is stated in the Treaty of Rome and aim for sustainable development. They also want the principle of precautionary action to prevent damage to the environment to be embodied into policies and actions as they are developed.

Although the EEA will commence on 1 January 1993, some of the flanking measures will be delayed. For example, the EFTA members will not participate fully in the education, training and youth programmes until 1995 since the Community wants a transition period to occur. The area of social policy is very complex but the EFTA countries will incorporate Community laws into their rules in areas such as health and safety at work, workers' rights and labour law, the equal treatment of men and women, and action for the elderly. The cooperation is intended to extend what is called the 'social dialogue' between management and workers. Some areas are explicitly excluded. These include health, including nutrition, and programmes dealing with Aids and cancer. The EFTA states have had a declaration included in the treaty stating their wish to contribute actively to the social dimension of the EEA as embodied in the Community Charter of Fundamental Social Rights for Workers (see page 17). The United Kingdom, which alone refused to sign this Charter in 1990, and also opted out of the Social Chapter at the Maastricht decisions on the new Union Treaty in 1991, will be even more isolated once the EEA becomes effective.

Flanking policies will be accompanied by what are called 'horizontal' policies, which means the broadening of cooperation into new areas such as company law, information services, social policy, consumer policy, tourism, the audio-visual sector, and civil protection. Both flanking and horizontal policies come under what is called 'mixed competence', that is the main responsibility remains with the individual member state and not with the institutions of the Community. The principle of subsidiarity also applies, that is, an action should only be undertaken at Community level if it cannot be done better at national level.

The Cost of the Agreement

Entry to the benefits of an enormous free trade area is not free and the EFTA countries have had to pay a high price for the agreement. The main price is through their acceptance of the proposal that they should establish and manage a fund to help the development of some of the less favoured regions within some countries of the European Community, that is, Northern Ireland, Greece, Ireland, Spain and Portugal. This is a version of the so-called 'cohesion' fund established by the richer members of the Community at Maastricht in 1991 to persuade its poorer members to accept monetary union and other aspects of the Union Treaty. In the case of the EEA they will put 500 million ECU into the fund for grants over five years, and make another 1.5 billion ECU available as soft loans over five years.

Another cost will be that of resolving the problem of road transport over the Swiss and Austrian Alps. The Swiss have very severe restrictions on lorries in order to protect their environment and way of life. Greece, which relies very heavily on road links, used its bargaining power to force an agreement which will maintain its competitive position. The solution will also benefit Switzerland and Austria in the long run and is extremely impressive in its farsightedness and vision. The Swiss are going to invest about 24 billion Swiss francs in building two tunnels under the Gotthard and Loetschberg Passes, and Austria will build a new tunnel under the Brenner Pass. These rail tunnels will take lorries through the Alps and keep them off the roads and will enable Switzerland to keep its 28-tonne limit on lorries and Austria to keep its severe anti-pollution laws. Greece will, in the short term, be given up to a further 2000 transit permits for lorries provided that they are matched by additional rail traffic.

On the Community side there is likely to be a growing demand from the fishing industries of some countries for subsidies to protect them from decline as a result of increased competition from the EFTA states. It will be very hard to separate the effects of the creation of the EEA from those of the recent changes on the Common Fisheries Policy which are aimed at conserving stocks.

Implications of the Creation of the EEA

The statistics speak for themselves to some extent. The nineteen members of the EEA, including some of the richest countries in the world, have a population of 380 million and are responsible for over 40 per cent of world trade. The free trade area will be larger than that of the nineteen because EFTA, for example, has negotiated a free trade agreement with Turkey in October 1991 and is planning further agreements with Hungary, Poland, and Czechoslovakia. It has started discussions with Bulgaria and Romania, and the three Baltic Republics have been invited to ministerial talks on trade. In addition, the Community has numerous agreements with non-member countries on trading conditions for a wide range of items as well as with the Lomé Convention countries. It too is busy negotiating new relationships in Eastern and Central Europe, and, in December

1991, signed an association agreement with Poland, Hungary and Czechoslovakia which will lead to free trade over a period of ten years, with the Community lowering its barriers to industrial imports more quickly than the other three. This type of agreement has been called a 'Europe Agreement' and signals an intention to apply for membership of the Community in the future.

Although some of the members of EFTA such as Sweden, Switzerland, Austria and Finland have applied to join the Community and others are on the brink of applying, there is unlikely to be a reduction in the role of EFTA because of its value as a 'half-way house' for the countries of Central and Eastern Europe in the adaptation of their economies to the free market model on the route to full membership of the European Community. Jacques Delors has already referred to a 30-nation 'Greater Europe'. There has been a bitter debate about whether to deepen the Community before widening it. Membership of EFTA prior to a full membership of the European Community could prove a useful compromise route.

The Institutions of the EEA

No sooner have we learned to cope with the names and functions of the institutions of the European Community than the EEA is created and we have to comprehend a new set of initials, functions and relationships. Apart from seeing people referred to as 'Eftans' we shall have to become used to 'The EEA Council', which will comprise ministers from the nineteen states and a representative from the European Commission. Its job will be to provide a political oversight to the EEA, and not to legislate. Under the EEA Council, a Joint Committee of officials will meet roughly monthly to take care of the practical running of the agreement. The Joint Committee will be able to make decisions by consensus and will have the important role of settling disputes. The original Treaty proposed to create an independent EEA Court of Justice from five judges of the European Court of Justice and three judges from EFTA. Its decisions would be binding. In addition EFTA will set up a body to police the agreement on its own side and the European Commission will exercise the surveillance role in the Community.

The EEA Treaty had to be vetted by the European Court of Justice and, in December 1991, the whole timetable for its adoption was put in jeopardy by the Court's ruling that the proposed EEA Court of Justice and its system of judicial supervision were incompatible with the Treaty of Rome. The judgment meant that parts of the EEA Treaty had to be renegotiated and the proposed EEA Court of Justice was abandoned. Instead there will be a new EFTA Court. Decisions of the EEA Joint Committee must not be contrary to rulings of the European Court of Justice. The EEA agreement was signed in May 1992 and must be submitted to the 19 national parliaments and to the European Parliament for ratification. The EEA becomes effective on 1 January 1993.

Governing the 4 One Europe

This chapter will be better understood if the details of the main channels of decision-making in the Community, as outlined in Chapter 1 under the heading 'Decision-Making in the Community' are consulted. Figure 4.1 summarises these relationships.

Such Figures as 4.1 give only a broad impression of where decisions are actually made. Ministers are advised by their civil servants. As a result, departmental policy refined over time is frequently more powerful than an individual minister who may have only a short stay in office. The officials of the Commission are also career civil servants who have a profound long-term effect on Commission policy. The Commissioners usually serve for four years and some serve more than one term. They may, however, switch portfolios because these are reshuffled every four years (until 1993 when it will be every five years). A very important role in decision-making is played by a committee called COREPER, the Committee of Permanent Representatives, which comprises the Ambassadors to the Community and their advisers and is the vital link between member governments and the Community. What may be said definitively is that no decision can be finally reached except by the Council of Ministers and how they reach that decision and whether they are sometimes a 'rubber stamp' depends on their personalities, the detail of the proposals and political factors.

FIGURE 4.1
How a Decision Is Taken in the European Community

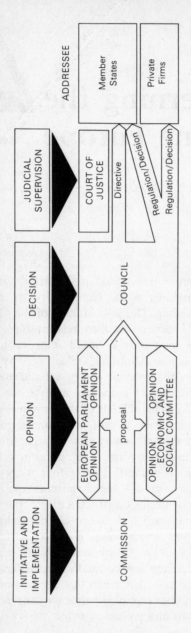

SOURCE Eurostat, *Europe in Figures* (Luxembourg: Office for Official Publications of the European Communities, 1988).

Unanimous or Majority Decisions?

The Treaty of Rome required decisions to be made unanimously in the Council of Ministers. This gave each nation an effective veto. The system which was intended to protect a nation's vital self-interest (as seen by itself) became less sensible as the Community was enlarged. The Single European Act which was signed in 1986 and came into force in July 1987 therefore included the provision for a qualified majority decision. This applies to measures which have as their object the establishment and functioning of the internal market and prevents delays imposed by a single reluctant member. The qualified majority system does not apply to every area of Community decision-making; the Council must remain unanimous when dealing with revenue, taxation and social policy. Majority voting does apply to transport, the environment and other matters related to the establishment of the internal market. The details of the qualified majority system in the Council of Ministers are shown in Table 4.1 and the proposed changes under the Union Treaty are discussed in Chapter 9.

TABLE 4.1
Qualified Majority Voting

West Germany	10
France	10
Italy	10
UK	10
Spain	8
Belgium	5
Greece	5
Netherlands	5
Portugal	5
Denmark	3
Ireland	3
Luxembourg	2
TOTAL	76
Qualified majority	54

These weighted voting powers enable a single important state to be outvoted but enable two large states together to prevent policies being implemented against their wills. The system prevents total obstructionism by one state but encourages dealing between nations to modify or promote policies.

The success of the qualified majority system of voting in the Council of Ministers has given rise to support for its extension to other decision-making areas and the draft treaties on European political union drawn up by Luxembourg in June 1991, and by The Netherlands in September 1991, contained provision for such an extension. This, combined with the proposals to reinforce the powers of the European Parliament, gave rise to a bitter dispute leading up to the meeting at Maastricht in December 1991 to agree the new Treaty on Political Union. The United Kingdom indicated that it would use its veto to prevent any extension of majority voting into foreign affairs or defence matters. The two draft treaties differed in the extent to which they would increase the powers of the European Parliament and the areas of application of majority voting. The Netherlands version, which was rejected in favour of a reconsideration of the Luxembourg proposal, was firmer in its intention to strengthen the democratic element of the Community, especially the Parliament. The Union Treaty adopted a 'negative assent' procedure which may, depending on how it is used, strengthen the Parliament. The details are discussed in Chapter 9 in the section on democracy.

What is the Problem of National Sovereignty?

Each nation, because it is an internationally recognised separate entity, has institutions which constitutionally have the power to make decisions on its behalf. This power of decision-making may be called sovereignty. Most nations have written constitutions and it is clearly laid out in them which bodies make laws and which court can vet those laws constitutionally. All nations at some time have chosen to subjugate this power of decision-making to some form of international agreement such as the Universal Declaration of Human Rights, or the European Convention on Human Rights, or the Geneva Convention on behaviour in war. Theoretically they retain the right to withdraw their agreement thus retaining their national sovereignty. In practice, however, such a withdrawal would be politically unthinkable in normal circumstances. This does not, of course, prevent some regimes ignoring or flagrantly flouting human rights. Yet they all, eventually, are subject to the international law to which they have subscribed.

In some forms of agreements some states have gone much further in surrendering the power of decision-making to other bodies. The best examples lie with the various federal governments that exist, as in the United States of America, the Federal Republic of Germany or the pre-1991 Union of Soviet Socialist Republics. In the American federal system the individual states voluntarily surrendered certain decision-making powers to the federal government consisting of President and Congress. The more important of these powers were the making of foreign policy, national defence, the currency and the regulation of interstate commerce. Note that the states gave the right. It is not a system where the federal government has all power and deigns to delegate some to the states. Some people persist in putting forward the view that the future for the European Community lies with a federal system and the suggestion arouses great antagonism.

The draft Treaty on Political Union produced at the Luxembourg summit in June 1991 referred for the first time in a Community document to the Community having 'a federal goal'. This phrase was repeated in the Netherlands version in September 1991 despite the great furore that the wording had caused in the United Kingdom. The row revealed a basic difference in the interpretation of the word 'federal' between the British government and political commentators and those on the continent. The British tend to see federalism in terms of a centralised power taking authority and decision-making away from the individual nations. They see the British Cabinet and Parliament as being neutered. Continentals see federalism as a looser concept with much less sacrifice of local powers. They emphasise the principle of 'subsidiarity' which entails decisions being taken as close as possible to the point of application of a policy, that is at local level where relevant and at Community central level where appropriate. The words 'federal goal' were removed from the Union Treaty and replaced by a phrase that has basically the same meaning, 'the process of creating an ever closer Union among the peoples of Europe'. There is a deep inconsistency in the approach of the United Kingdom government because it has systematically centralised powers since 1979 (a case could be made for earlier dates), and has steadfastly refused to delegate authority to regional bodies in Wales, Scotland or England. On the contrary, it has removed a whole tier of local authority, the Metropolitan Counties and the Greater London

Council, and reduced democratic participation in bodies such as Health Authorities. It has even removed most of the financial independence that local authorities once enjoyed. It has also established direct rule from Whitehall of Northern Ireland. It is on firmer ground when it argues that a federal structure would probably make it harder for the Community to absorb the other nations who are queuing up to join.

There seems to be relatively little support among European governments for federalism except as a long-term objective expressed as a general aim in the preamble to the Political Union Treaty but it is significant that some of them were willing to resist strongly any attempt by the United Kingdom to have the reference removed, although that may have been a negotiating ploy. Germany in particular has been keen to reduce the 'democratic deficit' in the Community and strengthen the European Parliament and extend majority voting in the Council of Ministers. Many would say that there is no real need to quarrel over the word 'federal' because the Community has been developed in a unique way which makes federation unnecessary.

Most of the members of the Community have suffered from foreign occupation, whether from Napoleon or from Prussia and Hitler's Germany. Most have experienced the need for coalition governments and compromise in decision-making. Some are small states which have always existed under the shadow of their larger, more powerful neighbours. Too much dwelling on theoretical ideals of sovereignty is, to them, a waste of time. They all took the pragmatic line which led to the signing of the European Coal and Steel Community (ECSC) Treaty and the Treaties of Rome. In these they set up institutions which made decisions affecting wide areas of their national lives, especially in the economic sphere. They set up the Court of Justice to judge the constitutionality of decisions made by member states, the European Commission, Parliament and Council of Ministers. This 'surrender of sovereignty' was made with open eyes and in frank recognition that the sacrifice of some degree of independence was essential if the great ideal of a Europe without strife and poverty was to be achieved. Opinion in the United Kingdom was not influenced by the same historical factors and was less pragmatic. 'Sovereignty' is still an important issue in some areas of British political debate.

The United Kingdom has no written constitution although certain laws and documents are part of its constitution. There is a great contrast in the United Kingdom between the 'formal' parts of the constitution, Queen and Privy Council for example, and the 'effective' parts, namely the Prime Minister and Cabinet. The role of the United Kingdom Parliament is very debatable nowadays. It has become increasingly 'formal' as its willingness to check the executive has waned and as the ability of the government to control through the whip system has increased. Yet, in the final analysis, Parliament, or the 'Crown in Parliament' to be pedantic, is sovereign. A Parliament can, in theory, undo any Act of any of its predecessors. No Parliament can bind its successors. In practical politics, however, things are different. The United Kingdom government and Parliament are irrevocably committed to those international conventions which are compatible with what all Britons are alleged to hold dear – freedoms of expression, property, religion and so on. They accept international law and generally follow United Nations edicts. The room for genuine independence or sovereignty had been increasingly constrained over the centuries. All this did not prevent a major outcry about 'loss of sovereignty' if the United Kingdom signed the Treaty of Rome and joined the European Community. This outcry was repeated, less forcefully, when the Single European Act was passed in 1986. It seems to be very difficult for some groups of British politicians and journalists to accept the idea that the United Kingdom can give, and has voluntarily given, powers of decision to European institutions in which it may have only one-twelfth of a say. The United Kingdom Parliament is then relegated to a rubber-stamping function. It has failed to create sufficiently good vetting and criticising committees to monitor European legislation so that it might have a more positive role.

The United Kingdom government has, for the sake of an easy life in getting its measures through Parliament, connived at this emasculation of the British legislature. Yet, in the hypocritical way of governments, leading United Kingdom politicians have not hesitated to wave the stick of 'threats to British or parliamentary sovereignty' when their policies are frustrated on the European mainland. There has been a tendency to resort to sovereignty as an excuse for stalling or obstructionism when the eleven other members of the Community have agreed on a policy. Patriotism is said to be 'the last refuge of a scoundrel'. It also could be said that sovereignty is the penultimate refuge.

It is possible to defend the British government's approach in pushing the Single European Act through Parliament yet, later, arguing on the grounds of sovereignty and national interest against the logical outcomes of the Act. The defence is on the grounds of expediency. The government was fully aware of the extent to which it was surrendering sovereignty to the Council of Ministers, the Commission and the European Parliament but it knew that public opinion could easily be whipped up against such a surrender. It therefore played this aspect down and concentrated on the positive economic benefits of harmonisation and the removal of barriers. Once the necessary legislation was passed, it has found it expedient to calm public fears about specific measures by quoting the national interest and sovereignty in its arguments with its European partners. It has done this over sensitive proposals about border controls, VAT, harmonisation, and joining the Exchange Rate Mechanism of the EMS. Increasingly, however, in a multitude of day-to-day decisions the issue of sovereignty is becoming irrelevant. The legislation has been agreed to, the power delegated and the individual nation's veto is largely a thing of the past although the United Kingdom Foreign Secretary told the Conservative Party Conference in October 1991 that he would apply a veto if his government considered that the sovereignty of the United Kingdom Parliament was at stake.

Will Sovereignty be an Issue in the Future?

The issue of sovereignty will never go away completely because groups of people and nations will always come to feel at some time that they could do better if they made all their decisions for themselves. There is, for example, a Basque separatist movement, a Walloon independence movement and similar aspirations in Cornwall, Wales, Scotland and the Italian Alps. It is easy to dismiss these trends as the stirrings of adolescent independence. They represent attitudes which arise in any arrangement that has dominant partners. It is inevitable therefore that, as the effects of the creation of a genuine single European market are understood, two major strands of opinion are developing. The first has come to dominate and is incorporated in the Union Treaty.

The first says 'things have worked out well, and look what can be achieved by close cooperation and common objectives – let's try to achieve even closer political harmony in a federal structure'. They want a common currency, a single central bank, a Community police force and perhaps a Community defence and foreign policy.

The second strand of opinion says, 'look at the negative effects, the growth of regional disparities, look how badly we have done and see how the big nations dominate decision-making at our expense. Let's go our own way.' The Treaty of Rome is rather exceptional in that it does not provide any means by which a signatory can leave the Community. It appears to be an irrevocable decision. Despite this Greenland chose, after a referendum, to separate itself from Denmark in this context and to negotiate a separate associate status. The Community is not likely to wish to restrain a member who wants to leave.

Such polarisation of opinion is, of course, somewhat exaggerated and a great deal will depend on how the Community institutions perform over the next few years, particularly the Parliament. We should always bear in mind however, the seemingly endless ability of groups in society to splinter into smaller groups. Events in the Balkans are a constant reminder of this.

Will the European Parliament be Adequate in the Future?

The European Parliament has become more effective since its powers were extended slightly under the Single European Act of 1986 and, more particularly, since its indirect election system was replaced by direct universal suffrage in 1979. Many British MEPs (Members of the European Parliament) take the rather parochial view that it was the advent of the British with their long parliamentary tradition that changed the nature of the European Parliament.

The Parliament has 518 members elected by proportional representation, except in Great Britain where the election is still by the traditional first-past-the-post method. Northern Ireland uses the single transferable vote system of proportional representation to elect its MEPs. In October 1991 the European Parliament voted in favour of all elections of its members being held by proportional representation but this has yet to be confirmed by the Council. Many

MEPs, except from the United Kingdom, do not have a specific constituency to which they are directly accountable. This reduces their work burden and their direct contact with the people. The Parliament divides into groups by political tendency rather than by nationality. MEPs are increasingly subjected to the approaches of pressure groups of different types despite the fact that their powers are very restricted.

The European parliament's powers are very much less than those of national parliaments. Its main job is to oversee and approve the work of the Commission. It can vote the Commission out of office with a two-thirds majority but the relationship between Parliament and Commission is such as to make this event extremely unlikely. Parliament has relatively little control over the budget although it must give its approval and can propose certain increases. It cannot itself create new sources of revenue. Since 1979 the Parliament has become more effective in criticising the Commission and Council of Ministers through its questions and committee system. It has been helped in the area of the budget by the twelve-member Court of Auditors which supervises the implementation of the budget.

The above is necessarily a brief analysis of the European Parliament's power but more details are given in Chapter 9, especially with regard to the Union Treaty. MEPs tend to give a rosier picture of their effectiveness and that of the Parliament. Some critics would be much more damning and allege that the Parliament is a self-important talking shop with the minimum of influence over decision-making. Its quaint movements between Strasbourg, Brussels and Luxembourg do not help its efficiency, although this may eventually be ended and the Parliament may settle in Brussels.

The European Parliament has gradually tried to increase its role and influence. There is plenty of evidence since 1986 to show this trend. Proposals to increase its powers were at the centre of the arguments over the Treaty on Political Union in 1991. If the United Kingdom introduces proportional representation in European elections, as it should eventually do, then there may be an injection of more 'democratic' blood into the Parliament. As the single market extends and intensifies, the electorate of Europe and pressure groups will increasingly look to the European Parliament rather than to national Parliaments. Each national bureaucracy will also increasingly work through European channels. Over time the European Parliament will be seen to be more important and will almost certainly want more powers. It may prove to be the best defence of democracy for the British people whose own Parliament has become decayed and ineffectual.

Is the Community Bureaucratic?

The word 'bureaucratic' is often used as a term of abuse by critics of an institution or system. It is frequently used with reference to the Community. Articles which dwell on the 'bureaucratic' nature of the Community usually include a picture of the Berlaymont Building in Brussels which houses the headquarters of the Commission. This is a cross-shaped office block of about twelve storeys with a circular helicopter pad on top at the intersection of the cross. It was decided, in 1991, to demolish it because it was contaminated by asbestos and replace it completely, but the decision was changed and a complete refurbishment began in early 1992. Near it is the smaller Charlemagne Building which is used for the Council of Ministers. Articles on a similar theme about the United States frequently include a photograph of the Pentagon.

The word 'bureaucratic' has two main meanings when used critically. The first is that the number of employees engaged in administrative tasks is excessive in relation to the size of the whole organisation or to the task in hand. (A classic case is the British Navy which now has more admirals than large surface ships.) The implication is that many will be engaged in pointless and repetitive clerical tasks which hold up the implementation of policy. The Community definitely does not suffer from this kind of bureaucracy. It employs only about 23 000 employees, 16 000 in the Commission, 3500 in the Parliament, 2200 in the Council, 700 in the Court of Justice, 500 in the Economic and Social Committee, and 400 in the Court of Auditors. Of those employed by the Commission an estimated 2 700 are language staff. The administrative cost of the Community is only about 4.6 per cent of the budget of which the Commission takes up 2.98 per cent, the Council 0.41 per cent and Parliament 0.81 per cent. These figures may, of course, be regarded as simply the tip of the iceberg. The individual member states employ many others on Community-related work and the implementation of its policies. They are, however, counted as national civil servants and not as Community employees.

The other meaning given to the word 'bureaucratic' is more nebulous and implies a ponderous, labyrinthine decision-making process with a complex hierarchy that causes decision-making to be delayed. It is obvious that the Community, comprising twelve nations, might lend itself to this type of bureaucracy because proposals and decisions have to be constantly referred back and forth between the individual states and the Community institutions. There is no real evidence, though, that the Community is more bureaucratic than it need be. It can be argued that it is highly efficient and effective in its decision-making processes, even allowing for the inevitable time delay required for compromises. Its achievements in meeting deadlines in the drafting and passing of directives for the coming of the single European market by 1992 have been impressive, achieving most of the 282 measures well on schedule. There have been some major areas of dispute such as merger policy, banking regulation and border controls that delayed matters but compromises have always been achieved, in most cases without sacrificing the spirit of the single market. In this sense of the word 'bureaucratic' as discussed in this paragraph it may be said that Europe is nowhere near as bureaucratic as the United States or the defunct Soviet Union.

In the context of the 'bureaucratic' criticism some people hope that the creation of the single European market will remove a great deal of administrative work. This has already happened with the use of a single document for commercial vehicles crossing internal frontiers of the Community and even that will be discontinued in 1993. The abolition in many sectors of such controls as those on capital movements and the harmonisation of regulations should both help reduce bureaucracy. There is a fear, though, that a new structure of rules, regulations and controls will actually establish a tighter and, eventually, more extensive bureaucracy. Mrs Thatcher and the Bruges Group expressed this fear especially in the context of social policy and tax harmonisation. Their view of an extension of free market forces is at variance with the common European and Community view of a benevolent guiding hand or direct interventionist role for the state.

A Budget Problem – Where to Get the Money?

Community budget problems have changed in nature over the years. The most persistent, until 1988, was that revenues never matched the levels of expenditure required to meet all the desirable objectives. The Community budget is fundamentally different from national budgets in that it is not an instrument of economic policy using deficits or surpluses to achieve economic objectives. As expenditure under the agricultural programmes got out of control, especially on the price guarantee side, there were less resources available for regional, social and technological programmes. The budget became the cause of annual conflicts between the Commission and the European Parliament and between nations at the Council of Ministers. All sorts of expedients and varieties of creative accountancy were adopted as temporary palliatives. When, eventually, the issue of controlling agricultural payments was successfully met in 1987–8, there was more scope for sensible budgetary policies. Unfortunately the relief was short-lived because the agricultural surpluses returned.

At the same time, there was a welcome increase in revenues for the Community from January 1986. This resulted from the decision in 1984 to increase the VAT revenues payable to the Community by each member to the equivalent of a 1.4 per cent rate of a uniform basis of assessment. This decision, implemented in January 1986, has provided much-needed extra revenue and there may be pressure in the future to increase this percentage further. The percentage was originally 1 per cent from 1970 to 1983. Since VAT receipts constitute about 60 per cent of the Community's income they yield the greatest return if the rate of contribution is increased.

The Community's revenues also began to take a healthier turn after the Brussels agreement in February 1988. The national leaders agreed to have additional national contributions to the revenues based on relative national wealth (GNP). They allowed the Community to collect up to 1.2 per cent of GNP. This very welcome increase in potential revenue, together with the rise in VAT contributions, permitted a rise of up to 30 per cent in the revenues over time, compared with the 1987 budget.

In its early days, between 1957 and 1970, the Community's revenue was based on contributions from the six members paid in accordance with an agreed scale based on shares of Gross National Product and other criteria. As was always intended by the Treaty of Rome, the Community shifted its revenue base once the Common Customs Tariff (CCT) was introduced in mid-1968. After the 1969 Hague summit the Community developed a system of revenue from 'its own resources' – that is it was guaranteed money from specific sources. At this time the United Kingdom, Ireland and Denmark were in the process of joining so the changes took place over some years. These sources were: customs duties, agricultural levies, sugar levies and a percentage of the VAT receipts.

The change-over to 'own resources' financing was slow in several respects; it was only speedy in relation to sugar levies. These charges on the production and storage of sugar were transferred to the Community in 1971. They were extended to isoglucose in 1977. The money is used to finance support in the markets for sugar. In the case of customs revenue the complete transfer of all revenues to the Community was not achieved until 1975. Even then customs duties on coal and steel were not handed over to the Community.

Revenue from customs duties has been of decreasing relative importance because of the series of international GATT talks which have reduced tariffs – the Kennedy round (1962–7), the Tokyo round (1980–6) and, possibly, the Uruguay round (1986–92). Various other agreements have also cut customs revenues – the Lomé agreement, for example, and the agreement with the EFTA countries, and bilateral agreements with Mediterranean countries. The general rise in imports and their prices has not compensated for this general decline in tariff levels. If, as the single market develops, the Community successfully replaces imports with home-produced products then it can expect a further reduction in its revenues from tariffs. The member states keep 10 per cent of the revenue from customs duties and agricultural levies in order to meet administration and collection costs.

The transfer of agricultural levies also took place over the years 1971–5. These levies are placed upon imported agricultural products to bring their prices up to the level of the Community products' prices. The revenue from them depends on price movements and exchange rates. The United Kingdom, being a relatively large importer of food products, contributes disproportionately to agricultural levies. They are not a very good source of revenue because they tend to fluctuate unpredictably. The revenue from them goes to help support or intervention buying within the Community but it is nowhere near sufficient for this purpose. Table 4.2 illustrates the problem as it was in 1985.

It was decided in 1970 to make VAT the main source of the Community's own revenue, but it was not until the budget of 1980 that every member paid its full VAT payments. Proceedings before

TABLE 4.2
The Community Budget, 1985 (Percentage)

Receipts	%	Expenditure	%
VAT	55.5	Agriculture and fisheries	72.9
Customs duties	29.6	Regional policy	5.9
Non-repayable advances	5.9	Social policy	5.7
Agricultural levies	4.0	Development cooperation	3.9
Sugar and isoglucose levies	3.8	Research, energy, transport	2.6
Miscellaneous	1.2	Administrative costs	4.6
		Miscellaneous	4.4

Total payment appropriations + 28 000 million ECU

the Court of Justice were required to make Ireland, Italy, Luxembourg and Germany comply in 1979 with the sixth VAT Directive of May 1977. The members agreed to give the Community up to 1 per cent of a uniform basis of assessment of value added tax. This limit was raised to 1.4 per cent in January 1986 after the Fontainebleau summit resolved the United Kingdom's contribution problem. There is pressure to raise the figure further but the United Kingdom and Germany are reluctant because they think that the limit imposes more budgetary discipline on the Community, particularly on the agricultural budget.

VAT was chosen as a source of revenue because the sixth VAT Directive of May 1977 harmonised the turnover (or VAT) systems. The tax is paid by all Community citizens and its revenue closely reflects the economic capacity of each member state. This may be regarded as an equitable system and is, to a degree, progressive because high revenue from VAT reflects high levels of consumption which, in turn, reflects high disposable incomes. Spain would dispute this statement because it raises a higher percentage of its tax revenues from indirect taxes than most members. The amount paid is based on a uniform basis of assessment defined as 'the sum of all taxable supplies of goods and services to the final consumer in the Community'. This means that it does not depend on the VAT rates which continue to differ quite widely among member states.

As part of the progress towards the creation of the single European market in 1992 it was intended to try to harmonise VAT rates. In 1991 an agreement was reached which represented a compromise to overcome short-term conflicts between the members. It was decided to have a 15 per cent minimum standard rate of VAT by 1 January 1993 for a transitional period up to the end of 1996. There will also be minimum excise duty rates on fuel, tobacco and alcohol. If the market becomes a genuine single unit, market forces are likely to produce a close harmonisation of rates over time. Otherwise there will be considerable distortions of the market with tax considerations influencing the location of production. There are still many details to sort out in the context of indirect tax harmonisation over the next few years. The United Kingdom government has been opposed to full harmonisation of rates of VAT because it would have to impose the tax on goods at present exempt, notably food and children's clothing. It has, however, quietly extended VAT in 1988 and 1989 to some areas hitherto excluded, such as opticians' services and parts of the construction industry. In 1990 it raised the standard rate of VAT in the United Kingdom to 17.5 per cent as part of its policy of shifting the tax burden from income on to expenditure. The French too are opposed to full harmonisation because they would have to lower many of their rates and find alternative sources of revenue. The details of the 1989 budget and a comparative study of the changes in the budget between 1973 and 1989 are given in Tables 4.3 and 4.4 and Figure 4.2. The national contributions to the Community's revenues are given in Table 4.5.

How are the Budget and Exchange Rate Fluctuations Reconciled?

The Community needed to devise a system for payments between members and the Community to take account of changes in foreign exchange rates. Before 1977 budgets were drawn up and implemented in terms of 'units of account' (u.a.). Each u.a. was equivalent to a fine ounce of gold – this was the content of the US dollar between 1934 and 1972. In other words the exchange rate in relation to the US dollar was the basis of calculation. Between 1978 and 1980 the European Unit of Account (EUA) was used instead and was based on a 'basket' of currencies. Since 1980 the budget has been drawn up and executed in terms of the ECU (European Currency Unit). This is described and explained fully in Chapter 7. The ECU is based upon a 'basket' of currencies in which individual currencies are weighted according to objective measures such as a country's share of the Community's gross domestic product and share of Community trade. This weighting is reviewed every five years. From 1979–80 the ECU was used for all legal and financial purposes and in the budget from January 1981.

TABLE 4.3
General Community Budget: Revenue Forecast for 1989 and 1990

| | *1989* | | *1990* | |
	Million ECU	*%*	*Million ECU*	*%*
Customs duties	9 954	22.2	11 399	24.4
Agricultural levies	2 462	5.4	2 289	4.9
VAT	26 219	58.5	28 124	60.2
GNP resource	3 907	8.7	1 962	4.2
Miscellaneous	274	0.6	327	0.7
Balance from previous year	2 025	4.5	2 616	5.6
	44 841		46 717	
	(or 1.03% of		(or 0.97% of	
	Community GNP)		Community GNP)	

SOURCE European File, *The European Community Budget* (Luxembourg: Office for Official Publications of the European Communities, 1989), and Eurostat, 1991.

TABLE 4.4
European Community Expenditure by Sector (per cent)

	1981	*1986*	*1988*	*1990*
Agriculture and fisheries	65.1	67.2	71.8	65.3
Regional policy	12.6	7.6	7.3	11.1
Social policy	4.7	7.1	6.4	7.8
Cooperation with developing countries	4.8	2.5	1.8	3.1
Research, energy, industry, transport	2.1	2.5	2.4	3.7
Reimbursement to member states	5.4	8.7	6.1	4.0
Administration	5.3	4.4	4.0	5.0

SOURCE Eurostat, *Basic Statistics of the Community*, 28th edn (Luxembourg: Office for Official Publications of the European Communities, 1991).

FIGURE 4.2
1. Development of the General Community Budget, 1973–89

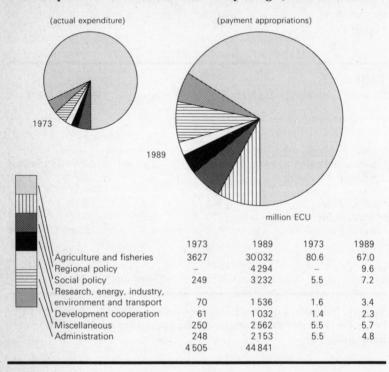

	1973	1989	1973	1989
Agriculture and fisheries	3627	30032	80.6	67.0
Regional policy	–	4294	–	9.6
Social policy	249	3232	5.5	7.2
Research, energy, industry, environment and transport	70	1536	1.6	3.4
Development cooperation	61	1032	1.4	2.3
Miscellaneous	250	2562	5.5	5.7
Administration	248	2153	5.5	4.8
	4505	44841		

The value of the ECU is worked out on a daily basis for each country's currency in relation to the currency's standing on the exchange markets. The Community budget is drawn up each year using the ECU rates for 1 February of the previous year. For example, the 1992 budget was drawn up on the ECU rate prevailing on 1 February 1991.

The use of the ECU was important in enabling monetary compensatory amounts (MCAs) to be calculated and adjusted. These were payments introduced in 1971 for agricultural products as they crossed frontiers to compensate for changes in exchange rates or the adjustment in central rates in the days before 1979 when the European Monetary System was introduced. The aim was to stabilise agriculture prices but they never achieved that satisfactorily. In fact

2. Financial Forecasts, 1988–92 (commitment appropriations, million ECU)

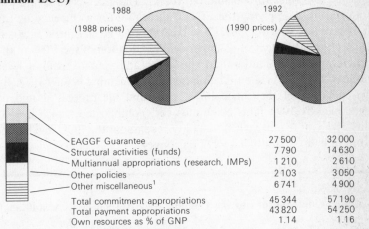

	27 500	32 000
EAGGF Guarantee	27 500	32 000
Structural activities (funds)	7 790	14 630
Multiannual appropriations (research, IMPs)	1 210	2 610
Other policies	2 103	3 050
Other miscellaneous[1]	6 741	4 900
Total commitment appropriations	45 344	57 190
Total payment appropriations	43 820	54 250
Own resources as % of GNP	1.14	1.16

[1] Reimbursements to Member States, monetary reserve, administrative cost, etc.

SOURCE   European File, *The European Community Budget* (Luxembourg: Office for Official Publications of the European Communities, 1989).

they created great opportunities for corruption and immense complexity in agricultural pricing. By 1988 there were 49 separate 'green rates' within eleven currencies. The system was extremely complicated and involved the calculation of a 'green' rate for each currency – hence talk of the 'green pound', or the 'green mark'. The whole system created great problems at the annual discussion of the level of agricultural support prices. There were positive and negative MCAs depending on the movement of currencies. MCAs were a large burden on the Community's budget. The balance between positive and negative MCAs constituted about 10 per cent of the expenditure on price guarantees.

In 1984–5 a new system for MCAs was adopted. This aimed at the dismantling and eventual elimination of positive MCAs. Under the new system for compensatory payments the strongest currency with the highest revaluation rate (usually the German mark) was used as the basis for calculating the new 'green' rates. The pound sterling was not considered here because it did not participate in the Exchange Rate Mechanism of the European Monetary System until 1990. After March 1984 a green central rate was established, replacing the old EMS central rates for calculating MCAs. The green central rate was obtained by multiplying the ECU central rate for a currency by the monetary factor of 1.033651. The creation of a green central rate was usually the equivalent of a 3.4 per cent revaluation of the ECU in the agricultural sector and raised the levies and refunds paid. It was decided that MCAs should be phased out, beginning in July 1987. By the end of 1991 they had almost gone and the process should be completed by 1993. This all sounds very complicated, which it is! It may make more sense when you have read about the ECU in Chapter 5 on agriculture and Chapter 7 on money.

TABLE 4.5
National Contributions to the Community's Revenues (ECU millions)

Country	1988 Forecast	% of Total Revenue
Belgium	1 880	4.4
Denmark	965	2.2
France	9 332	21.7
West Germany	11 677	27.2
Greece	422	1.0
Ireland	328	0.8
Italy	6 771	15.7
Luxembourg	87	0.2
Netherlands	2 775	6.5
Portugal	432	1.0
Spain	3 158	7.3
United Kingdom	5 182	12.0

SOURCE Eurostat, *Basic Statistics of the Community*, 25th edn (Luxembourg: Office for Official Publications of the European Communities, 1988).

Another Budget Problem – the Winners and Losers

Some countries are net gainers and some are net losers from the financial transactions of the Community. The gainers tend to keep quiet and hope that their luck continues. They are usually the poorer members such as Greece and Ireland although Italy has frequently been a substantial winner. Portugal has become a net beneficiary. The net contributors or 'losers' have been Germany, the United Kingdom and France. Germany and France, on the one hand, have usually accepted the 'losses' as a reasonable payment to maintain peace and stability in Europe and as a means of helping economic development in less favoured regions. The United Kingdom, on the other hand, made loud, continuous, and aggressive complaints about its net contributions. In Mrs Thatcher's words 'we want our money back'. Indeed, the problem of the United Kingdom's contributions persisted so long that it threatened to become the bore of the century.

Fortunately for us the matter was largely resolved following the Fontainebleau summit in June 1984. The leaders agreed that expenditure policy is at the heart of any method of controlling budgetary imbalances. This agreement led to subsequent controls on agricultural spending. They also agreed to a system of abatement or correction for excessive budgetary burdens with a specific formula for the United Kingdom. These corrections are deducted from the United Kingdom's share of VAT payments in the year following that for which the correction is made. The repayment, rebate, or correction obviously places a burden on the other members – the cost being shared among them according to their normal VAT share – but it is adjusted to allow Germany's share to move to two-thirds of its VAT share. In other words, Germany bears a disproportionate part of the burden of the United Kingdom's rebates despite the fact that it is the largest net contributor (loser) to the Community.

It became apparent very soon after the United Kingdom's accession to the Community that there was likely to be a growing problem of excess budgetary contributions. Denmark, in contrast, was a major net beneficiary. The United Kingdom wanted a closer relationship between payments and receipts. Its wishes were partly granted when the terms of entry were renegotiated. In 1975, the European Council agreed on a corrective mechanism which was to apply for an experimental period of seven years until 1983. This financial mechanism was inadequate since the net debit was not removed and the growth in the size of the United Kingdom's net deficit balance continued. By 1979 the situation was extremely bad. In 1980, it was agreed to reduce the net United Kingdom contribution for 1980 and 1981 from an aggregate of 3924 million ECU to

1339 million ECU. This reduction of 2585 million ECU was financed by the other members, partly by direct payments to the United Kingdom Treasury and partly by generous extra payments from the Regional Fund. This did not satisfy Mrs Thatcher who wanted a long-term solution and a control on expenditure. There followed several years of wrangling and almost every summit was soured by this until the 1984 Fontainebleau summit, as previously mentioned. There were some signs from leading Conservative ministers in early 1992 that they were beginning to resurrect the United Kingdom's grievance over net contributions to the Community's budget. Fuel was added to their fire when, in February 1992, President Delors told the European Parliament that the Community would need another 20 billion ECU added to its budget by 1997 in order to pay for the decisions made at Maastricht. The groans of economists throughout the Community will soon be heard as the budget debate is restarted!

Is the Community a Tower of Babel?

The Community of Twelve has nine official languages – English, Danish, Dutch, French, German, Greek, Italian, Portuguese and Spanish. This presents a significant financial burden (about £30 million a year in 1991), and a personnel problem. All important meetings, about fifty per day, have to be provided with facilities for translation out of each of the nine languages and into the other eight. In addition all the documents have to be translated into all the official languages. It is estimated that the advent of a new official language created a demand for up to 250 translators. Interpreting into and out of nine languages gives 72 potential combinations. This number may be reduced by translating at second hand from a language into which the original language has already been trans-lated. Even then at least thirty translators are needed for nine languages.

There is no chance of the number of official languages being reduced because of political and legal reasons. Formal meetings and documents will, therefore, continue to be available in all nine languages. If Turkey, Norway and Sweden ever join it will be even more like the Tower of Babel. The possible addition, in the more distant future, of the various Eastern/Central European languages, such as Polish, Hungarian and so on, has led to suggestions that new entrants should be asked to forgo their right of translation in some meetings or for some documents. In day-to-day practice, however, the usual working languages of the Community are English and French. The cultural imperialism or encroachment of English is resented and resisted by the French but it is in such a strong position internationally that it is likely to dominate in the long run. Its use by the Americans, the old British dominions and colonies and its adoption by the Japanese and Russians as their second language makes this inevitable. There has, however, been a recent surge in the popularity of German as a second language in Central and Eastern European countries. It will be interesting to see, over the next twenty years, what effect satellite broadcasting has on language use. Will it help to perpetuate local languages and dialects through local stations or will it extend English over a wider area?

Agriculture – Too Successful for its Own Good?

5

Has the Common Agricultural Policy been Successful?

There is no doubt that the answer to this question is 'yes' *if* the policy is seen in the light of its aims. The critics of the Common Agricultural Policy (CAP) tend to take short-term, oversimplified views. They can see no further than the so-called 'food mountains' and usually feel no need to put forward constructive alternatives to the policies that they wilfully caricature. They condemn the whole policy, in all its complexity, out of hand. What they should be doing is suggesting positive improvements in terms of the CAP's flexibility and ability to respond to changing circumstances.

The CAP was conceived against a history of eighty years of cyclical fluctuations in demand, prices and rural prosperity. Rural poverty in Europe was a mainspring of political and social unrest. The United Kingdom, which tends to take a piously superior attitude to the CAP, was spared much of this because of its earlier shift of resources away from the land into industry. Even so, the agricultural depressions of the 1918–39 period were devastating in the United Kingdom. The stereotype of the Jarrow hunger marchers obscures the reality of this rural deprivation.

The CAP was also founded against the immediate backdrop of over ten years of food shortages in Europe. These were particularly severe from 1943 into the early 1950s, many Europeans dying from malnutrition and its side effects. The foremost aim of the CAP, therefore, was to remove any threat of food shortages. In this the policy has been triumphantly successful.

The other objectives explicitly stated in Article 39 of the Treaty of Rome were: to increase agricultural productivity, to ensure thereby a fair standard of living for the agricultural community, to stabilise markets and to guarantee reasonable prices for consumers.

In order to guarantee food supplies farmers have to be offered secure markets and a fairly high degree of certainty in price levels. This makes some form of state intervention essential. It is the form that this intervention should take that creates division of opinion. Several types of policy are possible and each type can be tailored to the specific characteristics of a country. The CAP, covering as it does twelve nations with widely differing climatic conditions, is bound to be less appropriate to some countries than to others. This is not an argument for abolishing it, rather it is a reason for improving its application by fine-tuning to fit national conditions. There is no doubt whatsoever that free competition without state intervention would have resulted in market chaos in Europe with appalling social and economic consequences. It would be flying in the face of all human experience of the last 200 years to advocate free market competition in agriculture.

Why would Free Market Competition in Agriculture Cause Chaos?

'Chaos' here means successive food gluts and shortages with wide and rapid price fluctuations. It also means cyclical booms and slumps, with concurrent movements in agricultural incomes and employment.

The reasons lie in the nature of agricultural products and their production conditions and in the traditional responses of farmers to changes in markets and prices. These factors, when combined, tend to contradict the simple price theory of elementary economics textbooks, where supply and demand are brought into a neat equilibrium in response to price changes. In agricultural products there is just as likely to be a series of short-run diverging price equilibria, as shown in the 'cobweb theorem' (see Figure 5.1), and no long-run equilibrium.

Farmers' responses are of paramount importance. There are two main behavioural patterns that can be seen. The first is embodied in what has usually been known as the 'pig cycle', or as the 'hog cycle' in

American writings. Pigs are chosen to illustrate this idea because of their ability to reproduce quickly and to be fattened for market in a short time, although there is still a time-lag between planning and achieving production. The same principle now applies to 'lamb' although the cycle is longer and ewes usually have only two lambs a year. It can also apply to arable crops if farmers can quickly enter or leave production. Modern production techniques may cause it to apply to eggs and poultry meat production. The cycle is one of buoyant demand in relation to supply pushing up prices of pig products. Farmers see the high prices and apparent profitability. Existing producers quickly expand their output and newcomers begin production. The result, if demand fails to rise sufficiently, is an excess supply which tends to depress market prices. The fall in price forces marginal producers out of business and reduces profits for the more efficient. The consequent decline in output creates a deficiency of supply in relation to demand. Prices tend to rise and we are back at the starting point. This cycle may take less than two years. Its length, and the range of fluctuation of output and price depends on a number of imponderables such as international price movements, animal feed prices and the movement of the prices of substitutes. Although there may be a similar cycle in some sorts of manufactured goods it is not as intense, partly because many major markets are dominated by oligopolies.

An interesting comparison might be made with the silicon chip market for mass-produced chips for electronic devices. These markets have displayed a 'pig cycle' aspect in the 1970s and 1980s. In agricultural markets the 'pig cycle' effect, if unchecked, can destabilise markets and create wider fluctuations in demand, supply and price of products and factors such as labour, transport, animal feed, packaging materials and professional services. It should be remembered, however, that as in all spheres of business some clever entrepreneurs make their profits by anticipating the cycle and bucking the trend. One of the benefits of the CAP has been to remove most of the effects of the cycle in those areas where intervention prices have been applied.

Those readers who are familiar with supply-and-demand analysis will realise that the above explanation fits the so-called 'cobweb' theorem. This shows how some markets are subject to price destabilisation instead of tending towards an equilibrium. In these conditions the price oscillates around the potential equilibrium but does not settle at it. It may diverge more and more from the equilibrium over time. In diagrams this can be drawn to show a 'cobweb' effect although the 'web' is nowhere near as geometrically accurate as that made by the humble spider! See Figures 5.1 and 5.2.

In principle, then, farmers have always tended to enter markets where prices have been high in the recent past and to leave those where prices have been low. This may be a movement of 'marginal' producers only or may be a shift of a significant proportion of producers. Not all farmers have the luxury of choice as to what to produce. Their land conditions, expertise and machinery may all be specific to one type of production. (There has been a great growth in specialist contracting firms for various types of harvesting. This cuts the costs for farmers entering a new line of production.) In this case, a policy such as the CAP may be used successfully to finance the transfer of land to other uses or to pay farmers to stop producing. The policies adopted need to be flexible and to bear in mind the needs of the individual farmer as well as their effects on aggregate supply.

The second main behavioural pattern of farmers is linked to the first but, to some extent, contradicts it. It consists of farmers, especially those who have a limited range of output options, responding to a fall in their incomes by trying to produce more and to cut their costs. Thus, for example, a typical American Midwest wheat farmer, faced by a falling price of wheat and therefore a falling income, can only compensate by growing more wheat. If all his fellow producers do the same the aggregate supply expands. If demand fails to rise proportionately, excess supply is generated and prices fall even further. This is followed by another fall in net income unless the farmer has managed to cut costs even more. The possible causes of the initial fall in prices and farmers' incomes are many, for example good harvests in the Ukraine and elsewhere, or falling real incomes of consumers, or a change in the tastes and preferences of consumers. Once again, this response of farmers can be forestalled or controlled by the CAP setting target prices for current and future years and by setting output quotas.

These responses of farmers are partly a reflection of the nature of the demand for agricultural products, part of which comes from industry and part from domestic consumers. 'Industrial' demand for the products of agriculture has always been important but modern technology has modified this or provided substitutes via modern chemical processes. The main demands, historically, have been for

FIGURE 5.1
'Cobweb' Effects

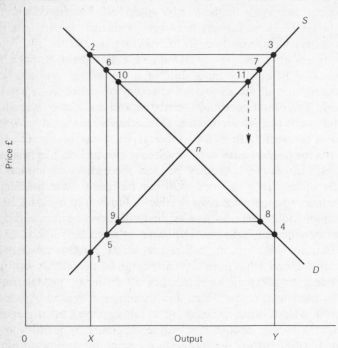

D shows the relationship between the quantity produced in a production period and the price that needs to be charged in order to sell that amount. S shows the relationship between the price in one production period and the quantity that will be produced in the succeeding production period.

If output in period *A* is 0*X*, the price will be at level 2. The price 2 will cause output in production period *B* to be 0*Y* (point 3) and the price will be at level 4 (where the demand is). Output in production period *C* will be at level 5 and price at level 6; and so on. Given the relative slopes of these two curves there will be an euilibrium at *n*. If, however, the curves have a different slope, as in Figure 5.2, this is not the case. Price may diverge further and further from the equilibrium unless the curves shift to a new position.

FIGURE 5.2
'Cobweb' Effects

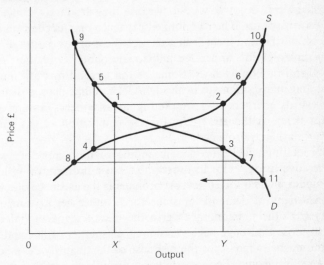

leather, wool, cotton and other fibres such as flax, dyes, alcohol, starch, oils from seeds, timber and products for brewing. Another aspect is the manufactured food processing industry which cans, packages and bottles products after dehydration, freezing, pickling, and smoking as a means of preserving the food. Food processing has several effects of great importance to agriculture. Preservation, in itself, can help to smooth out seasonal fluctuations in supply. It can, together with rapid modern transport systems with specialised carriers, make available all sorts of products from all over the world throughout the year, and provides the consumer with substitutes and variety. It also enables surpluses to be extended over time and widely distributed around markets.

Another very important effect is to enable value to be added to what are intrinsically cheap products. This partly explains the great growth since the 1920s of packaged, branded foods. The effect on the market has usually been to create oligopolistic conditions with a few major firms each taking a large share of the market within a given country. They may leave a small proportion of the market to be shared among a larger number of much smaller sellers. These smaller producers survive by supplying a specialised product to a narrow section of the market or by giving outstanding personal service or quality. They may enjoy low costs because they are family concerns with fewer overheads. Their continued existence may depend on the larger firms abstaining from trying to take them over because of the threat of investigation under the individual country's, or the Community's, anti-monopoly laws. Some of the larger firms are multinational and many originate in the USA. There has been a distinct trend towards mergers and marketing arrangements among the dominant firms as the 1992 date for the completion of the single European market approached.

The processing, packaging and branding of food, together with extensive advertising, helps to overcome a basic problem of agriculture in higher-income societies. This problem is the existence of a low income elasticity of demand for some foods and a negative income elasticity for others. Economists give the quaint name of 'inferior goods' to those that have negative income elasticities of demand.

Income elasticity measures the response of the quantity demanded to a change in income. Economists use a formula to measure it:

$$\frac{\text{Income elasticity}}{\text{of demand}} = \frac{\text{Proportionate change in quantity demanded}}{\text{Proportionate change in income}}$$

Theoretically this can vary between minus infinity and plus infinity. Most products show a modest increase in demand as income rises. This gives an income elasticity between zero and unity. Thus income may rise by, say, 5 per cent and the demand for bacon might rise by 2 per cent giving a measurement of 0.4. Bacon producers could, therefore, expect a slowly expanding demand as society became richer. Many products or services, mainly in the leisure fields, such as sports equipment, restaurant meals or foreign travel show a positive income elasticity above unity. Thus a rise of 5 per cent in income might produce an 8 per cent increase in demand for foreign travel, skis or restaurant meals, giving a measurement of 1.6 per cent. In contrast, there are many foods where a 5 per cent increase in income may be followed by a decrease in demand as people shift their consumption to higher-priced, higher protein content, foods. Hence a rise in income of 5 per cent may be followed by a decline in demand for potatoes, sliced white bread, offal and cheaper cuts of meat. The post-1950s' decline in demand for bread and potatoes can be explained in terms of this negative income elasticity of demand. This has had a profound influence on agriculture in terms of incomes and patterns of production. We are, of course, talking in aggregate rather than individual terms and with reference to Europe, North America, and higher-income countries. In most low-income countries an increase in income is reflected fully in increased demand for basic foodstuffs, but even there a greater proportion of income may be spent on widening the variety of foods consumed.

The nature of the income elasticity of demand for food products in Europe has led to shifts in the pattern of production. There is greater emphasis on meat production of all types, on dairy products and on fruit and horticultural products, while there has been a relative decline in demand for basic arable crops except as animal feed. As will be seen below, the implementation of the CAP has accelerated some of these changes and delayed others. The food processing industry is fully aware of the implications of income elasticity and, with an eye on its profits, has concentrated on products which reflect a higher income elasticity. The relationship between the grower and the food processor has sometimes tended to become one of servant and master. Many farmers have avoided this risk by creating their own cleaning, packaging and branding systems, often in a producers' cooperative.

In terms of conventional price theory the nature of income elasticity of demand for food means that the demand curve is only slowly shifting to the right as incomes and population increase. Indeed, for individual products, the demand curve may be shifting to the left.

Another major problem for farmers, food processors and policy-makers is that the demand for most foods is price-inelastic although the degree of inelasticity differs enormously between products. Price elasticity is a measure of the responsiveness of demand to a small proportionate change in price. A simple formula for measuring it is:

$$\text{Price elasticity of demand} = \frac{\text{Proportionate change in quantity demanded}}{\text{Proportionate change in price}}$$

If the quantity changes proportionately more than the change in price then demand is said to be elastic. This usually means that there are close substitutes at existing market prices.

If the quantity changes less than proportionately compared with the price change then the demand is said to be inelastic. This usually indicates a lack of close substitutes or that the product has a very low price in relation to the average income, or that its purchase is habitual. Looked at from a seller's point of view, an elastic demand means that total revenue (price times quantity sold) from sales will decline as price rises and increase as price falls. Alternatively an inelastic demand means that his total revenue from sales will increase as price rises and decrease as price falls. These statements are generalisations because price elasticity will, under normal conditions, vary considerably at different price levels. Thus the consequences of agricultural price changes on farmers' revenues will depend, to some extent, on the original price from which the movement occurs. Frequently, a price fall (assuming no state intervention) is the result of increases in supply rather than of any long-term decrease in demand. This creates a tendency to surpluses whose existence exerts a downward pressure on price. If the demand for the farmers' produce is price-inelastic the price reduction does not call forth a commensurately larger demand. This is because we have a physical limitation on our consumption of food. There may, however, be a shift in the pattern of consumption. The overall result of increased output and price inelasticity of demand will, therefore, be a reduction in revenues from sales. This does not necessarily mean that profits fall because production costs may have fallen faster than revenues. Often, however, farmers' incomes have fallen in years of good harvests and risen in years of bad harvests. These general points about the effects of relative inelasticity of demand and supply on price can be seen in Figure 5.3.

It is a reasonable conclusion then that a free market in farm products will be a rapidly fluctuating market with periodic shortages and gluts. Prices will be unstable and employment will be uncertain and there will be a greater risk of political instability. This is borne out by the history of agriculture in pre-intervention days. The destabilising forces are very strong indeed. They are income and price inelasticity of demand (with qualifications), the nature of the 'pig cycle' and the psychological reactions of farmers to falling incomes. It should be borne in mind also that agriculture is a very large consumer of capital goods in the form of buildings, machinery, raw materials and of items such as energy, fuel, and chemicals. Reverses in agricultural prosperity have a severe knock-on effect.

FIGURE 5.3
Effects of Relative Inelasticity of Demand and Supply on Price

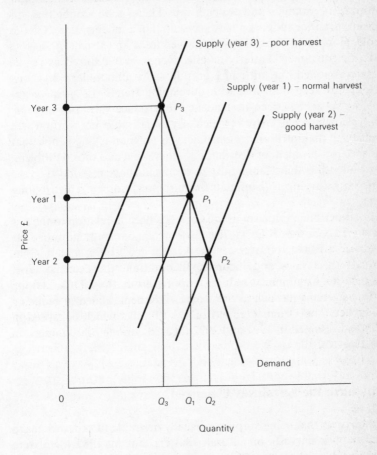

The steep gradient of the curves illustrates the relative inelasticity of supply and demand conditions for this agricultural commodity. Relatively small changes in output produces disproportionately large changes in price.

The figure also illustrates the change in revenue from the sales of this product over the three years. Compare the three rectangles of selling prices multiplied by the quantities $0Q_1$, $0Q_2$, $0Q_3$ in the years 1, 2 and 3.

In recent periods of rising unemployment, the existence of a healthy farm sector has worked as a very welcome automatic stabiliser, preventing an even greater variation in employment, incomes, and government revenues and expenditure. There is no doubt that an agricultural price support policy is essential in a modern state. On the whole, in its early years, the CAP proved to be an extremely effective and efficient policy. Latterly its effectiveness was reduced as politicians postponed the difficult, or politically unpopular, decisions required to keep it in line with developing trends. Its great weakness, however, has been its tendency to produce surpluses of some products, which has proved particularly undesirable in a world where famine and malnutrition are endemic. It is no good telling people that it is simply a problem of distribution – they see it as a moral problem. The evidence is that Community governments have responded to the criticism by trying to eliminate the surpluses, not by redistributing them.

The other main criticism of the CAP has been in relation to the less developed countries (LDCs). The CAP system of export subsidies has adversely affected the overseas markets of the LDCs, and this has reduced their sales and incomes. In addition, the external tariff around the Community reduces imports from the LDCs, despite various agreements such as the Lomé agreement, aimed at reducing its impact. The Uruguay round of GATT talks which collapsed in 1990 and resumed in 1991 and 1992 focused, among other things, on this aspect of the CAP.

Why have the Surpluses Occurred?

It is obvious that some surplus is usually desirable in order to guard against poor harvests or natural disasters, but by 1987 there were unacceptably large quantities of several products in store in the Community. By 1989, several of these excessive surpluses had been eliminated, although some had returned again by 1991. The main products in surplus were grains of various kinds, especially wheat and barley, beef, dairy products such as butter and skimmed milk powder, wine and vegetable oils. These stores of produce were very expensive to maintain and were sometimes disposed of in controversial ways, such as in sales of butter to the USSR at very low prices, or in the cheap distribution of beef and butter to pensioners or institutions. In financial terms the surpluses were a great drain on resources and imposed an excessive burden on the consumer. The impact varied from country to country. The seemingly bottomless pit of expenditure on agricultural support was the cause of most of the budgetary problems of the Community. Once the nettle of controlling agricultural price support was grasped, however, the budget problem altered. Indeed, in 1988–9 the Community moved into a budget surplus for the first time. Figure 5.4 shows the principle behind the operation of stock purchases and sales. These are frequently called 'buffer' stocks.

The main cause of the ever-growing surpluses lay in the method of setting prices for products. This method varied between products but usually involved setting a target price which would provide a reasonable return for the farmer in an area where the product was a marginal one – that is, where in some years profits were made and in others losses. The idea was to keep such marginal producers in being by giving them a market price that was certain. In order to achieve something like this target price it was necessary to fix an intervention price which was effectively a floor price, somewhere near, but below, the target price. If the producer could not obtain a price better than the intervention price he could sell his product, if its quality were acceptable, to an intervention board at the intervention price. The board would then store the product and hope to release it on to the market if the market price ever rose above the target price. In theory, therefore, prices would not normally ever fall below the intervention price or rise above the target price for long.

There were, in addition, various rebates or subsidies to exports of some food. There was also an external tariff or levy which, according to a complex sliding scale, 'taxed' imports in order to raise their price, together with transport costs from the ports to the market, to prevailing market levels or above to the target price. Since the United Kingdom was a larger importer of food than its fellow members of the Community, particularly of American hard wheat, it appeared to contribute excessively to these levies. The general effect of the pricing system was, and is, to place the burden of agricultural support on the consumer in the form of higher prices. This, it may be argued, is not good in terms of the high burden on lower-income groups.

The detail of the price support system differs enormously from product to product. These details, and the way in which the

FIGURE 5.4
A Simplified Illustration of a 'Buffer Stock' System in Operation

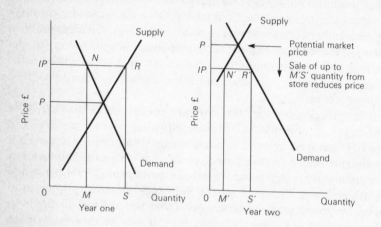

Year one

Year two

Year One

Supply exceeds demand at the proposed intervention price (*IP*) so the market price woud settle at *P*, which is below the intervention price *IP* guaranteed to the producer by the government, EC, or commodity agreement. The relevant authority buys up enough of the surplus to keep the price up to *IP*. This 'costs' the rectangle *MNRS*, that is the price *IP* times the amount bought, *MS*. Effective demand at the price *IP* is being created by the purchases.

Year Two or some future year

Demand exceeds supply at the intervention price (*IP*), perhaps because of a poor harvest. Thus the free market price (*0P*) without intervention would be above the price guaranteed to the producer, so the authority releases quantities of the product from store. Releasing the quantity *M'S'* would keep the price down to the intervention price. Releasing a smaller quantity would create a price around the target price for the commodity.

NB   The CAP intervention system has a target price above the intervention price, which is based on producers' costs. The intervention price is, therefore, a 'floor' price which the producer is certain of getting *if* his product is of the correct quantity.

regulations are interpreted by the Community bureaucracy and by national governments, matter a very great deal to the individual producer. Until 1987–8, however, the general effect, in which we are interested, was to encourage marginal farmers to continue in production on a regular basis. This was the intention and has helped to maintain prosperity in some regions. The other general effect has been to encourage non-marginal farmers to produce more and for the most efficient to invest large capital sums in expanding output. For many of these farmers the intervention price guaranteed a very healthy profit per unit of output. In pursuit of profit maximisation, they did all the things which now outrage conservationists and created joy among the manufacturers of machinery, chemicals and fertilisers. Banks joined in the fun by lending large quantities of money to farmers. Their lending was safe because of the guaranteed prices of the products. The ownership of land became a desirable investment for institutions such as pension funds because high agricultural prices enable farmers to pay high rents for leased land. This is Ricardo's theory of rent in operation. To quote the old examination question, 'rent is price-determined' (see Figure 5.5).

The quest for higher profits from the expansion of output has been accompanied by technological changes which have also generated extra output. These changes have taken many forms. There have been outstanding improvements in productivity from new varieties of arable crops, from the introduction of new breeds of animals and from the adoption of better techniques of animal husbandry. There have also been new fertilisers, better pesticides, improved veterinary practices and medicines. All this has been accompanied by larger, quicker, more versatile and more specialised machinery. There have been notable improvements in buildings and plant as well. The costs of applying these new methods and equipment have been a spur to the creation of larger farm holdings.

The EAGGF

The European Agricultural Guidance and Guarantee Fund (EAGGF) is divided into two parts. The Guarantee part creates the market and price structures needed to maintain and raise farmers' incomes. The Guidance section, which has undergone several transformations since it began, is aimed at financing the restructur-

FIGURE 5.5
Rent is Price-Determined

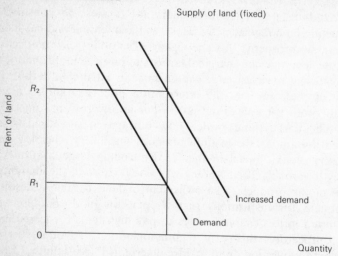

The demand for the product of the land determines the rent paid for the land if it is assumed that land is fixed in supply. If the demand for the product grown on the land, and therefore the product's price, rises then the rent of the land will also rise. The assumption is that the land user can afford to pay more for the land when prices are higher. This assumes that costs remain the same or rise less than the rise in price of the product. It should be remembered that the demand for land is what economists call a 'derived demand'; that is to say, it is derived from the demand for the product of the land whether it be turnips, wheat or office space.

ing of agriculture and helping the less favoured regions. The fund usually provides about 25 per cent of the cost with the remainder coming from the national governments. It has had most impact in France and Germany but will have increasing impact in the newer member countries such as Portugal and Greece. The trend towards larger holdings has been encouraged by this Guidance part of the CAP. It has given financial rewards to hundreds of thousands of small farmers as an encouragement to leave the industry or to alter their production patterns. The land of those giving up farming has usually been swallowed up into larger holdings. The trend to greater output has also been helped by direct subsidies from governments to farmers who wish to drain, plough, build, improve and modernise fields and buildings.

The nature and extent of these improvement grants has altered considerably over the years depending on what the government and Commission see as priorities. One of their main uses has been to give direct financial assistance to Less Favoured Areas (LFAs), or special cases such as hill farmers. In their very nature, however, many of them are also available to big 'agri-businesses'. Such grants are partly responsible for the disappearance of traditional meadowland, the ploughing of downland, the grubbing up of hedges, the reclamation of moorland, the drainage of wetlands and the sprouting of industrialised farm buildings. An alternative viewpoint is that they have helped to keep the hill farmer in place, thus maintaining the essential character of what is, in reality, a man-made landscape. They have, it is argued, contributed to the maintenance of the economic and social quality of life in the mountains, hills and border lands.

Other Reasons for Oversupply

Oversupply sometimes originates in the close production relationships of products or in what economists call 'joint-supply'. There is, for example, a direct relationship between an increased demand for dairy products such as butter, cheeses, cream and yoghurt, and the output of skimmed milk and beef. As incomes and population rise there is a greater demand for dairy products. Therefore, more milk must be produced. This can be achieved up to a point by feeding cows with better food (adding to costs) and by improved technical efficiency. But it can also be done by keeping more cows which will normally have a calf each year in order to maintain their milking capacity and to produce a valuable 'by-product'. The extra calves are either kept as future milking cows, or for beef, or slaughtered for veal, depending on their breeding sire. In practice, of course, a mixture of improved productivity and an increased number of cows is employed. The end result of the attempt to produce more milk for dairy products is the probable output of more beef, although this may not be a problem if the increased population and income also create a greater demand for beef products. It does, however, present problems for farmers who need to feed, house and market the beef cattle because this requires land for growing feed, and, probably, an increased import of animal feed. An alternative policy is the early slaughtering of animals but this tends to reduce their market value and may present problems to the intervention boards. This argument can have a different line if one starts from a situation of an increased demand for beef which may then create excess milk production, depending on how the industry reacts in using the milk of the cows which bear the calves.

Most of the above discussion about the causes of overproduction has been in the context of traditional Northern European products such as grain, meat and dairy produce. There has also been a major difficulty with products such as wine, olive oil and vegetable oils and some fruit and horticultural output.

How have the Surpluses been Dealt with?

Initially the surpluses were no real worry since they acted as a traditional buffer stock against future shortages. It was, and remains, sensible to have some surplus. The surplus of output over consumption of cereals, excluding rice, began in 1980–1. It became excessive in 1982–3, declined in 1983–4 and became exorbitantly high in 1984–5 but from then until 1989 it was controlled to reasonable levels. After 1989 the problem returned. Butter surpluses of output over consumption began in 1975-6 and reached a peak in 1983. This coincided with a peak yield for dairy cows and a low level of consumption as diet-conscious and unemployed people shifted their purchases to non-milk fats. The actual stocks in intervention stores did not move exactly in line with excess output. They reached a peak in 1986 but fell temporarily in response to the introduction of quotas on milk output. The wine lake has grown steadily as output has expanded and consumption of ordinary wine has declined. Consumption of wine in Europe fell from an annual average of 50 litres per head in the early 1970s to 40 litres in the late 1980s.

The methods of dealing with surpluses up to 1991 varied with the product but some general attempts were made. There was, for example, the belief that paying small farmers to give up farming would reduce the output of some food, especially in France and West Germany. It did sometimes have this effect but the long-term result was often to increase output, as land which had been inefficiently farmed came into the hands of larger, more efficient farmers. As self-sufficiency has been achieved in some products another general approach has been to encourage the export of food by the use of rebates. These are of immense complexity and have caused much international disquiet. The USA usually regards them as a breach of the General Agreement on Tariffs and Trade. Countries such as Australia and New Zealand see them as creating unfair competition for their products in markets such as Japan. Development economists attack them for creating unfair competition for indigenous producers in developing countries. They are also, allegedly, a gold-mine for fiddlers, twisters and cheats of all descriptions, or for those who understand and can exploit loopholes in the regulations.

Another method adopted to cut the amounts in intervention stores has been the direct sale, in large quantities, of products such as beef, butter and sugar to the Soviet Union and now to the Commonwealth of Independent States. The prices obtained for these bulk sales have often been exceptionally low. They are items which are supposed to have been close to the end of their storage life and any revenue is regarded as beneficial, as is the reduced cost of storage. These sales are politically unpopular. Akin to them are 'gifts' of food to famine-stricken countries. The gift of skimmed milk to impoverished people has been criticised on the grounds that it is harmful to young children because it lacks essential nutrients and requires hygienic preparation. This defiency, it is said, is not always emphasised and it is not always possible to achieve adequate standards of hygiene because of polluted water supplies.

One major device for using intervention stocks has been to make them available at low prices to institutions such as hospitals, residential homes, and higher education establishments. The assumption is that the demand for these products in the normal, high-priced market, is not affected by the offer of low prices for bulk purchase to these bodies. In effect the intervention board is taking advantage of the differing price elasticities of demand in the two markets – that is, the higher elasticity in the institutional market. This is a form of price discrimination. Similar schemes have been aimed at pensioners in distributing beef and butter. An unusual version of this made cheap butter available to all consumers for a short period in 1987. All these schemes have to be used very carefully in order not to destroy the existing orderly market for the product.

The methods mentioned so far failed to attack the basic problem of overproduction and its causes. There was a marked reluctance to tackle the issue by reducing target and intervention prices because of the political ramifications. It would probably not have cut output very much because of the tendency, explained above, of farmers to raise output as prices fall in order to maintain their income levels. The most effective technique, therefore, was to impose quotas on output. A quota is a fixed, legally enforceable limit on the output of a product from each production unit. Quotas were applied to milk in 1984 and they were strengthened in 1986. Despite the enormous political furore and the great hardship imposed in an arbitrary fashion on many farmers, the quotas have been very successful. United Kingdom farmers felt particularly ill-used, with some justification, because they were the most efficient. Thousands of farmers have ceased dairy production and the milk quota has become a saleable and transferable financial asset. The quota system, accompanied by 'fines' for overproduction and a gradually imposed price restraint, removed most of the milk product surpluses. There have since been several modifications to the system to make it fairer and less arbitrary and to prevent a return of the surpluses.

The methods used to cut surpluses of grain were also successful initially. They began with a 'coresponsibility levy' on output. This is, in effect, a tax on output and is therefore in direct conflict with the price support principles of the CAP. It has been varied and falls most heavily on large-scale producers. Then, in 1988–9, an upper limit, called a 'maximum guaranteed quantity' (MGQ), was placed on the total output quantity on which the intervention prices were payable. (This was similar to the United Kingdom system that existed before 1972. That limited the financial commitment of the government to a certain preordained volume of output.) Beyond this quantity the producers have no guaranteed price or sale. Moreover, if the MGQ is exceeded intervention prices are cut by 3 per cent in the following marketing year. The checks on quality were also tightened so that intervention prices became more related to quality. In addition, intervention buying for cereals and oil-seeds is restricted to months outside the normal harvest period. This forces producers to look harder for buyers in the market before offering their cereals for intervention buying. Some were in the habit of selling their harvest directly into intervention without bothering to look elsewhere.

Thus, with milk and cereals, the Community has managed to get away from the stranglehold of unrestricted price guarantees. It can now limit the guarantee to a predetermined amount and can affect the price received by the farmer by 'fines' and 'coresponsibility levies'. The problem of surplus output of oil-seeds was tackled by fixing a MGQ which, if exceeded, triggered a reduction in the market support prices and, presumably, a cutback in production in the following year.

Several other minor attempts at dissolving surpluses have been made. Some of them have been marginally effective. Others have been ludicrously expensive to implement. For example, wine growers have been paid to destroy vines. This has been worthwhile because mainly inferior vines were destroyed. One scheme which turned excess wine into industrial alcohol and another to turn butter into a condensed cooking fat were extremely expensive. Yet another scheme ended up feeding surplus milk products back to cattle.

Eventually, in 1986, the Community adopted a version of a policy that was first adopted in the USA in the 1930s, which consisted of paying farmers to leave land fallow. The European scheme is called 'set-aside' and is more complicated, sophisticated or cumbersome according to your viewpoint. In return for a cash payment per year, a farmer undertakes to remove a percentage of his land from the cultivation of certain arable crops. This policy is accompanied by inducements for what is called 'extensification', broadening the use of land into a greater variety of crops and into non-agricultural uses. The environmental lobby has high hopes that set-aside will be a stimulus to reafforestation with broad-leaved trees and to the establishment of new footpaths, bridleways and recreational areas. However, American experience does not give much cause for optimism about the effectiveness of set-aside. In that case there were massive improvements in productivity from the land that remained in cultivation, but the result was that overproduction reappeared. In the United Kingdom the risk of this happening has been somewhat reduced by the removal of fertiliser subsidies and various land improvement grants. The diversification of land use and employment in rural areas in the United Kingdom will be gradually extended because there has been a relaxation of planning controls on the use of agricultural buildings. It is hoped that old buildings will be converted for small enterprises and workshops. Tourist boards and enterprise agencies are also encouraging a diversification of farm activities. Similar policies are also being applied in other Community countries.

All these policies, taken together, were initially effective in removing the excessively large intervention stocks. Consequently, the financial burden of the CAP was lightened and the Community budget was in surplus in 1988–9. The food surpluses began to reappear in 1990 and this gave added impetus to the demands for a major reform of the CAP. It remains to be seen whether these policies can be sustained because, for example, farm incomes in the United Kingdom fell by about 20 per cent in real terms between 1985 and 1990, with further falls expected in 1991. There were similar falls in other countries. The main reasons for this were the 'low' levels set for target prices and the rise in production costs. Farmers are a particularly strong political lobby, especially in mainland Europe. In France, for example, in 1990–1 the farmers organised a large number of powerful demonstrations against government ministers and imported animals and foodstuffs. It is unlikely that farmers will meekly accept a permanent reduction in their standard of living. Having said that, the number of people engaged in agriculture has steadily declined over the past twenty years and the lobbies which have interests in opposition to the farmers' have been growing in strength and influence.

Reform Proposals

In early 1991 the Commission published what it called a 'reflection paper' stating its position on fundamental reform of the CAP. This was done against a background of the breakdown, mainly on the issue of the Community's agricultural policies, of the Uruguay round of GATT talks. There had also been an unwelcome reappearance of large surplus stocks of beef, cereals, butter and skimmed milk in intervention stores. These stocks were well above the levels required for protection against sudden disasters. There was also the very uncomfortable fact that farmers' incomes were falling rapidly whilst record amounts of money were being spent on the CAP.

The proposals were aimed at bringing the markets back into balance and controlling surplus production whilst maintaining rural communities and protecting the environment. Their general thrust was to cut guaranteed prices across a wide range of products and to compensate farmers with 'income aid'. In the cereals sector, for example, the payment of this aid would be per hectare, fixed annually in relation to market prices, and in relation to the size of the holding. Beyond a certain size of holding the payment would be dependent upon the farmer withdrawing a proportion of arable land from production. This land could be used for non-food production. The coresponsibility levies on cereals, which are effectively a sliding-scale tax, would be abolished. In the livestock sector there would also be direct income support through a system of premium payments for certain types of producers as in the present hill farming areas. Any farmer who adopted 'extensification' by, for example, reducing the number of animals per hectare, would also receive compensation. For other products the proposals include a mixture of price controls, direct income support and set-aside and, in the case of milk, reduced output quotas. There would, in addition, be direct income support for using environmentally sound methods, together with a long-term set-aside programme aimed at encouraging forestry and protecting the rural environment. A revised programme called a pre-pension scheme, to recompense farmers for early retirement, was incorporated in the plan.

These proposals were modified and adopted by the Commission in mid-1991 but received a very mixed reception ranging from lukewarm to outright rejection. There are likely to be exceptionally tough bargaining sessions before a policy acceptable to all the member states is arrived at, especially if the deadline of 1993 for its implementation is to be met. The major obstacle to be overcome is that of accepting the idea that large numbers of farmers should be paid considerable sums of money to do nothing. The idea could catch on among other groups in the Community! It is a concept that may be wrapped up in images of farmers being paid to conserve the rural environment or maintaining the fabric of the countryside, but it will still be hard for politicians to sell the idea to urban voters who may justly feel that they are being discriminated against and, to add insult to injury, that they are paying over the odds (that is, the world market price) for their food. In order to make the politicians' task easier the proposals were intended to reduce European food prices by about 10 per cent over the years from 1993 to 1997.

The proposals eventually adopted in May 1992 were a modified version of the 1991 scheme. Over the three years from 1993–6 they will, for example, cut the prices paid to farmers for cereals by 29 per cent, and for beef by 15 per cent. Dairy farmers will have their output quotas reduced by 1 per cent in 1993 and 1994. Large cereal producers will have to set aside 15 per cent of their land. The total area of set-aside land will be roughly equivalent to the area of

Belgium. In recompense farmers will receive direct income support which will be extended to all farmers and not restricted to farmers of smaller farms as originally proposed. Expenditure on the CAP will rise initially but is expected to fall eventually. It is alleged that the food mountains will shrink and that average food prices to consumers will fall closer to world levels, by about 10 per cent. It is more likely that middlemen and retailers will retain most of these savings and prices to consumers may fall by far less than the predicted figure. The reforms are the most important for 30 years and will concentrate on supporting the smallest and poorest producers. Many of the 1991 proposals will be implemented to help develop rural enterprise and to encourage retraining or diversification. The proposed reforms provoked riots among French farmers but were generally welcomed because they made an agreement on the Uruguay Round of GATT talks more likely.

The trauma of the recent negotiations on agricultural policy has led to renewed demands for the quest for a *common* policy to be abandoned and for each country to return to having its own national policy. This reversion to an earlier age is probably impossible once the internal free market without barriers is finally accomplished after 1992, although it may be feasible for small sections of the policy to be hived off to national governments. Examples might be sheep or tobacco, or olives. We can be reasonably certain that any policy that is adopted will be full of compromises to meet individual nations' internal political pressures, that it will need a major overhaul within a few years, and that the necessary decisions for change will be delayed until the last minute or until the breakdown of the system is imminent.

What of the Future?

Demographic trends do not bode well for European agriculture. The population of the Community is expected to rise by 2 per cent from 1985 to 2005. The populations of the area of the old Federal Republic of West Germany and that of Belgium are expected to fall. There may be extra growth in world markets because the world population is predicted to grow by 36 per cent in the same period. Some changes may arise as a result of the creation of the European Economic Area between EFTA and the Community in 1993 and from the creation of new democracies in Central and Eastern Europe but the effects may simply be to increase the supplies of food available. Further embarrassing surpluses may arise. It is reasonable to expect, therefore, that within the European Community there will be little expansion of total consumption of staples such as wheat for flour, potatoes and bulk vegetables. Patterns of consumption will continue to change if real incomes rise as anticipated. Allowing for fashions in diet, there will be a continued shift of demand to meat products, dairy products and higher-quality fruit, vegetables and horticultural products. Land use will respond to the need to feed more animals.

In some areas, there will be a return to mixed farming and a shift away from monoculture. There is also likely to be an extension of afforestation and more land will be dedicated to recreational use of various sorts, including nature conservation areas. Moreover, there will be a continued drain of land into building development for housing and industry. This will be harder to oppose if the required level of food production can be achieved with a smaller area of land in cultivation. Some farmers will apply the benefits of the latest biotechnological developments in plant types, animal breeding and recycling of materials.

In the future, there are likely to be two conflicting trends. On the one hand, there will be pressure to produce standardised, quality-controlled products for a mass market. This will be assisted by established grading and packaging standards which will be extended under the single European market. On the other hand, there will be a growing market for high-quality, organically produced food from those who are able to pay the inevitably higher prices. It is in this sphere that the smaller, more localised producer will flourish. However, all these predictions will be invalidated if there is a major shift in climatic conditions over the next twenty years.

Economic Performance 6

Introduction

The measurement of economic performance is notoriously difficult and fraught with controversy. The comparison of the economic performance of two or more countries or trading blocs is even more problematical. When it is eventually agreed what to measure and with what units there may still be disagreement about the relative merits of various aspects of performance. An analogy of the problem may be seen in the task of a motoring correspondent who has to draw up a comparison of a Mini and a high-performance sports car. You can measure, fairly objectively, top speed, acceleration, petrol consumption, luggage room, seats and maintenance costs, but many of these are dependent upon the operating context – urban, rural or motorway. A traffic jam on a motorway reduces them to temporary equality in most respects except the comfort of the seats and the quality of the 'in-car entertainment'. Similarly, two or more economies can be compared objectively but only up to a point. The context of the comparison and the base from which it is made then becomes of paramount importance.

Much of the emphasis of comparison of economic performance is upon rates of growth of various indices or absolute quantity. The implicit assumption is that all growth is good and that higher growth is better. This is, of course, nonsense because the costs of the growth to society may be excessive. It may reduce welfare, increase ill health, raise death rates and exploit Third World countries. The growth may also be very unevenly distributed. The present fashion for market-driven economies tends to ignore these facts. Part of the argument about the policies to be implemented to achieve the single market is really about distribution of growth, although the main emphasis is on overall growth. President Mitterrand of France and Jacques Delors, President of the Commission, are both quoted as not wanting a Europe for bankers only but for workers as well, hence their emphasis on the 'Social Charter'.

Having expressed all these doubts it remains necessary to attempt some assessment of relative economic performance. We should, however, bear in mind that we cannot know what might have happened if a particular country had not joined the Community. We should also remember, when making comparisons, that the Community only partially determines or influences the environment in which it operates. Changes in the international trade cycle, international interest rates and in other countries' economic policies are beyond its control. So too are natural disasters, international conflicts and political upheavals. An added factor is the need to make allowances for foreign exchange rates and their movements.

What Measures of Comparison are Useful?

Almost all international, and for that matter national, comparison starts from the calculation of gross domestic product – that is, from national income statistics. The United Nations has a preferred method for this calculation and one of the best sources of data is the annual Statistical Yearbook. Some nations do not adhere strictly to this method; the United Kingdom, for example, does not put a monetary figure on the value of housewives' services.

This is not the place for a full description of national income accounting but a brief explanation is needed. When measuring the national income the economist is calculating the amount of money income obtained by the nation in the form of wages, salaries and so on, profits and rent, in return for producing consumer goods and services, investment goods and public goods. By definition, allowing for the niceties of the calculation, national income should equal the value added to the national output. In measuring the national output it is important to avoid 'double counting' of items and to measure only the value added at each stage of production. Also by definition, the national income equals the amount of money spent on the purchase of capital and consumption goods. In this third method of calculation which is called the 'expenditure method', care has to be taken to avoid double counting or miscounting, especially with respect to indirect taxation and subsidies. There is a 'factor cost adjustment' to take care of this. The statistics can be related to the domestic stage only or can be modified to allow for foreign payments, income and expenditure. The phrase 'national' is then applied to the statistics as in statements such as 'national income = national expenditure = national output'. A final adjustment is made to allow for capital consumption or depreciation because output undertaken simply to replace worn-out equipment is not a net addition to output. This calculation, deducting a figure for capital consumption, turns the figures from 'gross' to 'net'. The figures used for this item of capital consumption are estimates and are among the least reliable of the national income statistics. At the end of all this the economist concludes that national income = national expenditure = net national product (national output).

What then have we got as a basis of comparison? We have a fairly accurate measure of the value of new output in a year, of the income derived from producing it, and of its monetary value in terms of expenditure. If we then wish to compare changes over time we need to make allowances for changes in price levels. This is done by taking a base year and using a price index as a 'deflator'. For example, in order to compare the national income of 1992 with that of 1979 we need to use, say, 1979 price levels for both and convert the 1992 figures by the amount by which an index of general prices has risen over the thirteen years. This is called converting money national income into 'real' national income. It simply means that account has been taken of inflation. It is also necessary, sometimes, to take notice of movements in the level of population over time and to calculate money or real national income per head. This is only a rough guide to living standards and it is best to combine it with an analysis of the distribution of income per head, although these figures are among the least reliable of all those available. They are also capable of many different interpretations.

Other useful statistics for international comparison are crude output statistics or changes in them as measured by an index, and levels of possession of standard consumer durable goods such as telephones, video recorders or television sets per head. Interesting results can be obtained from studying how many minutes or hours an average worker must work to be able to buy standard goods or services such as a kilo of butter, a unit of electricity, a small car or a loaf of bread. Other statistics which are valuable for comparative studies are those of working hours, average earnings and productivity.

These then are some of the basic measurements of comparison. If we take account of all the warnings about their validity and usefulness, how has the European Community fared?

How has the Community Performed?

The two sets of figures given in Tables 6.1 and 6.2 are a rough measure of how living standards have changed. The first set measures gross domestic product per head. The figures are at current prices and at what are called 'purchasing power standards'. These take account of exchange rates and differences in price levels and are far too complex to explain in this context. Suffice it to say most economists think they are the best way of coping with changes in foreign exchange rates over time when using statistics. They should be considered in conjunction with the second set which gives figures of volume indices of GDP at market prices.

A mass of statistics such as Tables 6.1 and 6.2 show is capable of many interpretations or variations of emphasis. The figures for Turkey, Austria and Sweden have been included because they are potential entrants to the Community, and because the Austrian economy has sometimes been held up as something to be emulated. The Swedish experience in reducing unemployment can provide important lessons for those who choose to study them. It is clear that Turkey's economic position is well behind that of even the poorer members of the Community such as Portugal, Ireland or Greece, although its recent growth rate has been exceptionally high. Norway has been included because it decided, by referendum, not to join the Community when the United Kingdom did. Norway remained part of EFTA which has developed very close trading links with the Community and formed the European Economic Area in 1991 (see Chapter 3). It benefited from oil and gas discoveries at the same time as the United Kingdom but has made much better use of its oil revenues to restructure its economy. Norway is currently reconsidering applying for membership of the Community. It is interesting to compare growth rates. The figures in

Table 6.3 are at constant prices and, therefore, make allowances for inflation.

TABLE 6.1
Gross Domestic Product at Market Prices per Head (At Current Prices and Purchasing Power Standards, PPS)

Country	1981	1986	1989	*1990 (£000)
Europe 12	8 770	13 639	17 229	n.a.
USA	13 591	21 307	26 478	13.5
Japan	9 194	15 155	19 896	10.9
UK	8 764	14 158	18 402	9.4
Belgium	9 041	13 883	17 444	9.2
Denmark	9 535	16 025	18 478	9.7
West Germany	10 033	15 702	19 244	10.1
Greece	5 090	7 670	9 353	4.7
Spain	6 392	9 893	13 324	7.0
France	9 900	15 042	18 703	9.8
Ireland	5 808	8 537	11 534	6.2
Italy	9 042	14 037	17 841	9.3
Luxembourg	10 258	17 326	22 311	11.5
Netherlands	9 673	14 527	17 605	9.3
Portugal	4 775	7 196	9 452	4.8
Turkey	1 310	1 404	5 503 (1988)	3.1
Norway	14 473	20 612	20 635 ..	11.0
Austria	9 110	15 252	15 810 ..	9.1
Sweden	14 134	16 425	18 675 ..	10.1

*1990 measured at purchasing power parity, OECD figures.

SOURCE For Tables 6.1, 6.2, 6.3: Eurostat, *Basic Statistics of the Community*, 28th edn (Luxembourg: Office for Official Publications of the European Communities, 1991).

It can be seen that the growth performance of the European Twelve between 1981 and 1986 was inferior to that of both the United States and Japan and that the United Kingdom was among the better performers in the Community. The United Kingdom's performance should perhaps be compared with Norway's, in that both were affected by oil revenues from the North Sea. It should also be seen against the rapid deindustrialisation of the early 1980s when British manufacturing industry suffered a devastating decline. It would have been reasonable to expect that the enormous revenues

TABLE 6.2
Volume Indices (GDP at Market Prices; 1980 = 100)

Country	1981	1986	1989
Europe 12	100.2	110.3	122.0
USA	103.7	119.6	133.3
Japan	103.9	123.9	143.4
UK	98.8	112.6	127.2
Belgium	98.6	106.2	117.0
Denmark	99.1	116.7	117.6
West Germany	100.2	108.8	118.1
Greece	100.1	108.1	115.2
Spain	99.8	110.6	128.7
France	101.2	110.0	120.7
Ireland	103.3	109.3	125.4
Italy	101.1	111.3	123.0
Luxembourg	99.8	118.6	139.2
Netherlands	99.3	107.3	115.1
Portugal	101.3	109.6	126.2
Turkey	104.4	136.7	154.6
Norway	100.9	123.2	129.0
Austria	99.9	109.3	119.8
Sweden	99.7	110.6	122.5

SOURCE For Tables 6.1, 6.2, 6.3: Eurostat, *Basic Statistics of the Community*, 25th and 28th edns.

from North Sea oil would have been used to renovate and re-equip British industry. One cannot imagine the Japanese missing such an opportunity. Instead it appears that the advantage has been used to finance social security for the unemployed or, if you look at it differently, on investment overseas. The long-term opportunity cost of such a policy, or absence of policy, will be immense.

There were significant changes during the period 1986–90, as can be seen from the figures. Events since 1990 as the world economic recession affected different countries to varying extents has caused their relative growth patterns to change. The reader who wishes to keep up to date with these changes is recommended to consult the half-yearly *OECD Economic Outlook*. These reports also contain projections for two years ahead. The OECD information is also available through computer data bases.

TABLE 6.3
Annual Rate of Growth of GDP at Market Prices (at Constant Prices, 1984–9) %

Country	Total	Per Head of Total Population	Per Head of Occupied Population	Growth of Real GDP in 1990
Europe 12	3.1	2.8	1.9	2.9
USA	3.6	2.3	1.1	1.0*
Japan	4.4	3.9	3.2	5.6*
Belgium	2.6	2.4	1.7	3.7
Denmark	1.7	1.6	0.8	2.1
West Germany	2.6	2.3	1.6	4.5*
Greece	2.2	2.0	1.6	−0.1
Spain	4.2	4.0	1.3	3.7
France	2.7	2.2	2.3	2.8
Ireland	3.2	3.3	3.5	6.6*
Italy	3.1	2.9	2.5	2.0
Luxembourg	4.4	3.8	1.6	2.3
Netherlands	2.4	1.8	0.8	3.9
Portugal	4.3	3.8	4.5	4.2
United Kingdom	3.8	3.5	2.0	0.8

*Real GNP.

The causes of economic growth are not always easily identifiable or quantifiable, nor is the relative emphasis to be given to each. It is usually agreed, however, that investment expenditure, the application of new technology, research and development expenditure, improved education and training of the population, and the shift of workers from less productive to more productive employment are important determinants of the rate of growth of GDP. In recent years, more emphasis has been placed on the detailed nature of the research and development (R & D) expenditure. Japan spends a relatively small proportion of its R & D money on defence-associated uses; the United Kingdom and the United States spend a relatively high percentage. It will be very interesting to see, over the next few years, what the effects of disarmament agreements will be on the make-up of R & D. The available evidence from the 1980s and 1990s seems to demonstrate conclusively that Japan benefited greatly from her policy and that the United Kingdom suffered from hers.

The pitfalls associated with the use of statistics can be illustrated from the case of the United Kingdom government which produced sets of statistics emphasising the great improvement in the country's economic performance in the 1980s compared with previous decades. The figures were mainly based on productivity growth per person employed. These statistics, as presented, were impressive but were the subject of debate among economists about their validity and relevance. For example, they usually took 1980 or 1981 as their starting base and measured changes rather than the absolute figures for output, so that they discounted the drop in manufacturing output in the early 1980s. If they are taken in the context of the general use of statistics by the United Kingdom government since 1979, then they need to be treated with great caution. The government consistently manipulated the unemployment figures in order to reduce the recorded number. It also indulged in what some people saw as odd accounting practices with regard to the sales of nationalised industry assets, counting the proceeds as negative expenditure. The government use of statistics on the National Health Service has also been highly suspect – it is probably safer to use Eurostat figures. However, some of the relevant figures are given in Tables 6.4 and 6.5, 6.6 and 6.7.

TABLE 6.4

Output per Person Employed – Whole Economy (Average Annual % Changes)

	1960–70	*1970–80*	*1980–88*
UK	2.4	1.3	2.5
USA	2.0	0.4	1.2
Japan	8.9	3.8	2.9
West Germany	4.4	2.8	1.8
France	4.6	2.8	2.0
Italy	6.3	2.6	2.0
Canada	2.4	1.5	1.4
G7 average	3.5	1.7	1.8

UK data from Central Statistical office. Other countries' data from OECD except 1988 which are calculated from national GNP or GDP figures and OECD employment estimates.

SOURCE For Tables 6.4, 6.5, 6.6, 6.7: *Economic Progress Report*, No. 201, April (London: HM Treasury/HMSO, 1989).

TABLE 6.5

Output per Person Employed – Manufacturing Industry (Average Annual % Changes)

	1960–70	*1970–80*	*1980–88*
UK	3.0	1.6	5.2
USA	3.5	3.0	4.0
Japan	8.8	5.3	3.1
West Germany	4.1	2.9	2.2
France	5.4	3.2	3.1
Italy	5.4	3.0	3.5
Canada	3.4	3.0	3.6
G7 average	4.5	3.3	3.6

UK data from Central Statistical office. Other countries' data from OECD except France and Italy which use IMF employment data. 1988 data for France and Italy cover first three quarters only.

TABLE 6.6

Relative Productivity Levels (Whole Economy 1986)

	GDP per Head of Population	*GDP per Person Employed*	*GDP per Hour Worked*
UK	100	100	100
USA	150	141	132
Japan	106	94	67
West Germany	110	113	105
France	106	119	117
Italy	100		
Canada	140	131	116

Average annual hours worked per person employed supplied by
A. Maddison, calculated as in appendix C of his *Phases of Capitalist Development* (1982).

Figures for Italy incomplete because of uncertainties in the size of the hidden economy.

TABLE 6.7
Employment and Hours Worked, 1986

	% of Population in Employment	Average Annual Hours Worked per Person Employed
UK	43.0	1511
USA	45.4	1609
Japan	48.2	2129
West Germany	41.4	1630
France	37.8	1533
Canada	45.9	1704

What have been the Longer-Term Trends?

Over the thirty years from 1960 the GDP per head in Europe more than doubled. In contrast, that in Japan rose by nearly five times. In the United States, it grew over 60 per cent. In absolute terms, in 1989, the USA's GDP per head was 54 per cent higher than Europe's; Japan's was 16 per cent higher (using purchasing power standards for comparison). In general the more mature economies of Europe such as the United Kingdom (average annual growth rate 2.2 per cent in 1960–85 and 3.2 per cent in 1986–90) grew more slowly than the less mature such as Spain (4.6 per cent in 1960–90) and Portugal (5.1 per cent in 1960–85 and 4.5 in 1986–90). The more mature economies also showed less volatility in growth rates than, for example, Spain.

In terms of total output the United States still dominates. In 1989, the United States' GDP, in thousand million ECU, was 4658, the Community of Twelve's was 4407, and Japan's 2559. These average figures hide wide regional disparities within the individual nations. The broad national differences can be seen in the tables of GDP per head. The alleged North–South divide in the United Kingdom is one obvious example of the regional variations in income, employment and other variables used to measure the quality of life. Eurostat produces very detailed figures of regional incomes based on GDP at market prices and on PPS. These permit detailed analysis and comparison and enable maps to be drawn to indicate the areas of the Community which are extreme in terms of affluence or poverty.

In the future, in the longer term, it is expected that changes involved in creating a genuine single market up to 1992 and beyond will be a major stimulus to economic growth. Labour and capital should be more mobile and the costs of production and movement of goods should be significantly lower.

Employment Comparisons

Since 1975 both the United States and Japan have coped much more effectively with unemployment than Europe although there have been improvements since 1985 in the Community's record. Between 1982 and 1984 the average growth rate of the Community was 1.6 per cent per year and the number of jobs was falling by 600 000 each year. The annual growth rate has since risen to about 3.5 per cent and 8 million jobs were created between 1985 and 1991. The figures given in Table 6.8 show this clearly. We have to assume that 'unemployment' means the same thing in each area. This is a very simplifying assumption but the alternative is two pages of footnotes and definitions! The interested reader should consult the OECD half-yearly reports to understand the complexities of the definitions, or read *Unemployment and Job Creation* by Andy Beharrell (Macmillan, 1991).

TABLE 6.8
Unemployment Rate (%) (Annual Average)

	Europe 12	Japan	United States
1975	2.9	1.9	8.5
1981	7.8	2.2	7.6
1985	10.6	2.6	7.2
1986	10.7	2.8	7.0
1987	9.7	2.8	6.1
1988	8.9	2.5	5.4
1989	8.3	2.3	5.2
1990	10.8	2.1	5.4
1991	8.9	2.2	6.7
1992 (est.)	9.3	2.3	6.7

Source Eurostat, *Basic Statistics of the Community*, 25th and 28th edns, and *Theme 3 – Population and Social Conditions* (Luxembourg: Office for Official Publications of the European Communities, 1988 and 1991).

The European statistics represent an average of a very wide range of unemployment in the member states. In 1991, the unemployment rates, not seasonally adjusted, as a percentage of civilian working population were:

Belgium	9.4	Ireland	15.8
Denmark	10.3	Italy	10.9
West Germany	4.6	Luxembourg	1.4
Greece	8.6	Netherlands	6.1
Spain	15.9	Portugal	8.8
France	9.4	UK	8.7

A particularly worrying aspect of the unemployment figures is the high proportion of the unemployed who are under 25 and the growing incidence of long-term unemployment. In April 1990, for example, in the Twelve, 42 per cent of all unemployed persons were under 25. Of all women unemployed, 50 per cent were aged under 25. Moreover, 52 per cent of the overall total had been unemployed for more than a year. About a third had been without a job for over two years. Overall about 47 per cent of those without work were women but this average covered a range from 34 per cent in Ireland to 60 per cent in Belgium. The United Kingdom's proportion for female unemployment was 40 per cent of the total. In the United Kingdom 37 per cent of the jobless were under 25. Some of the statistics give cause for great concern and explain the emphasis in the Community on regional programmes and cohesion funds. In Spain for example, 25 per cent of males and 39 per cent of females aged under 25 were unemployed. In Italy the figures were 23 per cent for males and 35 per cent for females. At the other extreme, Germany had 4.1 per cent of its males and 5 per cent of its females aged under 25 unemployed.

Some economists and politicians prefer the emphasis to be placed on job creation rates rather than on unemployment. There is an increasing amount of literature analysing the number and type of jobs created over recent years in both the United States and Europe. The conclusions from the research are often ambiguous or even contradictory. The interpretation of such studies may result in value judgements about the new jobs in the tertiary sector, especially in personal services, as being 'inferior' to the lost jobs in manufacturing industry. The new jobs may be part-time, seasonal, low-wage and unskilled. The best test of whether such job creation is satisfactory is to look at the skill and experience of the remaining unemployed and see whether it is matched to any extent by the nature of vacant jobs. It may be that there has been a long-term structural decline in an industry, as in coal mining. This means that few relevant new jobs will appear and that retraining is the only solution to the problem. This retraining has been the role of the Social Fund and Regional Development Funds of the Community.

The Community's role with respect to unemployment generally until 1990 was peripheral because it was regarded as a function of national governments to control their own internal economies and thus their own levels of unemployment. Since the movement towards the single market, however, the Community has begun to play an increasingly important part in employment policy where it impinges on the Social Charter and in certain aspects of 'Europe 2000', which is a plan launched in 1991 to improve regional balance within the Community (see Chapter 10).

The Service Sector

The service, or tertiary, sector consists of commerce, transport, banking, insurance, administration, distribution and personal services. In the Community, in 1975, about 60 million people were engaged in the tertiary sector. This was about 49 per cent of the total civilian labour force. By 1989 the percentage had risen to 60 per cent. In the same period, 1975 to 1989, the share of the sector in the GDP rose from 47 to 61 per cent. These changes may appear rapid but they were even more pronounced in Japan and the United States. Employment in the tertiary sector rose by 17 per cent in the Community compared with about 20 per cent in Japan and 32 per cent in the United States. In 1989 about 70 per cent of American and 58 per cent of Japanese workers were employed in the service sector. Most of the increase in employment in the Community between 1986 and 1989, from 122 million to 129 million in total, was in the service sector where employment rose by 10 per cent from 71.5 to 78.7 million. The growth of this sector is often seen as a major sign of an economy moving into a post-industrial phase. This is something of an oversimplification because some undeveloped economies have large personal service employment simply because labour is exceptionally cheap. They do not, however, have large employment in banking and financial services.

Many of the manufacturing jobs have been lost through improvements in technology and through transfer to developing countries. The resultant decline of skilled and semi-skilled employment in manufacturing is a cause for concern because there is a limit to which the personal services sector can absorb the unwanted labour. We cannot all survive by taking in each other's washing. Once again, there is a need for a retraining programme to raise the level of workers' skill and mobility.

Trade Comparisons

The Community was formed with the intention of easing and stimulating trade between its members by reducing all barriers between them. The tariff barriers were quickly removed by 1968 and the non-tariff barriers should have been removed by the end of 1992. It was also expected that the Community's internal market would expand and enable firms to benefit from the considerable economies of scale available in a market rising to over 336 million relatively affluent people. The cost-reducing benefits from such a large internal market would, it was anticipated, enable Community firms to compete effectively in world markets. The Japanese, by comparison, have a home market of only 123 million, the United States of 246 million. The USSR had 287 million and the new Commonwealth of Independent States (CIS), formed in December 1991, has 275 million. These promised benefits have never fully materialised but the European Community is, by most standards, the most important trading group in the world. Table 6.9 shows the Community's share of world trade in 1989 compared with other important trading groups.

How has intra-Community trade developed?

Trade between members, intra-Community trade, has grown much faster since 1958 than trade with non-members. Between 1958 and 1987 trade between members increased by 37 times (8 times in real terms) whereas trade with non-members rose by 16 times (3.5 times in

TABLE 6.9
Share of World Trade, 1989

	Imports %	Exports %
European Community	16.2	15
United States	15.6	12
Japan	7.0	9.1
USSR	3.8	3.6

real terms). The pattern varies but for all members intra-Community trade accounts for over half their total trade. The details are given in Table 6.10. The countries most dependent on intra-Community trade are Ireland, Portugal, Belgium, Luxembourg and The Netherlands. The least dependent is the United Kingdom whose imports from the Community in 1989 were only 51.1 per cent of her total, and whose exports to the Community were only 50 per cent of her total. Despite the above figures, the United Kingdom has been increasingly dependent since 1958 on trade with Community members. In 1958, only about 16 per cent of her exports and 20 per cent of her imports arose from trade with the Community.

TABLE 6.10
Intra-Community Trade as a Percentage of Member States' Foreign Trade (1985–9)

	1985	1986	1987	1988	1989
Benelux	67	70	72	73	71
Denmark	49	53	54	53	52
West Germany	51	54	55	54	54
Greece	47	58	61	64	64
Spain	33	51	55	59	59
France	55	64	66	63	63
Ireland	71	73	71	73	72
Italy	45	55	57	57	57
Netherlands	54	61	62	68	68
UK	44	50	51	49	51
Portugal	46	59	63	69	70

SOURCE Based on Eurostat, *Opening up the Internal Market* (Luxembourg: Office for Official Publications of the European Communities, 1991).

TABLE 6.11
Total Imports and Exports by Partner Country (%), 1989

			Origin		
Importing country	*Europe 12*	*USA*	*Japan*	*Rest of world*	*Of which: ACP**
Europe 12	58.2	7.8	4.3	29.7	1.8
			Destination		
Exporting country	*Europe 12*	*USA*	*Japan*	*Rest of world*	*Of which: ACP**
Europe 12	60.0	7.5	2.0	30.5	1.6

*ACP = African, Caribbean, Pacific nations.

SOURCE Eurostat, *Basic Statistics of the Community*, 28th edn (Luxembourg: Office for Official Publications of the European Communities, 1991).

How has the Community's external trade changed?

There have been major changes over the years in the composition of the imports. Initially, the Community was predominantly an importer of raw materials and processed them into manufactured goods for consumption and export. Gradually the position altered and an increasing proportion of imports has been of semi-finished goods and manufactured articles. Thus, by 1989, more than half the Community's imports were manufactured goods, finished or semi-finished. The United Kingdom's trade has, of course, altered in the same way so that it now has a very large deficit on visible trade in manufactures.

One of the main variables in Community trade has been oil and natural gas. Some of this has been derived from within the Community, that is, from the United Kingdom and The Netherlands, but most is bought on world markets where the price is very volatile. Large quantities of gas are bought from Russia. In common with other countries the Community's trade volume has altered as oil and energy prices have fluctuated. The heavy reliance upon oil imports pushed the Community's overall visible trade balance into deeper deficit until the large reduction of oil prices occurred in 1985. On visible trade, the Community was in deficit from 1958 until 1986 when a surplus was achieved. The surplus in 1989 for the whole Community, seasonally adjusted, was $5.3 billion, and $2.7 billion in 1990. The OECD puts the 1991 figure at a huge deficit of $38 billion, with predicted deficits for the following two years of $37 billion. The oil price change also had an impact on 'invisible' payments in the form of interest, dividends, profits, and the purchase of financial and transport services.

The changes in the Community's current account balances

A country's balance of payments on current account is made up of two main components. The first is payments for visible imports and exports of goods and is called the 'balance of trade'. The second is called the 'invisible balance' and consists of payments into and out of a country for services and other transfers. The most important of these invisible imports and exports are payments for banking, insurance and other financial services. The other main flow of money is interest, profits and dividends from investments in other countries or paid out to foreigners who have made financial investments in the country. Tourism and travel give rise to large invisible flows and so does the purchase of shipping and air services. There are, in addition, private transfers to or from individuals living in different countries. Some countries such as the United Kingdom earn large surpluses on their invisible accounts because of the activities of their financial and commodity markets and because of the large holdings of property and financial investments abroad. This is despite the expansion of foreign holdings of assets in Europe which create an outflow of interest, profits and dividends each year. It should be noted in this context that, if one country's prevailing interest rate levels are high compared with those in other countries, there will tend to be an enlarged flow of foreign capital into that country. This will necessitate larger future outflows of interest payments unless the interest is reinvested in that country. Significant differences in national interest rates will disappear as the pace of economic and monetary union gathers pace in the 1990s as described in Chapter 7.

When the two components, the balance of visible trade and the balance of invisibles, are added together we have the 'balance of payments on current account'. There is also an account kept of movements of capital into and out of a country. These may consist of flows originating from individuals, firms or governments. They may be moved either on a short-term or long-term basis. The transfer of such funds affects the foreign exchange markets.

Visible trade

Each of the twelve members of the Community has its own accounts for visible and invisible trade and therefore an individual balance of payments on current account although there may come a time when these national accounts become unnecessary, or even impossible to calculate, as documentation for intra-Community trade becomes negligible after 1993. These accounts show great variety. In 1989, for example, only West Germany, The Netherlands, Denmark and Ireland had surpluses in visible trade outside the Community. The importance of Germany in the Community can be clearly seen from the figures in Table 6.12.

Invisible trade and current account balances

In 1989, Denmark, Greece, Spain, France, Ireland, Portugal and the United Kingdom had current account deficits. The United Kingdom and France had large invisible surpluses but they were not sufficient to match their visible deficits. This visible deficit has continued to widen into 1989. The Community as a whole had moved into current account deficit in 1978–9 and continued in deficit until 1983. Thereafter a surplus, which increased until 1986, was achieved. It reached 49 billion ECU in 1986 but has since declined to 5 billion ECU in 1989. A return to an overall deficit for the Community was seen in 1990 and 1991 and further deficits are expected in 1992 and 1993.

There are major influences on the trend of the current account. The most important are the value of the ECU against the dollar and the yen, and world oil prices. As these change the costs of production of European goods alter and their competitiveness in home and foreign markets is affected. The Japanese have been building up their balance of payments on current account surpluses ($87 billion in 1987, $35 billion in 1990), and the United States has been struggling to reduce

TABLE 6.12
Balance of Trade, 1989

Country	Imports Billion ECU	Imports % of GDP	Exports Billion ECU	Exports % of GDP	Balance Million ECU
Belgium/Lux	93	64	91	63	−2 157
Denmark	25	26	26	27	+1 219
Germany	245	23	308	29	+64 003
Greece	15	30	7	14	−7 800
Spain	62	18	42	12	−19 334
France	182	21	167	19	−14 867
Ireland	16	51	19	61	+3 066
Italy	139	18	128	16	−11 164
Netherlands	102	50	105	52	+3 540
Portugal	17	41	11	28	75 647
UK	179	24	138	18	−41 122
12, Intra + Extra	1 074	24	1 043	24	−30 263
12, Intra	447	10	413	9	−33 706
USA	430	9	330	7	−99 506
Japan	191	8	250	10	+58 497

SOURCE Eurostat, *Basic Statistics of the Community*, 28th edn (Luxembourg: Office for Official Publications of the European Communities, 1991).

its deficit ($160 billion in 1987, $92 billion in 1990, $4 billion in 1991, and an estimated $56 billion in 1992). The changes in these totals and the measures taken to disperse the surplus or reduce the deficit affect interest rates and exchange rates. It can be seen, therefore, that Community trade is partly at the mercy of Japanese and American policies. As a general rule countries with surpluses are reluctant to take swift action to reduce them. Countries in deficit are also slow to take remedial action.

Trade performance needs to be seen against the background of the Uruguay round of GATT talks which ground to a halt in late 1990, resumed in 1991, failed to reach a conclusion, and resumed again in the first half of 1992. Other background features are the unification of the two Germanys which affected the flows of capital in Europe, the Fourth Lomé Convention with ACP countries, the creation of genuinely independent Central European states and the breakdown of Comecon in 1990, the dissolution of the USSR in December 1991 and its replacement by the Commonwealth of Independent States, and the general world recession. The creation of the European Economic Area, the development of monetary union within the Community and the probable enlargement of membership will also have very important impacts on trade. On the horizon too is the creation of a six-member Association of South East Asian Nations (ASEAN), which may have considerable impact on world trade because of its high growth rate. In January 1992 they endorsed a plan to establish a regional free trade zone over the next fifteen years. ASEAN was formed in 1967 by Singapore, Malaysia, Brunei, Indonesia, the Philippines and Thailand. Vietnam and Laos may join this ASEAN Free Trade Area (AFTA), and it will, if it is ever accomplished, be a market of over 360 million people.

Money 7

What Determines the Value of the Various European Currencies?

A number of factors influence the value of a currency compared with another. These factors change in relative importance over time. They include the supply and demand of the currency in world foreign exchange markets, the extent and nature of official controls on movements of money in or out of a country, government policy and the possible existence of international agreements on foreign exchange rates. An example of this last factor was the Bretton Woods agreement on fixed parities which survived from 1947 to 1971. Another is the European Monetary System (EMS), or more specifically the Exchange Rate Mechanism (ERM) which is part of it.

Economists try to explain the fundamental relationship of two currencies in terms of the 'purchasing power parity' theory (PPP). This formidable title disguises a fairly simple idea, although, needless to say, it can be expressed in a variety of ways and with different degrees of sophistication. At its simplest the theory says that a given collection or 'basket' of goods will have a certain price in each of two countries. This price will, of course, be expressed in the two different currencies. The PPP then says that the foreign exchange rate between the two currencies will tend towards that existing in the prices of the basket of goods in the two countries. So, if our basket costs £20 in the United Kingdom and $30 in the United States, the foreign exchange rate will tend to be around £1 = $1.5. This is because the competitive nature of the markets leads to shifts in the supply and demand for goods and services as price differences become apparent.

How Well does the Purchasing Power Parity Theory Apply?

This theory seems to show basic common sense and can be seen in operation in cross-border trade between neighbouring underdeveloped countries. It does, however, become less applicable in the short term in developed economies although its long-run applicability remains valid. The PPP theory is much harder to apply when capital as well as goods and services enters into trade and when speculation is rife.

Another major problem which arises is the fact that certain important items of expenditure do not entail trade or international exchange. Such items may be power, such as electricity, housing services, a wide range of personal services and local or central government services. More sophisticated versions of the theory try to take this into account and there is sound evidence that the PPP theory of an exchange rate between two countries is valid over time, albeit with short-term aberrations.

Where does the Non-Speculative Demand and Supply of a Currency Come From?

It is easier to answer this question if we take one country, such as Britain, as an example. The demand for the pound, on the one hand, comes from foreigners who wish to buy British exports and need to pay British companies in sterling. This demand arises from both visible exports and invisible exports of services such as tourism, banking, insurance and so on. Obviously this demand relates to the volume of such trade which, in itself, is affected by comparative rates of inflation. Other things being equal, a high exchange rate for the pound will reduce the demand for the United Kingdom's exports. The extent of the reduction will depend on the price elasticity of demand for the exports. Price elasticity of demand measures the responsiveness of demand to price changes. In effect, within certain exchange rate limits, United Kingdom exports yield greater total revenue as the exchange rate of the pound drops.

The other non-speculative demand for the pound arises when foreign companies and individuals wish to transfer capital to Britain for investment purposes. This may be physical investment in the Keynesian sense of expenditure on capital goods such as factories or plant. It may, however, be the transfer of money capital for deposit in a wide range of short-term or long-term financial assets. This type of monetary flow is influenced by the interest rate levels prevailing within the United Kingdom compared with those in other similar economies. They also respond to changes in the comparative rates of inflation and to expectations of movements in foreign exchange rates in different countries. The money is used to buy bills of exchange, Treasury Bills, short- and long-dated government stock, local authority bonds, various types of certificates of deposit and company shares.

The United Kingdom has long been a major international financial centre although the preeminence of the City of London is fading. As a result of this role there are extremely large flows of capital into and out of sterling. The 'City', meaning the banks and financial institutions, earns large fees and commissions on such transfers. Those paid by foreigners are part of the United Kingdom's invisible earnings on the balance of international payments. Some of these flows into short-dated bills or bonds are very 'liquid', that is, convertible into cash, and are transferred easily and quickly, though at some expense, into other currencies if conditions change. These funds which move quickly for very short-term gains are sometimes called 'hot money' – an inescapable element in the foreign exchange markets. It is also frequently an undesirable element.

The supply of pounds, on the other hand, is produced by the reverse elements of the factors described above. That is to say, importers need to sell pounds in order to get the foreign currency required by their overseas suppliers. British tourists are selling pounds to buy the currency they need for their holidays. There is also a large supply of pounds arising from the great volume of investment abroad by British firms and individuals. This investment has, over the years, reached a huge total and economists take an intense interest in its destinations. In recent years, to 1992, North America has been a favourite destination for British overseas investment. Some of this transfer originates in the fashion for take-overs of American firms as a quick way of getting into the North American market.

What is the Role of Speculation in the Fixing of Exchange Rates?

Most of the currency bought and sold in the foreign exchange markets is dealt in with a speculative profit in mind or with the intention of avoiding loss. That is to say, the buyers and sellers do not want the currency to finance visible or invisible trade or capital movements. They are hoping for a profit after the costs of transfer are met from buying or selling. The simplest form of speculation is to buy in the hope or expectation of the price rising in the future so that a capital gain can be made. A more complicated alternative is to sell, at a high price, something that you do not yet possess in the hope that you can buy it at a lower price in order to meet your obligation to deliver it. Markets vary in the scope that they give speculators to operate.

Speculation is made a normal activity in the foreign exchange markets by the existence, side by side, of a 'spot' market and a 'forward' market. A spot market refers, as its name suggests, to a deal based on the current prices prevailing as the deal is fixed. A forward market is often called a 'futures' market when commodities are concerned. It allows dealers to reach agreement on price at one moment on a deal to be concluded in the future – days, weeks or months ahead. The bargain is made. The price to be paid is fixed and must be honoured when the date arrives. Such forward markets do serve a very useful function, enabling buyers and sellers of goods to fix their costs in advance. Thus, for example, an importer of raw materials makes his forward deal so that he can calculate exactly the costs of production arising from the purchase of foreign exchange to pay for the materials.

The existence of forward markets is a great stimulus to speculation but this does not necessarily create greater fluctuation in exchange rates. Indeed, some economists argue that an efficient, well-informed speculative market may iron out the peaks and troughs of foreign exchange rate movements. This will reduce the range of fluctuation because speculators need to take their profits while they can and there are always some who try to get out of a rising market by selling before it peaks. Alternatively, they may buy in a falling market before it bottoms out. By so doing they will, if they do it in sufficient volume, cause the rise to cease or the fall to halt. There is also an activity called 'hedging' which involves a loss of overall profit but ensures a profit or prevents a loss. Hedging involves precautionary buying or selling, contrary to the speculator's original expectations, if the market begins to behave differently from the manner anticipated. The currency speculator may be constantly adjusting his buying and selling and making new forward deals in order to avoid loss or to make certain of some profit.

Most speculation, especially in commodities, is fraught with danger since millions of pounds can be lost in a very short period. Financial institutions and banks need to keep a very strict control over their forward dealings. So do companies who buy commodities because they are forced to participate in the markets if they wish to remain in business.

Are There Any Controls in the Foreign Exchange Markets?

The United Kingdom abolished its exchange controls in 1979 as part of its efforts to reduce regulation and to expose the economy to free competition. Until then there had been a mixture of controls applied to the export and import of capital and the purchase of foreign exchange to finance deals. These controls stemmed from the war and the period of the postwar dollar shortage. Their intensity and extensiveness varied according to the nation's economic problems. At times, there were draconian restrictions on the amount that British tourists could take abroad. Most of the controls were aimed at outflows of capital. They inevitably generated a supervisory and regulatory bureaucracy and introduced an element of delay and uncertainty into commercial transactions. Most people were glad that they were abolished although there appeared to be a striking increase in the outflow of capital from the United Kingdom after they were ended. Some other countries have also abolished exchange controls on capital movements in accordance with a directive of June 1988, for example, Germany, The Netherlands, Belgium, Denmark, France, Italy and Luxembourg. They achieved this by the target date of 1 July 1990. Of the more advanced Community countries France had the most extensive controls on capital which limited the ability of its citizens to hold bank accounts abroad. They also required permission to open foreign currency accounts in French banks and there were restrictions on the ability of French banks to lend to non-residents. Some of these controls stemmed from the early period of socialist government under President Mitterrand when there was a flight of capital out of France. Inevitably, Greece, Spain and Portugal and Ireland, which have underdeveloped financial sectors, had a higher degree of control over capital movements. They were granted a reprieve until the end of 1992 for full implementation of the directive, but Greece and Portugal may be given a further extension until 1995. There is a safeguard whereby a country can control short-term capital movements if there is a serious problem with its monetary or exchange rate policy. This consists of medium-term financial assistance if balance-of-payments difficulties result from the liberalisation of capital movements. About £11 billion (16 billion ECU) is available to help members with such problems.

None of the Community countries, however, approached the now dissolved Eastern bloc system of complete control of the inflow and outflow of currency. It was this control that enabled the Soviet Union, for example, to impose a blatantly unrealistic exchange rate for the rouble on foreign visitors. Tourists quickly found that the 'free' market, or the 'black' market, exchange rate was many times more favourable, although taking advantage of it was illegal.

It is intended that this relaxation of controls over capital move-ments will extend outside the Community and the European Economic Area to movements to and from non-Community coun-tries. The long-term hope, therefore, is that trade, investments and financial markets will all benefit. Gradually the freeing of capital movements will help to integrate the financial aspects of the Community. It will introduce more pressure to harmonise the rules and framework under which the banks and financial markets operate. The achievement of that harmony is essential in the movement towards a common European currency and central bank as pro-posed in the 1991 Maastricht agreement.

Do Governments Allow their Exchange Rates to Float Freely?

Very few governments leave their foreign exchange rates to the vagaries of the international markets. Some, like the now dissolved

USSR, whose controls collapsed in 1991, went to the opposite extreme and tried to control them completely. Others intervene in the markets when it suits their policy, but generally leave their currency to find its own level. Some, like most of the members of the European Community, get together and operate a coordinated or linked scheme to influence their rates. This scheme is called the Exchange Rate Mechanism (ERM) of the European Monetary System (EMS).

Perhaps the most extensive and effective system of control of foreign exchange rates was that arising from the Bretton Woods agreement of 1944. This survived until 1971, although it suffered many vicissitudes. The agreement required countries to fix their exchange rates at a certain level which was notified to the International Monetary Fund (IMF). This rate was set at a level in relation to the price of gold but was, in effect, set against the dollar because the United States fixed the world price of gold in intergovernmental exchange. The country then needed to use its reserves to intervene in the foreign exchange markets to keep the rate within a band of 1 per cent above or below the central (par) rate. For example, the United Kingdom between 1949 and 1967 kept the pound between $2.82 and $2.78 with a central, or 'par' value of £1 = $2.80. For much of the time the rate was closer to the 'floor' price of $2.78 than to the 'par value'. In 1931, in the middle of the great international financial crisis, the United Kingdom had left the old gold standard. It set up the Exchange Equalisation Account which contained the country's gold and other currency reserves. This fund of reserves was used to enter the foreign exchange markets to buy and sell currencies, including sterling, in order to keep the rate against the dollar at the required level. The markets were usually aware of the intervention but not of its extent. This system is essentially the same as the operation of 'buffer stock' buying and selling as in some world commodity agreements or in the Common Agricultural Policy.

Under the Bretton Woods agreement all the signatories used equivalents of the Exchange Equalisation Account to intervene in markets to influence their own rates of exchange. If they got into difficulties in this respect, or into balance-of-payments problems, they could ask the IMF for short-term loans to give them time to correct the situation and restore equilibrium. In the last resort, they could devalue their currency. The United Kingdom, for example, devalued the pound, overnight, from £1 = $2.80 to £1 = $2.40 in

November 1967. The loans from the IMF were, and are, given provided that the country concerned took action to remove or reduce the fundamental causes of the problem. These might be high internal inflation, excessive government expenditure, or high costs of production reducing export competitiveness. The methods needed to tackle these problems – tax increases and cuts in government spending, were politically unpopular. The terms imposed by the IMF on the 1974–9 Labour government when it asked for loans were an important contributory factor to the unpopularity that led to its defeat in the 1979 election.

The Bretton Woods system of fixed parities which had to be defended gradually broke down. Some countries such as Canada floated their currency. Others, like the United Kingdom, were very slow to devalue until forced. Stronger economies, like the West German, were very slow to revalue, that is to raise the value of their currency. Governments increasingly felt that fixed foreign exchange rates imposed far too heavy a restraint on their internal economic policies. It was inevitable, therefore, that the growing international financial problems of the late 1960s and early 1970s should induce countries into trying a new panacea, freely floating foreign exchange rates accompanied by some intervention buying and selling.

This complete freedom was not, however, entirely suitable for the members of the European Community. They adopted temporary expedients of common exchange rate controls in the early 1970s. These were various versions of what became known as the 'snake in the tunnel'. This was a framework under which each country would have an upper and lower target limit for its exchange rate. Within this 'tunnel' the exchange rate could fluctuate. As the rate came near the outer limits the country needed to take corrective action. The rates of each participating country were interlinked or weighted in calculating the rates against the dollar. The system was modified over time but was not completely satisfactory because some countries were too slow, or ineffective, in taking remedial measures to correct problems. They were slow because the necessary measures were bound to be politically unpopular, since they usually included restraints on public and private expenditure. West Germany was sometimes slow to react despite the persistent strength of its economy and balance of payments. This was because it would have had to revalue the Deutschmark upwards which would have cut the competitiveness of its exports. It was therefore necessary to develop another, more effective system.

Floating Exchange Rates and Monetarism

The politicians of the major economies succumbed to the siren songs of the economists who recommended floating exchange rates. They had reached their wits' end on measures to control inflation, rising unemployment, growing balance-of-payments deficits and budget deficits. When they were told that they could, in effect, have their cake and eat it, they seized on floating rates as the panacea for all their ills. They thought that they would free themselves from the shackles of having to make unpalatable and unpopular decisions about their internal economies in order to restore a balance-of-payments equilibrium or to maintain a narrow range of exchange rates. At the same time the new priesthood of the resurrected theory of monetarism joined in the chorus.

This is not the place for a detailed explanation of what is called monetarism, a term that has come to have several meanings with the passage of time. In this context, however, we do need to know that the monetarists saw a direct relationship between changes in the quantity of money in circulation and the rate of change of the price level (inflation). Keynesian economists saw an indirect link because they allowed for excess demand and supply of money to be absorbed in a sort of 'buffer' in the shape of purchases and sales of bonds. The problem confronting the monetarists in practice was deciding what to count as 'money' and then how to control it. The financial world is such that as soon as you try to control something, the participants in the markets switch their assets or holdings into another type. Money takes many forms apart from the cash and notes with which we are all familiar. It includes all sorts of bills and bonds, bank deposits and liquid financial assets such as building society deposits, some of which are held in sterling and some in foreign currencies. In the United Kingdom one of the major problems of the pre-1979 period was that the government had a very large borrowing requirement which was financed by the issue of long-term stock and by the sale of short-term bills (Treasury Bills). Several other member states had similar debt burdens. The methods they adopted were, according to the monetarists, the equivalent, to some extent, of 'printing money'.

Thus any attempt to control the growth of the money supply involved the curtailing of government borrowing and, inevitably, cut-backs in public expenditure. This was successfully achieved in Britain by 1988 and the Treasury, with the help of the sale of public assets from the nationalised industries, enjoyed a large surplus of revenue over expenditure and was able to reduce the National Debt. This process was also supposed to have left extra funds available for the private sector to borrow for investment, that is, it ended what was called 'crowding out'. This was the name given to the process whereby the government, which was always able to pay as high an interest rate as was needed to get loans, could outbid the private sector.

From the perspective of the United Kingdom a major aspect of the money supply problem was the movement into, and out of, the country of foreign funds. This movement is heavily influenced by the rate of interest prevailing in the United Kingdom compared with that in other comparable countries. High rates, other things being equal, attract larger deposits, and vice versa. The other influence is the level of the foreign exchange rate and expectations about its movements relative to other currencies in the future. Higher rates attract more foreign money into the country and tend to raise the foreign exchange rate. This cuts the effective price of imports and is deflationary, and tends to cut the demand for exports. This has a detrimental effect on the balance of payments (depending on the relative elasticities of supply and demand of imports and exports) and can contribute to large current account deficits.

Worse still was the significance of exchange rate intervention. Positive official financing involved buying pounds and selling foreign currency from the reserves in order to alter the exchange rate. An inevitable result was for the domestic money supply also to be reduced, or to be increased by negative financing. Thus exchange rate policy constrained monetary policy in what, to monetarists, was an unacceptable way.

The United Kingdom adopted policies in the 1980s that were said to be monetarist, although many monetarists thought they were half-hearted and insufficient. The main remaining weapon left to the Chancellor by 1988 was the ability to influence the interest rate. This was aimed at affecting the demand for money. Almost all the other controls over bank lending and asset ratios were abandoned. This was in contrast with West Germany which had an extensive and powerful set of controls over its banking sector. It could, as a result, control the supply of money as well. Consequently, Germany was able to have a low rate of inflation, a low level of interest rates and a heavy inflow of foreign capital. Its position was strengthened by the existence of a sound labour relations structure that, until the public sector workers' strike and pay settlement of May 1992, kept wage demands within the bounds of what could be afforded from economic growth and increased productivity. Moreover, German banks used Luxembourg, which had a much freer banking regulation structure, as a base for some of their operations for capital transfers when their own home regulations became too oppressive.

The monetarists offered what appeared to be a simple explanation of inflation and an apparently straightforward set of solutions. All that governments had to do was to control their money supply and to reduce their government spending and borrowing and everything would be all right. At the same time, they should try to improve the underlying efficiency of the economy by reducing costs on enterprise. These 'supply-side' improvements would reinvigorate a flagging national economy and generate a climate in which enterprise would flourish. Governments would be absolved from responsibility for their balance-of-payments equilibrium and exchange rate levels. The system would be self-levelling and self-adjusting and no more politically unpopular measures resulting from balance-of-payments problems would be necessary.

These ideas were not equally well received in all European countries. Some were tried and rejected or modified. On the whole, the economic policies of Europe remained neo-Keynesian with some modifications. It can be argued, of course, that neo-Keynesian policies did not fail in the 1960s and 1970s but that the political will and nerve of politicians collapsed when it came to taking the remedial action required. They did too little, too late. The United States, which remained the power-house of the international economy, was embroiled in the Vietnam War. Its mounting expenditure and deficits at home and abroad fuelled international inflation and disrupted money markets. Another problem was the mounting volume of oil revenues seeking investment outlets. Third World debt was also increasing rapidly. The growing oil revenues resulting from the price rises of the early 1970s shifted about the world looking for high returns and security. Their existence and movement affected exchange rates and interest rates. In the circumstances, it is no surprise that freely floating exchange rates were not fully adopted since most nations intervene to influence their foreign exchange rate. This is often called 'dirty floating' and its effectiveness depends to some extent on the size of the reserves with which the country can intervene. The Community adopted its own system arising from the need to make payments between members and to achieve some stability of its currencies in relation to each other. The European Monetary System was born.

What is the European Monetary System?

The EMS comprises a European Monetary Cooperation Fund (EMCF), an Exchange Rate Mechanism (ERM) and a currency, or unit of account, called an ECU, and a very short-term facility (VSTF) whereby each central bank makes credit facilities available in its own currency to the other members. ECU stands for European Currency Unit in English but it was also a medieval French gold coin. The EMCF will disappear in the late 1990s as a single currency is achieved. The EMS was established in its present form in 1979. The United Kingdom did not join the ERM until October 1990 but participated from the start in the EMCF and ECU elements. The Spanish peseta and Portuguese escudo were included for the first time in the calculation of the value of the ECU when its base was recalculated in September 1989.

The European Monetary Cooperation Fund

The EMCF was set up in 1973 and acts as a mixture between the IMF and a Community central bank. The participants in the EMS deposit 20 per cent of their gold reserves and 20 per cent of their dollar reserves with the EMCF. In return they are credited with ECUs, the quantity of which credited to each country will change as the price of gold and dollars alters on world markets. The gold portion of the deposit with the EMCF is valued using six-monthly averages of London gold prices and the dollar portion is valued at the market rate two days before the date of valuation. Thus both the world price of gold and the price of the dollar affect the quantity of

ECUs created. Once credited to a country these ECUs can then be used to settle payments between members. The system is a foundation, via the ECU, for both a currency and an international reserve unit. The details of the deposits and their valuation in terms of dollars are reviewed every two years. The technicalities of the scheme are highly complex but there is no doubting the effectiveness of the institution. The number of ECUs in existence increases yearly and had reached 80 billion in 1987. The EMCF is at a disadvantage in that it cannot control the creation of ECUs because that is determined by the gold price and rate of the dollar.

The EMCF also has the function of making the Exchange Rate Mechanism work in the sense of facilitating payments between members. The intervention mechanism which is designed to make the ERM work obliges countries' central banks to give each other unlimited, very short-term credit facilities to finance required interventions. These loans and debts are paid through the EMCF in ECUs and interest is also paid in ECUs. As the single market developed to 1992 more and more restrictions on banking and on movements of money were relaxed. Under Stage 2 of the plan for monetary union regulations will be harmonised. The agreement reached at Maastricht in December 1991 shows that the EMCF and the ECU will both play an increasingly important part in the progress towards a new central bank and a currency for the Community as outlined below. The functions of the EMCF will no longer be required when the ECU is established as a single currency because there will be no exchange rate fluctuations between Community currencies.

The European Currency Unit

The ECU was a new name for the European Unit of Account (EUA),introduced in 1975, and has taken over all the functions of the EUA. From 1950 there had been a unit of account introduced by the European Payments Union (EPU) which was very straightforward in that it was based on the weight of gold in one US dollar. It was converted into national currencies at the official central rate for a member's currency, as determined by the Bretton Woods agreement. When that agreement began to break down in the early 1970s a number of different units of account were adopted, based on a variety of measures, some relatively stable, some fluctuating. The EUA replaced all these and was based on a specific quantity of each of the members' currencies. This was a copy of the special drawing rights (SDRs) introduced by the IMF in 1969. The value of the SDRs was based upon an agreed 'basket' of sixteen different currencies weighted according to their relative importance.

The ECU then is a 'basket' currency which is used in the Community's budget, in payments between members and between them and African, Caribbean, Asian and Pacific members of the Lomé Convention. It is also used in Common Agricultural Policy payments, in the European Coal and Steel Community and in the European Investment Bank and may be held as a reserve currency at the EMCF by non-members of the Community. Apart from these official uses there is a rapidly growing private market for the ECU: loans in ECUs can be raised by companies; you can buy travellers' cheques in ECUs; payments can be made in ECUs, and they are quoted on foreign exchange markets. In 1988, the United Kingdom government began issuing Treasury Bills in ECUs to finance some of its short-term borrowing requirements and in 1991 floated a foreign currency bond denominated in ECUs and amounting to 2.5 billion ECU. The ECU is a genuine currency in international payments. It is not available as notes or coins, except for collectors, but is a unit of account, a store of value and a medium of exchange, that is it performs the traditional functions of money. There is every possibility that, by the end of the century, it will be *the* currency of the Community or the majority of member states, although its nature will have changed and there will be a European central bank to control its issue. The United Kingdom made an attempt in 1990 and 1991 to have the ECU adopted as an *extra* currency alongside the others and usable at the individual's discretion as well as for interstate transfers. This proposal for the so-called 'hard' ECU never appealed to most of the other members because it showed a lack of commitment to monetary union and was regarded as a typical British attempt to stall the implementation of the programme recommended in the Delors committee report on economic and monetary union of April 1989.

How the ECU 'basket' is made up

The basket is re-examined every five years and was reconstituted in September 1989 to include the escudo and the peseta. The Greek drachma was included in September 1984. Table 7.1 shows the composition of the basket from September 1989.

TABLE 7.1
Composition of the ECU

	One ECU Comprises the Following Amount of National Currencies:	Weight %
Deutschmark	0.6242	30.40
UK pound	0.08784	12.60
French franc	1.332	19.30
Italian lira	151.80	9.70
Dutch guilder	0.2198	9.60
Belgian/Lux franc	3.431	8.10
Danish krone	0.1976	2.50
Irish punt	0.008552	1.10
Greek drachma	1.44	0.70
Spanish peseta	6.885	5.20
Portuguese escudo	1.393	0.80
		100.00

The weights are based on exchange rates on 30 October 1990.

You can look up the value of the pound in ECUs in the foreign exchange section of a newspaper. In June 1992 £1 = 1.42 ECU. The currency amounts given above have to be reviewed at the request of a country if its currency changes more than 25 per cent in 'weight' against the other currencies since the previous five-yearly review.

The ECU is bought and sold on the foreign exchanges just like any other currency and also features in futures and options markets. Over 10 billion are dealt in every day on the exchanges and their use is growing and extending. One of their attractions is their relative stability in the markets which tends to reduce some of the risks of international trading and financial transfers.

In order to calculate the value of the ECU, the central bank in each member state works out a representative market rate for its currency against the dollar. These rates together can then be used to calculate the dollar equivalent of the basket of Community currencies. The

ECU is thus valued at the sum of the dollar equivalents of the currencies in the basket.

The Exchange Rate Mechanism

The mechanism was designed to help create what was called, when it was introduced in March 1979, 'a zone of monetary stability'. Spain joined the mechanism in June 1989 and the United Kingdom joined, after intense debate, in October 1990; Portugal entered in April 1992. They entered with a wide 6 per cent band of permitted divergence from their central rates as opposed to the usual 2.25 per cent. Italy, which operated a wide 6 per cent band, adopted the narrower band in January 1990. Greece is not at the time of writing a member of the ERM but is expected to join shortly as part of the run-up to Stage 2 of economic and monetary union (EMU) which begins on 1 January 1994.

In order to create stability in the relationships of the exchange rates of the members, it was decided to replace the early 1970s' versions of the 'snake in the tunnel' systems referred to above with a grid system. Each participant establishes a central rate for its currency which is expressed in ECUs. The rate set has to be approved by all the members and is not set solely at the individual country's discretion.

The next step is to use these ECU-expressed rates to work out a grid of bilateral exchange rates, for example between the Deutschmark and the French franc. See Table 7.2 for details of the grid. Once these bilateral rates are established a restriction is put upon the extent to which the market rates may diverge from the bilateral rates – usually up to 2.25 per cent on either side. These margins on either side of the bilateral rate are accompanied by a central rate fixed against the ECU which enables 'divergence indicators' to be established (see below). It is likely that Greece will initially be given a 6 per cent margin on either side of its central rate when its currency joins the ERM. Before the United Kingdom joined there was considerable debate about the desirable level of divergence to be granted and the length of the transition period. The crucial question, however, was the level of the bilateral rate against the German mark, which was eventually set at £1 = DM2.95. Many economists regarded this as too high a rate and one which might prove indefensible in the long run.

TABLE 7.2

The Currency Grid: Bilateral Central Rates and Selling and Buying Rates in the EMS Exchange Rate Mechanism of Four Major Currencies from the Nine in the System, from 8 October 1990

	France Fr. 100	Germany DM 100	Italy Lire 100	United Kingdom £1	
France	——	343.050	4.58450	10.50550	s
Fr.f	——	335.386	4.48247	9.89389	c
	——	327.920	4.38300	9.31800	b
Germany	30.4950	——	1.36700	3.13200	s
DM	29.8164	——	1.33651	2.95000	c
	29.1500	——	1.30650	2.77800	b
Italy	22 817.0	76 540.0	——	2343.62	s
Lir	22 309.1	74 821.7	——	2207.25	c
	21 813.0	73 157.0	——	2078.79	b
United	10.7320	35.9970	0.481050	——	s
Kingdom	10.1073	33.8984	0.453053	——	c
£	9.5190	31.9280	0.426690	——	b

c = Bilateral central rate.

s/b = Exchange rate at which the central bank of the country in the left-hand column will sell/buy the currency identified in the row at the top of the table

SOURCE *Economic Briefing*, No. 1, Dec. 1990 (HM Treasury).

Although the narrow band is fixed at 2.25 per cent on either side of a central rate this does not mean that a particular currency can necessarily fluctuate against another by a full 4.5 per cent. This is because it is part of a grid against all the other currencies within the ERM. For example, the lira might reach its limit against the peseta before it could make full use of its range against the French franc. The consequence of this impact of the grid is that the band in practice is less than 4.5 per cent and appears nearer half that.

Since 1979 there have been periods in which one or more countries' currencies have got into difficulties, leading to twelve realignments of the central rates between 1979 and 1991. These have usually involved revaluing the Deutschmark and guilder and devaluing the lira and French franc. Such readjustments must be done by agreement because every country's ECU-related central rate is dependent on the rates of the other countries. The sequence of events, therefore, is for the bilateral rates to be renegotiated first, after which the central rate is recalculated. There will probably be a final realignment of currencies during Stage 2 of EMU after 1 January 1994 as all member states move to narrower bands within the ERM. An earlier realignment may have occurred before then because an adjustment of the pound's central rate against the Deutschmark was being speculated on in the foreign exchange markets at the end of 1991 and the start of 1992. The Chancellor of the Exchequer had reaffirmed the United Kingdom's intention of entering the narrow band in the future.

What are the divergence indicators for?

Divergence indicators are intended, first, to act as an early warning that a particular currency is deviating too much from the average, and, second, to provoke an early response before the gap grows too large. It is presumed in the EMS that a country will take appropriate action to restore the level of its currency and to remove or restrain the cause of it divergence. The system should encourage economic discipline and make governments work harder at controlling their inflation rates and public sector spending. They have not been completely successful in this because of the political reluctance of some governments to take the necessary measures. This is one reason why there have been realignments over the years.

What happens if a divergence indicator is reached?

If a currency touches its 2.25 margin above or below its bilateral rate against another country, it must take specific actions in its economic policies to readjust the relationship over time. The divergence indicator is set at a level within these outer limits to give it early warning to take action. In the short run it will indulge in intervention buying and selling, and is helped by the other country involved. In addition the central bank with the strong currency buys the weak currency, and the central bank with the weak currency sells the strong currency. It may borrow from the 'strong' central bank if it does not have enough reserves to sell. These manipulations are conducted with the help of the EMCF and all the dealings are in ECUs. Any interest on loans is also paid in ECUs. The use of ECUs has the effect of sharing between the two countries the risk of any loss on the foreign exchange dealings. This intervention is compulsory once the divergence thresholds are reached but a country may choose to take earlier action and indulge in what is called *intramarginal* intervention.

What has been the Effect of the Exchange Rate Mechanism since 1979?

The participants have very diverse economies with varying degrees of reliance upon foreign trade, and their balance-of-payments positions and rates of inflation differ greatly. Germany has dominated the ERM because of its low inflation, steady growth and very healthy balance-of-payments surpluses. Italy has tended to be a problem, despite the greater 6 per cent range of latitude for the lira until 1990. The French economy has gone through bad patches but has recovered. In the face of this variety the ERM has, on the whole, achieved a remarkable degree of stability of exchange rates for its participants in a period when world exchange rates have been volatile. The study of comparative exchange rate movements is beset with statistical problems, but the rates of the currencies within the grid seem to have been less subject to the extremes of fluctuation than those outside it. This is not necessarily entirely due to them being in the ERM but the supporters of the EMS believe that it is. It is interesting to note that Sweden tied its currency to the ECU in 1991, thus effectively joining the ERM.

Why did the United Kingdom Not Join the ERM until 1990?

The Labour government of 1974 to 1979 was a weak government reliant on the support of minority parties. Despite the referendum which strongly supported the United Kingdom's continued membership there was a powerful element in the party and Cabinet which regarded the Community as an alien authority. They feared deeper involvement in any enterprise which appeared to them to be non-socialist in aspiration or from which they could not easily escape. The government faced severe difficulties in its economic management. The inflation rate and level of unemployment were rising rapidly. A succession of incomes policies was tried and found wanting, culminating in the breakdown of the 'social contract' and the subsequent 'winter of discontent'. The balance of payments and the value of the pound were both subject to unusual pressures because of the inflow of capital to exploit North Sea oil development. Large loans had been raised from the IMF and other groups of international lenders. It was thus not thought to be a good time to embark on what was seen as another uncertainty by joining the ERM. It may be that the government was not willing to accept the required levels of discipline to make the pound fit within the ERM, regarding it as a surrender of sovereignty over its economic policies.

Between 1979 and 1990 the pound fluctuated between wide extremes. As a result there was a sharp conflict between those whose interest was in having a low exchange rate, mainly against the dollar (that is, exporters), and those who favoured a high rate (that, is importers). For a time, the pound, on a tide of oil, reached the 1967 devaluation rate of £1 = $2.40. This had a devastating effect on manufacturing industry and was partially responsible, together with high interest rates, for the destruction of the United Kingdom's manufacturing base in the early 1980s. Then, for a while, the pound fell so low that experts were predicting a £1 = $1 exchange rate. There were, however, reasons for this greater volatility of the pound. Sterling is more important than the other European currencies in international trade and finance. The general point of importance, though, is that there was no real agreement on what is a reasonable, workable rate of exchange against the dollar and the yen. The United Kingdom government had no genuinely consistent policy with relation to the exchange rate except to let it float in accordance with market forces. It did, periodically, intervene to halt a movement or to nudge it in a certain direction and its interest rate policies sometimes had an exchange rate dimension, that is, influencing the flow of capital into and out of sterling.

Although there was a lack of a coherent, interventionist policy, a consensus of opinion grew up that strongly favoured the United Kingdom's entry into the ERM. Thus, by 1987, it appeared that Mrs Thatcher, with a few loyal supporters, was the only obstacle to joining, and there was a major difference of opinion between her and the Treasury and the Bank of England. This position gradually changed after mid-1988 as more economists analysed the hypothetical effects of the United Kingdom's joining. They became more cautious in their support and some became critical of the possible effects. One cause of the change was the revelation that Mr Lawson, the Chancellor of the Exchequer, had been following a policy of keeping sterling in step with the German mark for about a year, with a view to joining the ERM. A number of economic events undermined this policy and Mrs Thatcher disapproved of the degree of intervention required in the foreign exchange markets.

In the final analysis, however, the main reason why the United Kingdom did not join the Exchange Rate Mechanism was the fear of loss of economic sovereignty and the reluctance to accept externally imposed discipline over economic policy. There was, and remains, a lack of agreement about what level to set for the pound against the mark, and there were problems about the percentage allowed initially for divergence from the central rate. These were resolved when the United Kingdom joined the ERM on 8 October 1990 at a central rate against the Deutschmark of £1 = DM2.95, within a wide band of 6 per cent. After some initial difficulties the pound settled down within its band and did not come under real pressure until the end of 1991 when the United Kingdom showed a lack of commitment to the EMS in choosing to demand an opt-out clause from the Union Treaty draft at the Maastricht summit in December 1991. The pound was unsettled by the failure of the economy to rise out of its recession and by the strength of the US dollar and, in mid-1992, by its weakness. The difficulty for some sections of British opinion in adopting a full commitment to the European monetary union is a psychological one related to national pride, independence and sovereignty. There has also been some disenchantment with the price that has had to be paid for membership of the ERM in terms of externally imposed discipline that has resulted in an inability to manipulate aggregate demand or interest rates in preparation for a general election in 1991 or 1992 and an ominous rise in unemployment.

Will the Single Market after 1992 have Much Impact on Money and Banking?

There will be enormous changes as the directives establishing the single market are implemented although they are in some respects weaker than originally envisaged. It is the intention that the movement of services and capital should be freed from artificial restrictions as well as that of goods and people. This has involved the dismantling, in most states, of a range of restrictions on the holding and transfer of capital and currency. The United Kingdom had relatively few controls except those required to prevent fraud and to protect the customer, the shareholder and the depositor. It was partly this lack of controls, matched only by Luxembourg, that enabled the City of London to retain its preeminence in European financial markets. However there is a long-term threat to this position as the European markets are also freed. The French stock exchange and other financial markets are being modernised. German banks are becoming more international. There is a real risk that the City of London will fail to put enough resources into European financial centres to exploit the new markets. A proposal for an early linking of major financial centres with a common electronic dealing system has foundered but it is a matter of dispute as to whether this will help perpetuate London's preeminence or allow the other major European centres to prosper more quickly. There is also a threat to the City in that the new Community rules may, in some respects, make London less attractive to non-European banks such as the Japanese, Arabian and American. A decisive influence may prove to be the location of the new European Central Bank during Stage 3 of the movement to monetary union. The development of information technology may mean that its head office where decisions are made will be in a different place from the dispersed centres in which its activities occur. Its head office is unlikely to be in the United Kingdom since Mr Major opted out of commitment to Stage 3 of monetary union at the Maastricht summit in December 1991. He seemed remarkably blasé in the United Kingdom House of Commons at the prospect of not securing this important insurance to the continuing dominance of the City of London but a great deal of disquiet has been expressed at the long-term consequences of the Central Bank going to Amsterdam, Luxembourg, Frankfurt, or Bonn.

There will also be significant changes in the framework within which insurance services operate. These will, theoretically, provide great opportunities in Europe for British companies which already have a major international role. A general fear of some British commentators is that the single market will impose a more bureaucratic regulatory framework than exists in the United Kingdom today. This, it is argued, partly defeats the objective of freeing the Community from restrictions.

These rather mundane areas of advance were overshadowed by the row that developed in 1988 between Mrs Thatcher, then Prime Minister of the United Kingdom, and other members of the Community, notably Jacques Delors, the President of the Commission. This concerned the idea that the single market and the freeing of capital movements made inevitable the creation of a Community central bank and a single Community currency. Mrs Thatcher dismissed this idea as nonsense despite public opinion polls at the time that indicated that the British people would not mind a European currency. M. Delors was, of course, right. A single market for capital, a European Monetary System based on the ECU and an Exchange Rate Mechanism all indicate the need for a single, or super, European central bank and a single currency based on the ECU. Mrs Thatcher and her successor Mr Major may delay the introduction but they will arrive in due course.

We would all benefit from a single currency. A Euro MP once explained to the European Parliament that if you started with £100 in cash and changed it into francs and then into lira and so on until you had successively bought all the currencies of the Community, and then bought back pounds, you would only have £26 left. Thus £74 would have gone on commission without your having bought anything! (There seem to be a number of versions of this measurement and £45 is an alternative remainder that is quoted. Presumably the arithmetic depends on whether you are buying and selling at individual or corporate rates.) The logic of a single currency will eventually get through. Indeed, there has already been considerable growth in the use of the ECU by private business and some individuals. There is a danger of a two-speed Europe developing in the field of monetary union with some of the other major countries of the Community going ahead without the United Kingdom as is explained below.

The creation of a central bank for the Community might pose more problems, especially for economic nationalists. The United Kingdom is again very concerned about economic sovereignty. The Germans, for their part, are increasingly concerned about the prospect of sacrificing the strong Deutschmark to an uncertain ECU over which they will have significantly less control. The impartial observer might say that the European performance, especially that of the West German Bundesbank, is superior to that of the Bank of England in recent years. Thus the United Kingdom would do well to pool what little of the sovereignty remains to the Bank of England and Treasury with the Europeans. Many economists say that this sovereignty is, in any case, very severely constrained. It is impossible for the United Kingdom to operate an independent policy in the face of the other economic forces in the world, such as the Deutschmark, the dollar and the yen. Britain is, moreover, reduced to having only one shot left in its locker – interest rate changes – and even in this respect is largely constrained by the need to follow what is done by Germany. The City of London and leaders of commerce and industry, if not certain politicians of the Thatcherite persuasion, appear to be recognising that their future self-interest lies in a European commitment, including a single currency and European central bank.

Perhaps the most telling statement was made by Sir Leon Brittan, British Commissioner and Vice-President of the Commission, who said, in February 1989, that 'the EMS has succeeded in providing the structure within which movement between member currencies has been significantly limited. The role of the Deutschmark as linchpin of the system has led to a convergence on a low inflation level for those countries in the ERM: this has been a highly constructive development both for them and for the cohesion of the Community generally.' He went on to argue that it would be advantageous for the United Kingdom to join the ERM for three reasons: first, because joining the ERM now would be a clear signal to the financial markets that the United Kingdom's political commitment to low inflation had been given institutional form; second, the United Kingdom's full membership of the EMS would put it in a far more favourable position from which to help guide its future development; last, membership of the EMS would be of benefit to British business and industry by providing for the first time a framework within which receipts from goods exported to the Community could be planned in sterling terms.

Practical views such as this eventually prevailed over the more emotional, national sovereignty attitudes of Mrs Thatcher and her close supporters, and the United Kingdom embraced the Exchange Rate Mechanism. In the meantime M. Delors and the Community central bankers had met in committee and produced what came to be called 'the Delors Committee Report'. This was to lead to a powerful surge towards fuller economic and monetary union and to a new treaty. An incidental effect of the surge was to carry away Mrs

Thatcher from the office of Prime Minister in November 1990 as her opposition to monetary union caused her to adopt an embarrassingly strident tone which was out of tune with important elements in her party and Cabinet.

The Delors Committee Report

The Single European Act included economic and monetary union as a formal objective and imposed on the members an obligation to work towards a convergence of domestic policies in order to achieve it. The treaty, however, required any future institutional changes in respect of monetary policy to be done by amendment to the treaty, a process which required unanimity. Those who opposed or who were doubtful about a future common monetary policy thought that this would satisfactorily delay any change. They were disappointed and what followed is an object lesson for those who fail to take account of the steamroller-like capability of the Commission, and Community, to grind onwards to a conclusion.

In June 1988 the Hanover summit meeting agreed to Jacques Delors, President of the Commission, forming a committee of seventeen members including governors of central banks from members of the Community. The Governor of the Bank of England attended in a 'personal capacity'. Its task was to study the steps needed to achieve a monetary union as defined in the SEA though its terms of reference did not, at Mrs Thatcher's insistence, include mention of a single currency for Europe or a European central bank. The committee started meeting in September 1988 and produced a unanimous report in April 1989 which was submitted to the Madrid summit in June 1989.

The report defined monetary union as 'a currency area in which policies are managed jointly with a view to obtaining common macroeconomic objectives' and laid down three conditions for achieving one. These three points have been central to the discussions ever since and will remain so for the rest of the decade. They were, first, total and irreversible convertibility of currencies; second, the complete liberalisation of capital markets and the integration of financial markets; and third, the irrevocable locking of exchange rate parities. The committee said that once these three conditions had been achieved individual national currencies would become substitutes and that interest rates would tend to equalise between every member state. As a result it would be possible to have a single currency for the Community and that this would be desirable though not strictly necessary. The report went on to state the need for a common monetary policy with a new institution to implement it, that is, a federal European System of Central Banks (ESCB) which would have a Council appointed by the Council of Ministers and be independent of national governments. It would govern national central banks whose functions would gradually wither away as monetary union developed.

The report included a list of the four basic elements required for economic growth. Three of these caused no surprise because they were simply restatements of previously held beliefs, that is, a single market with free movement of goods, persons, capital and services, a competition policy and other measures to strengthen markets, and common policies directed at structural change and regional development. The fourth, however, was the coordination of macroeconomic policies including binding rules for budgetary policies. This raised all sorts of fears and spectres in the hearts of those who were concerned about economic sovereignty and the ability of national governments to use budgetary policies to steer the economic cycle for electoral purposes. It also led to the development of discussions about the nature and degree of convergence of national economies required before monetary union could take place.

The committee outlined a timetable for the attainment of economic and monetary union or EMU as it came to be called and proposed three stages. Stage 1, which actually started in July 1990 following an agreement at the Madrid summit in June 1989, involves concentrating on the completion of the single market from its starting date of 1 January 1993 and on increasing monetary cooperation. The coordination of policies would be improved through the working of the Council of Economic and Finance Ministers, which is called ECOFIN in Euro-jargon. Those members not in the ERM were expected to join and the United Kingdom, Portugal and Spain have done so, leaving only Greece outside. No time-scale was fixed for this stage but the committee thought that seven years would be sufficient. During Stage 1 each nation would supervise its own economic performance in the light of agreed economic objectives. Since July 1990 there has been an increase in cooperation and consultation and some countries such as Denmark and Belgium have begun to operate within a narrower self-imposed band within the ERM, trying to keep their exchange rates more stable against the Deutschmark.

Stages 2 and 3 were not given definite starting dates or time spans. During Stage 2 changes to the Treaty of Rome could be made, or a new treaty agreed. Decision-making would become collective and the European System of Central Banks (ESCB) would be set up. The emphasis would be on setting medium-term objectives by the use of majority voting but other collective decisions on budget deficits, exchange rate and other monetary policies would need unanimous decisions. Gradually, during Stage 2, fluctuations of currencies within the ERM grid would be eliminated. All this would involve a substantial transfer of economic power from national governments to the ESCB. It was this proposed transfer that most concerned the objectors to the plan. Stage 3 of the Delors committee plan would have given the ESCB the power to put constraints on national budgets in order to preserve monetary stability or to increase Community revenues or to force members to make their economic adjustments more effective. At this point the Community could adopt a single currency, such as the ECU, and national currencies could be phased out.

The Madrid summit meeting, in a compromise, decided, as stated above, to implement Stage 1 of the Delors report on 1 July 1990 and to establish an Inter-Governmental Conference (IGC) to plan for economic and monetary union. This IGC was to run parallel with another one on Political Union and both were to prepare reports and draft treaties for a final decision to be made at the Maastricht summit in December 1991. The discussion of economic and monetary union and political union side by side was essential because the proposals to have a single currency and single central bank for the Community seemed to produce the inevitable conclusion that some sort of a federal union would eventually develop, to replace the separate national states. Those who were dubious about the Delors report hoped that the IGCs would fail to produce an agreement that could be put into treaty form but they underestimated the political drive towards economic and monetary union that had been generated by the logic of the creation of the single market. They naively thought that they could settle for an enormous free trade area without any necessity for closer political and economic union. In practice, the decision to adopt Stage 1 of the Delors committee report was also a decision to adopt the later stages because the path to monetary union was clearly shown by the report, and by the earlier Werner report of 1970, to be a single, continuous one. This did not mean, of course, that there would not be any modifications of the Delors plan, and the Maastricht agreement produced several.

Maastricht and Economic and Monetary Union

Maastricht is a small town in The Netherlands built in a loop of the river Maas or Meuse close to the borders with Germany and Belgium. Many of its market traders accept any currency from the Community countries. The difficulty inherent in such multicurrency dealings highlights the reasons for the determination of many Europeans to aim for a single currency. Maastricht was the centre for the Council of Europe meetings in early December 1991 that agreed the draft Union Treaty on Economic and Monetary Union (EMU) and on Political Union because The Netherlands were currently holding the Presidency of the Community. The meetings were enlarged by the presence not only of the foreign ministers who usually attend such Councils, but also of the finance ministers. Representatives of the media attended in huge numbers. Most of the work had been done before the national leaders met and draft treaties were well-publicised beforehand and national political stances fully advertised. The nature of such meetings is that every leader must appear, for the benefit of the folks back home, to have negotiated strongly and effectively. 'Face' is very important and the media is massaged on a regular basis to ensure that the headlines reflect what the politicians desire. The truth behind the final outcome may take many years to emerge as the agreements are put into practice and the European Court of Justice interprets them.

The decisions in respect of economic and monetary union were as follows. In February 1992 the formal Union Treaty on economic, monetary and political union was initialled and will be ratified during 1992 by national parliaments. In June 1992 there will be a revision of the Community's financing to be discussed at the Lisbon summit. The single market with free movement of capital and services, and so on, comes into force on 1 January 1993. In January 1994 Stage 2 of economic and monetary union will start. (Stage 1 began in July 1990.) During this stage a European Monetary Institute (EMI) will be set up to prepare for the final stage of EMU. The EMI will be the forerunner of the European Central Bank (ECB). It will take over the short-term holdings of gold and foreign exchange reserves now held and pooled as part of the EMS. It may also hold and manage national reserves.

During Stage 2 of EMU the member countries will bring their exchange rates into narrower bands and will begin the process of making their economies converge to certain accepted limits in relation to some key indicators. These so called convergence tests are

1. *Inflation.* The country must have had an inflation rate which is no more than 1.5 per cent higher than that of the three members of the ERM with the lowest rates in the previous year.
2. *Interest rates.* The country must have had long-term interest rates (long bond rates) no more than 2 per cent higher than the lowest three members in the previous year.
3. *Exchange rate.* The country must have been in the narrow band of the ERM for two years and not to have realigned (devalued) in that time.
4. *Budget deficit.* The country's budget deficit must not exceed 3 per cent of gross domestic product.
5. *Debt stock.* The country's outstanding stock of public debt must be less than 60 per cent of GDP.

The extent to which the members of the Community matched these convergence criteria in early 1992 is shown in Table 7.3.

The American Investment Bank, Morgan Stanley, forecast at the end of 1991 that six countries would have met these convergence standards by the end of 1996: Denmark, France, Germany, The Netherlands, Spain and the United Kingdom. In 1992, however, the United Kingdom's predicted budget deficit rose to 4.5 per cent of GDP.

During the second stage the members will start the process leading to the independence of the Community's Central Bank by setting up the EMI. According to the treaty, 'The currency composition of the ECU basket shall not be changed, and from the start of Stage 3 the value of the ECU shall be irrevocably fixed.' The single currency will not be the present 'basket' ECU but a new currency representing the irrevocably fixed values of existing currencies. In theory Stage 3 could start as early as 1 January 1997.

TABLE 7.3
Are the Convergence Criteria Met? (1991)

Country	Inflation	Interest Rates	Exchange Rates	Budget Deficit	Debt Stock
Denmark	Yes	Yes	Yes	Yes	Yes
France	Yes	Yes	Yes	Yes	Yes
Ireland	Yes	Yes	Yes	Yes	No
Germany*	Yes	Yes	Yes	No	Yes
Netherlands	Yes	Yes	Yes	No	Yes
Belgium	Yes	Yes	Yes	No	No
UK	No	No	No	Yes	Yes
Spain	No	No	No	Yes	Yes
Italy	No	No	Yes	No	No

*Germany's budget deficit is temporarily high because of the costs of German reunification.

SOURCE Own work from available statistics.

By the end of 1996 the European Commission and the EMI will produce a report stating which members have met the agreed criteria for joining a full currency union. In the meantime, in June 1994, elections for the European Parliament will have taken place, and in January 1995 Sweden and Austria will probably have joined the Community. In 1996 also, the Community leaders will have reviewed the Union Treaty. After studying the report of the Commission and EMI, there will be a decision by qualified majority vote on whether to move to Stage 3 of EMU and the date for its inception. If it is agreed to start then exchange rates will be irrevocably fixed and a European Central Bank will take over the functions of the European Monetary Institute.

The United Kingdom is committed to all the clauses relating to EMU up to and including Stage 2, but was granted an opt-out protocol at Maastricht which enabled it to make a separate and delayed choice about Stage 3, the commitment to a common currency and to the ECB. Denmark was granted a protocol that enables it to submit any advance to Stage 3 to a national referendum. The United Kingdom made a great fuss over the need to consult Parliament about adopting a common currency but the real reason for the demand for an opt-out clause was the fear of a split in the Conservative party led by the Thatcherite 'Eurosceptics' in the run-up to a general election in 1992. The United Kingdom could have done what most of the other nations have to do, that is obtain their parliament's approval to the Union Treaty, including the EMU proposals. In any case, the United Kingdom government will require parliamentary approval of legislation implementing the agreements.

If it is decided in 1996 that it is too early for any country to embark on Stage 3 and no plan for a single currency has been introduced, then by the end of 1998, the Council of Ministers will decide, by a qualified majority, which economies are strong enough to begin on EMU. The designated countries will begin Stage 3 of EMU by 1 January 1999 at the latest. This does not mean that national currencies will immediately be replaced by the new Community currency because the task of replacing existing notes and coins is a mammoth one. Over time, however, a Community currency will be introduced after 1999 and will probably consist of different national note designs denominated in the common currency, which the treaty specifies as the (new) ECU, together with some reference to the original, established currency. The notes would be interchangeable in each participating country as Bank of England and Scottish notes are.

The protocol that the United Kingdom negotiated recognises that it 'shall not be obliged or committed to move to the third stage of economic and monetary union without a separate decision to do so by its government and parliament'. The protocol continues, saying that the United Kingdom shall notify the council whether it intends to move to the third stage, and that unless it does, it will be under no obligation to do so. If no date is fixed for the beginning of Stage 3 the United Kingdom may change its notification before 1 January 1998. The United Kingdom will retain its powers in the fields of monetary and exchange rate policy and be free to negotiate international agreements for itself, but it will have no rights to participate in the appointment of the president, vice-president and the other members of the executive board of the European Central Bank. If the United Kingdom changes its mind after the beginning of Stage 3 by other members it may notify its desire to join, but must meet the necessary convergence conditions and pay its dues in terms of capital subscriptions and the transfer of foreign reserve assets to the ECB. Some economists find it unthinkable that the United Kingdom would be able to remain outside the Stage 3 system if it gets under way with important members such as France and Germany and the Benelux countries. Others predict that the whole scheme will falter as various countries come to count the cost of convergence and the political unpopularity likely to be involved from deflationary policies and possible increases in unemployment. These pessimists are reckoning without the strength of commitment shown by the eleven members and the irrevocable nature of some of the contents of the agreement.

The European System of Central Banks

The Union Treaty goes into great detail about the establishment of the ESCB, the European Central Bank, their functions and the extent of their independence from national governmental interference. The treaty says that a ESCB and a ECB shall be established and that 'the primary objective of the ESCB shall be to maintain price stability'. It defines the tasks of the ESCB as: first, defining and implementing the monetary policy of the Community; second, conducting foreign exchange operations consistent with treaty provisions; third, holding and managing the official foreign reserves of the member states; and fourth, the promotion of the smooth operation of payment systems. It is expected to 'contribute to the smooth conduct of policies pursued by the competent authorities relating to the prudential supervision of credit institutions and the stability of the financial system'.

'The ESCB shall be composed of the European Central Bank and of the central banks of the member states'. The decision-making bodies of the ECB will be first, the Governing Council, which will comprise the members of the Executive Board and the Governors of the national central banks, and second, the Executive Board. The President, the Vice-President and the other four members of the Executive Board will be appointed for eight years by common accord of the governments of the members, on recommendation of the Council of Ministers and after consulting the European Parliament and the Governing Council of the ECB. They will not be able to serve an additional term. In an attempt to guarantee the independence of the ESCB the treaty says that 'neither the ECB nor a national central bank, nor any member of their decision-making bodies shall seek or take instructions from Community institutions or bodies, from any

Government of a member state or from any other body'. It goes further and says that Community and government institutions and bodies undertake to respect this principle and will not seek to influence the members of the decision-making bodies of the ECB. Some countries will have to rewrite the laws governing the roles of their central bank to conform with the treaty. In effect the treaty is creating a system which is even more independent than the Bundesbank has been.

Why have a Common Currency?

The potential financial benefits of full monetary union are enormous. A major saving would be the removal of the costs of exchanging the currencies of the members. It has been estimated that these costs are between £9 billion and £12 billion a year in the Community as a whole. A detailed analysis of the costs is given in a report called *One Market, One Money*, published for the Commission in October 1990. The report also states that monetary union will mean an increase of production in the Community of about 5 per cent of its gross domestic product arising from the greater confidence induced in investors who will no longer be deterred by exchange rate fluctuations. It also expects that the convergence of inflation rates would stimulate real output by 0.3 per cent of Community GDP. An additional benefit would be that the members of EMU would no longer need to keep currency reserves in relation to fellow members' currencies and this would save money. A further benefit is very hard to quantify but would arise from the greater ease with which trade could occur if there were no currency considerations.

Over the long term the greatest benefits would arise from the convergence of inflation rates and the tendency for interest rates to fall. It would be easier for enterprises to control costs and there would be greater certainty in their investment decisions. There would still be international currency dealing costs against, for example, the yen or the dollar, which would continue to fluctuate on a free foreign exchange market, assuming that the present floating rates prevail.

There are, however, significant costs in creating a monetary union. The experience of France, Belgium and Spain in the 1990s as they brought their policies into a form that would maintain their currencies within the ERM bands, and the recent experience of the

United Kingdom, show that the progress towards economic convergence can be very painful. The evidence from the difficulties of transition in the monetary union of East and West Germany emphasises the point. The pain arises from rising unemployment as the economy adjusts to the fact that slow depreciation of the currency can no longer be used to maintain international competitiveness and to absorb rising production costs, especially wage costs. There is also a painful loss of sovereignty over interest rate changes. Members of the ERM have found it very difficult to avoid following the interest rate changes introduced by the German central bank. The criteria for convergence referred to above will impose great budgetary, and therefore political, constraints on governments. It is predictable that unscrupulous politicians of all persuasions will use the ERM and EMU as a scapegoat for their inability to resolve national or sectional problems. EMU will produce long-term benefits whereas politicians are faced by short-term imperatives. On a gloomy note, those with experience of the French introduction of the 'new' or 'heavy' franc and of the United Kingdom's introduction of decimal coinage can only blench at the thought of the tide of ignorance and prejudice that will flood the popular press as the new currency is introduced.

The Future

In 1970 the Community said that it would create a monetary union by 1980. It failed, and on the basis of that experience many people think that the Maastricht agreement will also fail to produce EMU. Such thinking fails to appreciate the subtlety and significance of the Union Treaty details. Assuming that national parliaments accept the treaty, the third and final stage of EMU will start definitely by 1 January 1999, and the European Central Bank will have been set up by 1 July 1998, or at least six months before a single currency comes into existence. The economic convergence criteria are given great weight by the treaty and, in 1996, a majority of the twelve members must be 'fit' for the currency union to proceed. Later on, however, there is no need for this so-called 'critical mass' of fit countries to be achieved. All that the Community leaders must do in 1998 is to decide which countries are ready for EMU, which will proceed anyway six months later. The number of qualifying states then will be at least three because of the way the convergence criteria are stated. In practice more are likely to be fit to proceed, especially those who have been aligning their economies closely to Germany's.

It should be remembered that Germany was a powerful supporter of the Maastricht agreement on monetary union although it wanted greater progress on the political front, especially an increase in the democratic controls exercised by the European Parliament. The proposed management structure of the European Central Bank appears to guarantee its independence from outside political interference and some commentators say it will be even more independent that the Deutsche Bundesbank. Chancellor Kohl has, however, a hard task ahead in selling the agreement to the German people who will insist on the new European currency being at least as good as the present Deutschmark. As for the United Kingdom, whose leadership has been surprised at the degree of commitment of the other eleven, and which has been isolated by its opt-out clause, it will either be a member of the group in the slow lane to EMU, with the considerable disadvantages that entails, or, as many commentators think, it will find the pressures to join the full EMU irresistible. In the background is the important influence of how multinational companies will react if a single currency zone is created within Europe and from which the United Kingdom is excluded. They are likely to transfer their new investments and some of their activities into that zone. The United Kingdom's opt out would then be seen as short-sighted and lacking in vision.

The Social Integration of Europe

8

Introduction

The nations of Europe are likely to retain their distinctive characters for many centuries to come, but the very existence of the Community will tend to create greater uniformity of approach in vital areas of daily life. This will happen largely because of institutional and legal pressures to conform, but there will also be a considerable informal pressure arising from the natural human characteristic of copying successful methods and procedures. The process has already gone a long way in the original Six members despite the differentiating marks of language and history. It is continuing with the subsequent groups of members. In this context two areas in particular are worth looking at in greater depth, social policy itself and environmental policy. Closely linked with these are law and justice which are dealt with in Chapter 9.

The Social Policy of the European Community

The social policies of the European Community originated in the European Coal and Steel Community (ECSC). This intended to rationalise the two industries so it was inevitable that the social implications should be considered. Thus one of the ECSC's objectives was 'to promote improved living and working conditions for the workers'. This involved provisions for redeployment, safety, retraining, resettlement, guaranteed adequate wages, free movement of workers and safeguarded entitlement to social security benefits.

The European Community took over these objectives although they were not always expressed in exactly the same form. There were also important additions, notably the adoption of the principle of equal pay for equal work for men and women and an emphasis on harmonisation of standards among member states. The Community also set up a Social Fund whose objective was to promote employment opportunities and geographical and occupational mobility for workers within the Community. An area of particular interest was social security for migrant workers. Minimum health and safety standards were also established by the Euratom Treaty.

The European Social Fund

The ESF was set up by the Treaty of Rome in Articles 123 to 127. The Fund has been reformed on several occasions since, in 1971, 1977 and 1983. In 1988 a major review led to the introduction of new rules from January 1990 not only for the ESF but also for the Regional Fund and the Farm Fund. The three funds have been given five principal objectives:

1. Helping less developed regions, that is those with a gross domestic product per head of less than 75 per cent of the Community average. This definition covers the whole of Ireland including Northern Ireland, Portugal, Greece, large areas of Spain, southern Italy, and the overseas territories of France.
2. Helping to restructure regions in serious industrial decline where unemployment is high and new jobs are difficult to create.
3. Reducing long-term unemployment.
4. Helping the entry of young people into work.
5 (a) Helping to adjust production, processing and marketing structures in agriculture and forestry.
   (b) Assisting development in rural areas affected by structural decline.

The Social Fund concentrates on objectives 3 and 4, reducing long-term unemployment and integrating young people aged under 25 into work. The map, Figure 8.1, indicates the areas to which the funds are directed.

FIGURE 8.1
Community Regions Entitled to Assistance under Objectives 1, 2 and 5b of the Community's Structural Funds Document

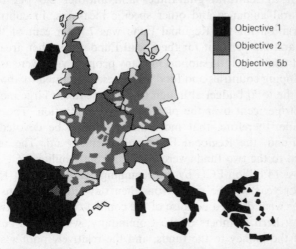

Objective 1
Objective 2
Objective 5b

SOURCE   EC Commission, *Guide to the Reform of the Community's Structural Funds* (Brussels/Luxembourg, 1989).

The Fund obtains its money from the Community budget. In 1988 the ESF budget was the relatively low figure of £2122 million. Usually, the money is allocated to match that put up by public bodies in the country concerned. The Social Fund, and for that matter the Regional Fund, has to compete with the Common Agricultural Policy (CAP) for money. The CAP has its own fund for 'guidance and restructuring', the European Agricultural Guidance and Guarantee Fund (EAGGF in English or FEOGA in French). This has helped to finance the less favoured areas of farming and has provided money for small farmers who wish to leave the industry. In the 1970s and the early 1980s the demands of the CAP expanded rapidly, especially on the price guarantee side, and prevented any significant growth in the Social or Regional Funds.

The European Parliament and Community politicians found this increasingly frustrating. Their frustration partly explains the willingness to curtail agricultural spending. There was a slow growth in expenditure by both funds but this did not match the problems that arose from widespread unemployment and industrial decline after 1973. The difference in emphasis on the programmes can be seen from the 1985 budget which appropriated about 67 per cent of the total for agricultural guarantees and another 2.5 per cent for agricultural guidance and other specific measures. In contrast, the appropriation for the Regional Fund was 7.5 per cent of the total budget and 6.5 per cent for the Social Fund. The other areas which received relatively little support in many people's view were assistance to developing countries and food aid. These amounted to about 3 per cent of the total budget although this represented a large increase of about 30 per cent over the previous year's allocation. The decision was made, therefore, that more money should be devoted to the Social Fund, the Regional Fund and overseas aid. The resources allocated to the two funds were doubled from 7 billion ECU in 1988 to almost 14 billion ECU by the beginning of 1993. About 15 billion ECU per year will be spent from then onwards. Decisions on the increases were delayed because of the conflict of interest between the 'rich' northern members of the Community, who would contribute most of the money to the funds, and the relatively poorer southern states.

On the financial side of the social policy, one of the recent problems has been created by the accession of Greece, Spain and Portugal. These have, in varying degrees, higher unemployment, lower incomes per head and lower standards of social provision. The same conditions apply in some areas of Italy. The Community responded by raising the budget for expenditure from the Regional and Agricultural Guidance Funds from £5 billion in 1985 to £9 billion by 1992. Between 60 and 70 per cent of the total funds have been spent in Portugal, Greece and parts of Spain and Italy. Ireland is also included in this group. In 1985 some special schemes called Integrated Mediterranean Programmes were also established. These are used to develop the Mediterranean areas of France, Italy and Greece. They are aimed at reducing high unemployment and economic weakness, and raising living standards. They provide training facilities, protect the environment and improve agriculture, fishing and the infrastructure. There is another programme to help Portugal. This is called PEDIP and is intended to improve Portuguese productivity and the quality of its goods.

One of the strengths of the Community is the way in which it can muster resources and target them at disadvantaged areas. The assumption is, of course, that market forces will not in themselves rectify the economic backwardness of the regions mentioned. The new 'Cohesion Fund' to be set up in 1993 is a good example of channelled assistance.

What areas does social policy cover?

The following list will give some idea of the pervasiveness of the policy. These items cannot be discussed individually in any depth and the reader is recommended to obtain, free, copies of *The Social Policy of the European Community* and *1992 – The Social Dimension*, from the Office for Official Publications of the European Communities, if detail is required. It will be obvious, however, that simply listing the items reveals a great possibility of conflict between governments and the Community. Most members are able to accept these policies with little difficulty and eleven signed the Social Charter in December 1989. But the prevailing pro-market, anti-interventionist policy in the United Kingdom was very different from the social democratic, interventionist tone of the Community's social policy and the United Kingdom refused to sign. The difference of opinion was a problem in the negotiations at Maastricht in 1991 leading up to the Treaty on Economic and Political Union.

The areas covered by the policy include:

Free movement of workers
Social security for migrant workers
Promotion of workers' geographical and occupational mobility
Equal pay for men and women
Safety at work
Health protection in the nuclear industry
Working hours and holidays
Vocational retraining
Handicapped persons, elderly workers
Youth unemployment
Full and better employment-coordinating national policies
Redeployment of workers in declining industries
Leisure of workers, housing
Accident prevention and health protection
Integration of migrant workers
Help for the neediest – homeless, old, vagrants, one-parent families

Industrial democracy, workers' participation
Rights of working women

The penultimate item in the list, industrial democracy and workers' participation, created problems for the United Kingdom government. Having 'defeated' the unions between 1979 and 1986, it faced the unwelcome prospect of the Community putting trade unionists on the board of management of all companies above a certain size. The fact that most European countries saw this as right, sensible and constructive seemed to escape the British government.

From the lengthy list given above it may be useful to examine one area in detail, the rights of working women.

How has the social policy affected the rights of working women?

Article 119 of the Treaty of Rome said that pay differentials between men and women should be abolished by the end of 1961. This deadline was not achieved and it was reset at the end of 1964. This delay was despite the fact that most of the written constitutions of the members include guarantees of the equality of the sexes. It became apparent as time passed that women remained in a relatively unprivileged position both in the labour market and socially. In 1975, therefore, the Council of Ministers adopted a directive which required member states to repeal all laws, regulations and administrative provisions that were not compatible with the principle of equal pay. They were also ordered to ensure that the principle was integrated into collective agreements and individual contracts. They were to enable any woman to claim her rights before the courts without fear of dismissal. A year later, in 1976, a supplement to this directive gave members two and a half years to give equal treatment to men and women in access to employment, vocational training, promotion and working conditions. They had to abolish all legal provisions and any terms of collective agreements that were prejudicial to working women. These directives led to extensive changes to British law.

There still remained, however, areas of discrimination, for example in the application of social security. At the end of 1987 member states were given a six-year period in which to introduce equality of treatment. This includes the abolition of discrimination in respect of sex, marital or family status, the coverage of social security schemes, the obligation to pay contributions and the calculation of benefits and allowances.

Since then the Commission has insisted on receiving regular reports from each country on its progress in implementing the directives. It has followed up any failures to do so by threatening reference to the Court of Justice and has, on several occasions, brought actions against recalcitrant member states. Private individuals have also brought cases before their national courts and later appealed to the European Court of Justice.

As an extension of its efforts the Commission organised an action programme between 1982 and 1985 on promoting equal opportunities for women. Another programme was implemented between 1986 and 1990. The adoption of the Charter of Fundamental Social Rights for Workers (the Social Charter) in 1989 led to a third action programme aimed to run from 1991 to 1995. It is intended to produce a more integrated and comprehensive strategy for action and to develop new schemes to help women in vocational training and employment. This includes the protection of pregnant women at work and of those who have recently given birth. The United Kingdom objected to some of the provisions relating to the remuneration of pregnant women during their time off work because the other members, in order to circumvent the United Kingdom's veto, made proposals for the Social Charter under the 'health and safety' rules which required only a qualified majority in the Council. The United Kingdom resented this manipulation of the Single European Act. No one pretends that equality has yet been achieved especially when the evidence of inequality of earnings and so on is seen, but the Community has made effective progress towards creating a proper legislative framework for equality. This has probably gone much further than it would under some individual governments, including that of the United Kingdom.

The Social Charter

It quickly became apparent after the passing of the Single European Act in 1986 and its implementation after July 1987 that the removal of barriers to trade needed to be balanced by some progress towards the harmonisation of social conditions and social legislation in the member states. The Commission, therefore, asked the Economic and Social Committee (see page 5) to draw up a 'European Charter of Basic Social Rights'. The committee, made up of representatives of employers, workers, professions, farmers, and small and medium-sized businesses, produced a draft in February 1989. Its efforts were supported by a resolution in the European Parliament in March 1989 calling for significant advances on the social aspects of the Community.

The draft proposals were considerably modified in the version produced by the Commission in its submission to the Council of Ministers in May 1989. The ministers responsible for social affairs and employment discussed the proposed Social Charter in June 1989 and it was the subject of further consultations with industry and trade unions before its final version was accepted by eleven members of the European Council at Strasbourg in December 1989. The United Kingdom refused to adopt it despite important changes made during the discussions. In 1990 the Commission put forward an action plan to carry out the charter. It is fair to say that very little was achieved before the Maastricht summit in December 1991 and this partly explains why the eleven 'opted themselves out' in the Social Chapter protocol of the Union Treaty.

There was a significant change in the title of the charter as it passed through the consultative process but the media still call it the 'Social Charter'. The name adopted was the 'Charter of Fundamental Rights for Workers'. The substitution of the words 'rights for workers' for 'basic social rights' reflected a narrowing of the scope of the charter. The original conception was of a charter that would apply to all, irrespective of whether they were actually in work or not.

A second important alteration was to shift the emphasis from providing solutions at a Community level to increasing the role of the member states. This was partly a recognition of the principle of 'subsidiarity', that is, legal changes being instituted at the level of decision-making most appropriate to the matter involved. In other words, responsibility for most of the rules and legislation affecting workers' rights will devolve on to the individual member states. There will still be plenty of scope for Community action but a great deal of national variation in provision will remain. The European Parliament criticised this change of emphasis away from citizens to workers and the general vagueness of the charter itself.

The impact of the Social Charter

The Charter is based on the fundamental principles relating to twelve main themes, or rights:

1. Free movement of workers based on the principle of equal treatment in access to employment and social protection.
2. Employment and remuneration based on the principle of fair remuneration, that is a decent basic wage, receipt of a fair wage, and fair treatment for part-time workers.
3. Improvement in living and working conditions. This is concerned mainly with working hours, holiday entitlement, shift working, rest periods and redundancy procedures, among other things.
4. Social protection based on the rules and practices proper to each country. It is this section that makes the controversial reference to a guaranteed minimum wage and to social assistance to those who lack adequate means of subsistence although there is not an intention to *impose* a minimum wage across the board.
5. Freedom of association and collective bargaining.
6. Vocational training. This refers to the right to continue vocational training throughout one's working life, including the right to leave in order to undertake such training.
7. Equal treatment for men and women. This aims at equality of access to employment, social protection, education, vocational training and career opportunities.
8. Information, consultation and participation of workers. This has proved to be a very controversial proposal because it aims particularly at those employed in transnational companies. It intends that they be given the right to be informed and even consulted about major events affecting the company that may influence working conditions and employment.
9. Protection of health and safety in the work-place. This area will lead to the issue of several directives to national governments over the next few years in an attempt to create Community-wide standards of good practice. The fishing, mining, and construction industries are the major targets for improvements in health and safety practices.
10. Protection of children and adolescents. This aims at a minimum working age of 16 with youth employment being subject to labour regulations geared to the needs of young people. It also

intends to establish the right to two years of vocational training after the end of compulsory education.

11. The elderly. This asserts that those reaching retirement, or early retirement ages are entitled to a pension which provides a 'decent' standard of living. Those not entitled to a pension should be given a minimum income, social protection, and social and medical help.

12. The disabled. This aims at giving every disabled person the right to benefit from measures for training, rehabilitation, and social and occupational integration.

The action plan put forward by the Commission includes a list of directives, regulations, decisions and recommendations under each of the twelve headings. (See Chapter 1 for an explanation of the different applications of these terms.) Its intention is to concentrate on areas where it thinks legislation is required to create the social dimension of the single internal market or to contribute to the economic and social cohesion of the Community. The Commission is playing a very minor part in the sections relating to freedom of association and collective bargaining, preferring to leave changes to the decision of individual governments. The intention is to present all the proposals before the end of 1992 and to follow up with further measures as necessary after 1993.

Conclusion

The Social Charter has a basic weakness in that it uses terms such as 'decent', 'fair', and 'equitable' without adequate definition or reference to monetary levels. This is bound to cause problems in the future because such use of subjective terms always starts off a discussion in confusion. Eventually, no doubt, a consensus will develop about the meaning of these terms in relation to absolute levels of income, benefits and provision but, in the meantime, there is ample scope for the development of several interpretations based on national or party self-interest.

Underlying the demand for a Social Charter is a fear which is prevalent in the more affluent countries with better social provisions, that the advent of the single internal market will, if unchecked, cause what is called 'social dumping'. This phrase, like all community jargon, takes on several meanings, but two predominate. The first is the idea that workers and their families, given free movement within the Community, will gravitate to those countries with the highest standards of provision, thus placing a heavy burden on those countries' budgets for social provision as well as creating housing, employment and educational demands. These workers would 'dump' themselves in the affluent regions and be willing to work for lower wages and in worse conditions to the detriment of the existing local work force. The second aspect of 'social dumping' is that, if the differences in wage levels and working conditions persist among Community members, industry and commerce will tend to shift its location to those countries with the lowest levels, such as Portugal, Spain, and Greece, or to areas with labour forces from outside the Community. This process, of which there is already some evidence, would adversely affect those nations with better provision in the areas covered by the Social Charter. The critics of the argument say that the multinational companies who set up plants in countries such as Spain and Portugal do not run down or close their existing plants elsewhere in the Community.

The United Kingdom refused to sign the Social Charter in 1989 on the grounds that the areas covered by it were the responsibility of individual governments and that the Community was an economic institution, not a social one. Its opposition was important in establishing the greater application of the principle of subsidiarity to the Charter. It also, by its opposition, forced the other eleven members of the Community to take the proposed Social Chapter, which would have put the Social Charter into a new treaty context, out of the Union Treaty and to place it in a separate protocol for the eleven to operate under Community institutions (see below).

In spite of this the United Kingdom will find itself forced into implementing some regulations and modifying its own laws to give effect to directives passed under the qualified majority voting system applied to measures to implement the single market. The evidence is that the United Kingdom had already, before 1990, been forced or dragged along by the Community at a pace faster than it would have adopted on its own. The United Kingdom is still near the bottom of the European league in terms of social security provision, hours of work, inspection of health and safety at work, and overall social welfare. The United Kingdom also remains far behind in relation to worker participation in management and decision-making. It is probable that the changes required under the Single European Act and the harmonisation of the social market will eventually work wonders for the British economy. The powers of the Council were and are limited in respect of social policy under the Single European Act. Unanimity is required in the Council of Ministers. Decisions by majority are not allowed in all areas of social policy but, once again, the other members intend to go ahead without Britain wherever they can define the proposed changes as ones needed to complete the single market under the heading of 'health and safety at work'.

The Social Chapter of the Maastricht Agreement

The divergence between the United Kingdom and the other members in the field of social legislation is likely to widen if the Social Chapter opt-out protocol for the eleven in the Union Treaty does actually work as intended. It will permit the application of qualified majority voting by the eleven and speed up progress. Some observers find it hard to see how the United Kingdom can remain unaffected by this situation, especially as it seems as if multinational firms will have to apply common standards to their establishments in the eleven and in the United Kingdom. If the United Kingdom did go ahead with the same general approach as the other members, it might pull the United Kingdom's social policies out of the Victorian age. The argument against is, of course, based on the possible addition to employers' costs of the improved provisions for their employees and on an alleged potential reduction in employment of workers on low wages. The government is also reluctant to face up to the likely increases in its own expenditures and their tax implications.

During the Maastricht negotiations the United Kingdom insisted on the Social Chapter being removed from the Union Treaty. As a result it was removed into a separate protocol enabling the eleven to continue with the Social Charter's proposals. The assumption is that they will continue trying to get the agreement of all twelve to proposals. The arrangement is that agreements made under the protocol will continue to be reached within the framework of the Community's institutions which will be 'on loan' to the eleven members. If the United Kingdom cannot accept a proposal it will opt out of discussions and decisions. The present system of discussions of the Social Charter will continue until the treaty takes effect in 1993. The present voting procedures will also apply until then.

The eleven agreed that certain issues can be decided by qualified majority vote of 44 votes out of 66. These are: (1) health and safety at work; (2) working conditions; (3) information and consultation of workers; (4) equality at work between men and women; (5) integration of persons excluded from the labour market.

They also agreed to keep certain issues for unanimous vote. These are: (1) social security and social protection of workers; (2) protection of workers made redundant; (3) representation, and collective defence of workers and employers; (4) conditions of employment of third country nationals; (5) financial contributions for promoting jobs.

It is interesting to note that a major factor in Denmark's rejection of the Union Treaty in its referendum was the dissatisfaction of Left-wing parties with the commitment to social policies.

The Community and the Environment

The word 'environment' is usually used in a subjective as well as objective sense to refer to the quality of the air, the water, countryside, soil, sea and animal life around us. This quality is heavily influenced by the size of population and its density. This, together with income per head, determines the other major factor influencing the quality of the environment, that is, energy use. These three forces, population size, population density and energy use tend to predetermine the nature and scale of environmental problems. These difficulties can, of course, be alleviated or aggravated by Community policy. Some people allege that the Common Agricultural Policy is responsible for considerable ecological damage with its stimulation of arable farming and the 'excessive' use of fertiliser and pesticides.

It should always be remembered when discussing environmental issues that they nearly always have an international aspect. The United Kingdom's power-station gases may be Western Europe's acid rain. A chemical works putting effluent into the Rhine affects the quality of the North Sea. A Chernobyl disaster, or atmospheric test of a nuclear device, spreads a radioactive swathe across several continents. It is this international feature of environmental affairs that makes the European Community peculiarly valuable because it has the administrative machinery already in place to act quickly in pursuit of a coordinated policy.

What is the population background?

In 1989, the population density of the twelve members of the Community was 144 per square kilometre. This compares with 328 in Japan, 26 in the United States and 13 in the USSR. It is expected that all these figures will rise by the year 2000, the Community figure by about 2. The figures for European countries show a wide range as is clear from Table 8.1.

TABLE 8.1
Population Density

1989	Population million	Inhab km²	Total Area km²	Agricultural Area in Use approx. %
Belgium	9.9	324	30 500	46
Denmark	5.1	118	43 100	66
West Germany	62.0	249	248 700	48
Greece	10.1	77	132 000	44
Spain	39.2	78	504 000	54
France	56.1	102	549 100	57
Ireland	3.5	50	70 300	81
Italy	57.6	191	301 300	58
Luxembourg	0.4	143	2 600	49
Netherlands	14.9	355	41 785	54
Portugal	9.8	106	92 389	48
United Kingdom	57.1	234	244 100	76
Europe 12	325.6	144	2 260 680	59
World		37	135 837 000	–
United Germany	78.7	220	356 700	–

Source   Eurostat, *Basic Statistics of the Community*, 25th edn (Luxembourg: Office for Official Publications of the European Communities, 1991).

Crude measures of overall density are only a start to analysing basic pressures. We also need to have data on urbanisation and population movements over time. It is urbanisation which produces the undesirable concentrations of atmospheric pollution from vehicles and industry, creating the need for extensive systems for the collection and disposal of refuse and sewage. The very act of creating urban areas destroys natural habitats, trees and hedgerows. It requires large volumes of raw materials such as timber and aggregates like sand and gravel. Urban growth is accompanied by extensive road building, power lines, pipelines, reservoirs, pumping stations, sewerage works and railways. This process involves the exploitation of natural resources, many of which are from the Third World. Since there is relatively little stress on the recycling of materials this represents a high level of new demand.

The growth of communications and the ownership of the private motor car now ensure that no area is free from exploitation. There has been a remarkable expansion of urbanisation, for example, in the areas of the Community blessed by sun and sea. High incomes and the trend to early retirement have accelerated this movement, nor are inland or mountain areas safe if they are suitable for leisure developments. As a result, seas and lakes are prone to many forms of pollution. Since water touches or crosses many frontiers and derives from rain or melting snow, even a nation which actively pursues a sound environmental policy may be at the mercy of its 'dirty' neighbours. The United Kingdom had the unenviable reputation in the 1970s and 1980s of being the 'dirty man of Europe' because its atmospheric pollution drifts on the prevailing westerly winds over to Scandinavia and Western Europe. Excuses are uttered and the United States is also blamed but only gradually have effective countermeasures been taken. In the autumn of 1988, Mrs Thatcher donned a 'green' mantle in a major speech and more action has been taken in the United Kingdom on atmospheric pollution from industry, on exhaust emissions, water quality and the disposal of waste into the sea although the environmental lobby is still not satisfied with the depth of the commitment or with the speed of the implementation of measures.

The European Court has not been satisfied either. In January 1992 the Advocate-General issued a preliminary opinion saying that the United Kingdom was failing to meet Community purity standards for drinking water and specifically that it had failed to implement a 1980 directive setting standards to be met by a 1982 deadline. There were excessive nitrate levels in 28 water supply zones in the United Kingdom. The Commission is taking similar action against all the member states except Denmark, Greece and Portugal.

Fortunately, the expected population growth of the Community is marginal although that of some countries in Eastern Europe gives cause for concern. This provides an opportunity to implement effective policies that are built into all areas of agricultural, commercial and industrial expansion. It is perhaps as well to keep the issue in perspective. In the Community, in 1987, only 8.5 per cent of land was classified as 'built up'; 58.8 per cent was agricultural; 22.1 per cent 'wooded'; 1.6 per cent was 'inland water'; 9 per cent had 'other uses'. If enough money and political will is forthcoming then those elements which arise from within the Community can be controlled. Those elements arising outside the Community, such as the destruction of tropical rain forest, require international action. Again, it is fortunate that 'green' politics have become very important, especially in West Germany and Scandinavia. The unification of Germany has had a major beneficial effect and has led to the closing down of a large number of East German plants responsible for pollution, although the financial cost has been huge. The political will seems to exist to make environmental considerations paramount, although in The Netherlands the government was brought down in May 1989 because it tried to push control of the private motor car too far.

How significant is energy use in the Community in the environmental context?

Of the Community countries only the United Kingdom has an energy surplus – of approximately 15 per cent above its consumption. The Netherlands, which is the next country in terms of energy self-sufficiency, has a deficit of 5 per cent. The United Kingdom's surpluses arise from oil and natural gas but they will probably give way to a deficit at some time in the 1990s. As a result the Community in 1987 imported 43 per cent of its primary energy requirements. In contrast the United States imported only 12 per cent while Japan, at the other extreme, imported 82 per cent. The USSR produced a surplus of 20 per cent. The Community worked very hard to reduce energy imports after the first oil crisis of 1973. Imports were then 60 per cent of consumption (see Table 8.2).

Oil accounts for about 45 per cent of European primary energy requirements. The transport and burning of oil is probably the major environmental hazard. Nuclear power is growing in importance especially in France where it is used to generate about 70 per cent of the electricity. By 1986 nuclear energy was being used to generate 37 per cent of the electricity in the Community. Over the years since

TABLE 8.2
Production and Consumption of Primary Energy: Europe 12

	Production %	Consumption %
Oil	25.6	45.0
Coal and Lignite	28.7	23.1
Natural gas	21.6	18.0
Nuclear energy	21.3	12.2
Hydroelectric	2.8	1.7
Total	589 million TEP	1029 million TEP

TEP = tonnes of oil equivalent.

SOURCE Eurostat, *Basic Statistics of the Community*, 25th edn (Luxembourg: Office for Official Publications of the European Communities, 1990).

1973 industry has managed to reduce its share of energy consumption from 35 to 29 per cent. In the household and services sector consumption has been a static share of the total. In the field of transport, however, there has been a rise from 18 to 25 per cent. This is largely accounted for by the growth of private car ownership, despite the greater fuel efficiency of modern vehicles.

Energy consumption has several main implications for the environment. The extraction of coal is usually environmentally harmful. The extraction and transport of oil is accompanied by potential risks as with the *Torrey Canyon*, *Amoco Cadiz* and *Piper Alpha* disasters. Nuclear energy for electricity generation carries the greatest long-term hazard to the environment although enormous expenditures and engineering skills go into reducing this risk factor. The greatest immediate hazards, however, come from the burning of hydrocarbon fuels, coal, oil and natural gas. The emissions from this burning pollute their immediate environment and, through the atmosphere, the environment hundreds or thousands of miles away. In addition, the production, use and dispersal of chemicals and plastics sometimes has an accumulative deleterious effect on the environment.

In 1985 the Community put forward a series of objectives to be achieved by 1995 for energy use. A review in 1988 showed that these aims would be only partly met. It should be remembered that projections of energy use are notoriously unreliable, especially over long periods. The objectives included the improvement of the efficiency of final energy demand by at least 20 per cent. The 1988 review shows that this is unlikely to be achieved. Another aim was to cut oil consumption to around 40 per cent of total energy consumption and to keep oil imports at below 33 per cent of total energy consumption. A cut to 43 per cent is more likely and the import share will remain at about one-third. Other objectives included an increase in the use of fossil fuels and a reduction in the share of gas and oil in the production of electricity to below 15 per cent. Both of these are likely to happen but only to a small degree. The final aim of increasing output share from new and renewable sources of power will probably result in 2 per cent of total energy deriving from these sources. The depressing conclusion of the 1988 review was that the Community's total energy consumption by 1995 would rise by between 70 and 110 million tonnes of oil equivalent more than the target set in 1985. This would make the Community more vulnerable to any interruptions of world energy supplies and would probably have a detrimental effect on industrial costs.

One consequence of the review was an increased emphasis on the promotion of energy efficiency in a new programme introduced in 1989. The *Thermie* programme provides money for spreading technological information on energy efficiency, renewable energy sources, clean coal technologies, and oil and gas prospecting and development. In December 1991 45 nations signed a new European Energy Charter incorporating proposals aimed at creating a legal and financial framework to exploit Eastern European energy resources more efficiently. Western members will install modern, environmentally cleaner power-stations and equipment.

Has the Community developed a coherent policy on the environment?

The answer to this question is a qualified 'yes'. There is still a debate about the detail and the timing of initiatives but the need for a policy was recognised as long ago as 1972. The Single European Act of 1986 established legal requirements in the environmental sphere and by 1991 over 100 pieces of legislation applied to the environment. The Community undertook action programmes and the fourth, between 1987 and 1991, shifted the emphasis from simply preventing environmental deterioration to incorporating environmental considerations into the basic agricultural, social, regional and economic policies.

Fine words are not always carried into action but a positive step was made when the European Council made the 'Dublin Declaration' in June 1990 agreeing that the Community had a special responsibility for the environment both to its own citizens and to the wider world. They called for special protection for Antarctica, and a treaty preventing development there has since been signed. They also urged the acceleration of efforts to reduce depletion of the ozone layer and to revise the Montreal Protocol of 1987 which deals with that issue. They adopted some popular concerns and sought combined efforts to check the destruction of tropical rain forests, soil erosion and the spread of deserts. To give credence to their fine words, they said they were willing to put additional financial and technical resources into the effort. They congratulated themselves on the inclusion of such environmental considerations in the Fourth Lomé Convention and expressed great concern at the environmental problems being revealed in Eastern Europe.

The Commission made detailed proposals in 1989 for the setting up of a European Environment Agency to include, if they wished, neighbouring non-Community countries. The European Parliament wanted it to be given greater powers than those proposed so its role will be reviewed after two years. The decision was made in May 1990 to adopt the scheme and the Agency was given the job of providing reliable data, objectivity, and the information needed to monitor the application of Community laws on the environment. The hope was expressed that it might eventually become the basis of an *international* agency.

Some countries appear to be more susceptible than others to pressure from industry to delay and procrastinate. The United Kingdom has lagged behind in terms of water purity standards, beach cleanliness, the control of vehicle exhaust emissions and the use of unleaded petrol. There is considerable argument about Community standards for food, food processing and animal husbandry. Another serious dispute concerns the treatment and disposal of toxic waste. Once again the United Kingdom was called the 'dustbin' of Europe because it placed stress upon private enterprise controlling disposal sites and the provision of incinerators for all sorts of dangerous chemical waste. To the intense anger of the environment lobby much of this waste was imported. Sellafield in Cumbria has now been expanded to become the major European nuclear waste processing plant.

It is hard for the lay person to find a way through the labyrinth of statistics and propaganda that emanates from governments and pressure groups. It is to be hoped that the new European Environmental Agency will make the task easier. Environmental and ecological pressure groups have multiplied over the past twenty years. They all want government, Community or international action of some sort. Frequently, this involves large expenditure or additional costs on producers or users. The scene is then set for a clash of pressure groups. Usually, the producers' lobby is financially stronger and more skilled at manipulating the political decision-making process. Eventually, the environmental lobby may triumph in whole or in part through the persuasion of public opinion, as in the suspension of whaling by most countries, or in the international agreement in May 1989 to suspend the use of CFCs by the year 2000. Gradually, governments may see votes in appeasing the 'green' lobby. Alternatively reports from its research institutions may provoke them into belated action as in the banning of CFCs in plastics and aerosols in order to protect the ozone layer, as mentioned above. It is probably fair to say that the United Kingdom has rarely been at the forefront of environmental progress in the Community, Its role, despite recent protestations, has been a cautious, tending to a negative, one.

How has the Community policy developed?

In 1972, there was a major United Nations Conference on the Environment in Stockholm. The Community heads of government later in 1972 acknowledged that economic growth had to be linked to improvements in living standards and the quality of life of its citizens and to protection of the environment and natural resources. They concluded that 'economic expansion is not an end in itself'.

The heads of government laid out a thirteen-point programme and asked the Commission to formulate a Community environment policy. This was done and in late 1973 the Community's first programme began. It lasted four years and was followed by a second and third. The fourth programme began in 1987 and operated until the end of 1991. Over 100 pieces of legislation have been enacted although not all the tight deadlines specified have been met. The programme adopted outlined three main spheres of action:

1. the reduction and prevention of pollution and nuisances;
2. the improvement of the environment and the quality of life;
3. action by the Community, or where applicable, by united action of the members, in international organisations concerned with the environment.

The Commission had tried to define 'the environment' as 'the combination of elements whose complex interrelationships make up the settings, the surroundings and the conditions of life of the individual and of society, as they are, or as they are felt'. This broad definition includes the man-made environment such as the architectural heritage as well as the natural world.

The heads of government had agreed on some very important principles that have been included in subsequent statements. For example, the Single European Act of 1986 endorsed those principles mentioned. The main decisions were that preventive rather than curative action should be taken over pollution, that environmental damage should be rectified at source, and that the polluter must'pay the costs of prevention and rectification. The SEA included the phrase that 'environmental protection requirements shall be a component of the Community's other policies'. This could be regarded as simply a bland form of words but the Act also said that any future Commission proposals about health, environmental protection and consumer protection would 'take as a base a high level of protection'. This partly explains the wide-ranging measures and disputes over environmental policy that emerged after 1986. The main focus of attention in the 1990s is likely to be the role and effectiveness of the European Environment Agency described earlier.

The concept that 'the polluter must pay' is frequently voiced. It sounds clear, straightforward and just. In practice, however, it is by no means simple. It is not always easy to identify a polluter although scientific tests are improving so much that it is now possible to identify the origins of most oil spillages, Even then it is not always easy to identify the spiller. Atmospheric pollution cannot always be traced to its source. Moreover, there is a code of legal practice for waste disposal. People often exceed these legal limits in an undetected or accidental fashion. Even water authorities are sometimes forced to pollute waterways with excessively toxic levels of discharge. There is also a major disagreement sometimes about the safe level of pollutant or discharge. One of the functions of the Community policy is to fix standards of emissions, discharges and additives.

Who should pay to protect the environment?

The phrase 'the polluter should pay' frequently means, in practice, that the consumer pays in the form of higher prices. This is the case with water supplies, emissions from power-station flues and car exhaust controls. If the supplier is a 'natural monopolist', as with water and electricity, most of the burden of increased cleanliness is passed on to the consumer. If the industry is oligopolistic, as with petroleum, then most of the burden will be borne by the consumer but its extent will depend on the effectiveness of the collusion among sellers.

The principle of the polluter paying may depend upon the state creating a very effective inspection, supervision and monitoring service backed by effective punishment for malpractice. Most of the costs of this will fall on the taxpayer because the regulatory system, if effective as a deterrent, will produce insufficient income to pay for itself. The principle eventually boils down to the fact that an industry has to pay for any of the costs needed to equip itself to comply with minimum standards.

The alternative to the consumer paying is for the government to cover some costs out of taxation. Another possibility is to identify the polluter and make him pay. At present, many 'polluters' are undetected. They are, in effect, keeping their production costs down by not having effluent or emission control and treatment. They are managing to make someone else pay some of their costs in terms of dirt, noise, unusable land, dead rivers and plant life, or dead animals. These costs are called 'external' costs by economists and are foisted on to the community at large or in particular. Occasionally, there can be external benefits when a firm improves the environment and reduces other people's costs or raises the quality of their lives. The result of the existence of these external costs and benefits means that there is often a divergence between the private and social costs of an economic activity. It may be profitable in terms of private costs and revenues alone. But if externalities are taken into account the deficit between social costs and benefits may outweigh the private profit. That is to say, the private firm is profitable commercially but society as a whole is losing more than the firm's private profit.

The Community has recognised this fact and has implemented a directive which says that major public or private development projects in agriculture, industry or infrastructure (for example, road building) must produce an environmental impact assessment before the work begins. The instigator must analyse potential pollution or other impacts such as noise, on soil, air and water. The effects on wildlife habitats must also be considered. Permission for the project is only granted, and then possibly with conditions attached, after these environmental considerations have been balanced against the social, economic and other benefits of the scheme. The Commission, in 1991, criticised the British government who, it alleged, had failed to observe this directive when preparing plans for the Channel Tunnel rail link and for new roads through ancient woodlands and down-lands. The United Kingdom government stated that it was in the right and would go ahead anyway.

Would energy taxes help?

In September 1991 the Commission produced discussion proposals on the introduction of a completely new tax on energy use in the Community. Shortly afterwards the environment ministers of the Twelve welcomed the suggestions and later accepted the principle of a tax to reduce carbon dioxide emissions. The proposals have to be discussed by three main groups of ministers, finance, energy, and environment. The final decision will probably be made in June 1992.

The taxes, if adopted, would be phased in from 1993 to 2000. They would apply to non-renewable sources of energy and would be most heavily applied to those fossil fuels which produce the highest levels of carbon dioxide emissions and contribute to global warming. The aim is to make the taxes 'fiscally neutral' by reducing other taxes. Even so, the Commission predicts that the taxes would raise inflation by about 0.5 per cent, and cut economic growth slightly. The hope is that the United States and Japan would follow suit, although it must be admitted that the USA is so tied to relatively profligate energy use that it will find it hard to shake off its old ways. The taxes would be levied by each individual member state and have two components, one on the non-renewable element, and the other on the degree of contribution to pollution. The figures envisaged would, by the year 2000, put a tax of $10 a barrel on oil (rising from a $3 tax in 1993), put up the price of industrial coal by about 60 per cent, petrol by 6 per cent, domestic heating oil by 17 per cent, and domestic electricity by 14 per cent.

One of the main objectives of the proposed tax is to meet the target of maintaining carbon dioxide emissions at 1990 levels in the year 2000. The United Kingdom has set itself a later target date of 2005. Other policies would have to be adopted, and suggestions include further speed restrictions on all vehicles, the use of the tax revenues to encourage energy efficiency, raising minimum standards for household appliances and equipment, and financing renewable sources of energy. Progress is being made along these lines. For example, transport ministers decided in December 1991 that, from 1994, newly registered lorries and buses should be fitted with speed-limiting devices (governors) which would prevent them exceeding 85km an hour and 100km an hour respectively. The limits will apply to all freight vehicles over twelve tonnes and to buses of over five tonnes carrying more than eight passengers. These limits will also be compulsory on all cross-border vehicles in these categories that have 1988–94 registrations from 1 January 1995. Vehicles operating solely within national boundaries will have until January 1996 to conform. The European Parliament needs to approve this proposal.

The Commission reckons that there is scope for improvement in energy efficiency in the region of 15 per cent throughout the Community as a whole on the basis of existing technology. The proposals will undoubtedly meet with fierce opposition from vested interests and from the governments of the poorer member states who stand to lose most from the rise in energy costs because of increases in their production costs. In December 1991 the Council of Environment and Energy Ministers agreed to the Commission bringing forward proposals for legislation to implement the energy tax, with May 1992 as a target date for a final decision. The commission did adopt proposals then but their implementation will be subject to reciprocal action from the United States and Japan.

The amount of revenue raised by such a tax would be a staggering 50 billion ECU each year, approximately. Since the Community is responsible for only 13 per cent of the world's emissions of carbon dioxide it is vital that the other nations be persuaded to follow similar policies. (The USA is responsible for 23 per cent, Japan for 5 per cent, and the USSR and Eastern European countries for 25 per cent.) It will take great political courage to adopt the tax strategies proposed by the Commission. Unfortunately, the politicians who govern our world tend to have short-term, electoral perspectives. Most of them do not expect to be alive when depletion of the ozone layer and global warming have their full effect! But, taking a more optimistic view, the energy tax proposals may mark the start of a new age in international cooperation.

Law and Democracy 9

Law and Justice

It is the application of law which distinguishes civilisation from anarchy. Thus a study of the European Community should probably start from a detailed examination of its legal base. The Community is unique – there has never been a national or international system like it – and is based on a new, autonomous and uniform body of law that is separate from national law. This body of law also transcends national law and is applied directly in all member states.

In order to make sure that there was a uniform interpretation and application of this law the Community set up the Court of Justice based in Luxembourg. Its job is to ensure that the law is observed when the treaties establishing the Community are applied and interpreted.

The origins of Community law

The major source of Community law lies in the 'primary' legislation created by the members. This consists of the Treaties of Paris and Rome in particular, plus various Conventions and the Treaties of Accession when new members join. It also includes the new Union Treaty whose draft was agreed at the Maastricht Council of Europe meeting in December 1991 and which was expected to be formally ratified by all members in 1992. Association agreements with non-members such as Turkey (1963) and the First Lomé Convention of

1975 with African, Caribbean and Pacific countries are also sources of primary legislation. These treaties and agreements have had numerous additions made to them as time has passed. These additions are called protocols, schedules or annexes and count as 'primary' legislation.

The other important written source is called 'secondary' legislation, and is the law created by the Community institutions. It usually takes the form of directives, regulations and 'decisions' which may be addressed to states or to individuals.

There are also some international agreements reached by the Community as a whole. The most important of these relate to tariffs and trade. These agreements are implemented by directives and decisions and thus become Community law rather than remaining as international law.

Community law has, in addition, an unwritten basis. Various articles of the Treaties of Rome say that the Court of Justice must look at the general principles of law as well as at the written law. The early treaties say nothing about fundamental rights so it is essential to apply general principles in this area. The Union Treaty of 1992 contains a new article on *citizens'* rights such as the right to citizenship of the Community, to move and reside freely within it and to have consular advice. It also says, 'The Union shall respect the rights and freedoms as guaranteed by the European Convention for the Protection of Human Rights and Fundamental Freedoms, and as they result from the constitutional traditions common to the member states as general principles of Community law'.

There is also what is called 'customary law' which results from established practice. The best example is the right of the European Parliament to question the Council of Ministers. This derives from custom.

The Court of Justice frequently applies the general rules of international law. These are regarded only as a supplementary source of Community law because they tend to be very generalised.

An important source of law in the Community stems from decisions made by the Council of Ministers. The ministers represent their governments so technically these 'decisions' are governmental agreements and, therefore, international conventions. These decisions are taken by the ability of each state to act under international law, not under power conferred by the Community treaties. There is still some debate as to whether these decisions, based as they are on international conventions, are technically Community law, but they are in practice which is what matters.

The Court of Justice

Since 1986 the court has consisted of thirteen judges assisted by six advocates-general. They each have two assistants, legal clerks who do research for them on the case and on procedure, and who prepare documents for them. The judges and advocates-general have their independence guaranteed by law. They are irremovable; they deliberate in secret and are immune from legal proceedings against them unless the court itself waives the immunity.

The appointment of members of the court is done by agreement by member governments. The judges sit for six years and may have their term of office renewed. Membership is arranged so that every three years there is a partial replacement of judges. There is no nationality requirement but there is one judge from each state, the thirteenth judge always coming from one of the larger states. The judges have a variety of backgrounds apart from recently practising law or being a judge. Some of them have been diplomats, some politicians, some academics and some senior officials. They must be chosen from 'persons whose independence is beyond doubt and who possess the qualifications required for appointment to the highest judicial offices in their respective countries or who are proconsuls of recognised competence'.

The judges choose a president from among themselves. He acts for three years directing the court, allocating cases, appointing a judge as rapporteur for each case and determining the schedules for hearings. He may act alone to give judgment in summary proceedings on applications for provisional measures but his decision may be referred to the full court.

The advocates-general are appointed on the same terms as the judges. They are assigned to cases and their job is 'to act with complete impartiality and independence and to make, in open court, reasoned submissions on cases brought before the Court in performance of the tasks assigned to it'.

The court conducts most of its business in plenary session, with a quorum of seven judges. Cases brought by member states or institutions of the Community must be heard in plenary session. The court may, however, operate in 'chambers'. There are four chambers composed of three judges, and two chambers composed

FIGURE 9.1
Structure of the European Court of Justice

THE EUROPEAN COURT OF JUSTICE

Governments of the
Member States appoint
the 13 judges
and six Advocates-General
by common accord for the term of six years

COURT OF JUSTICE

Full court of 13 judges

2 chambers with 5 judges

4 chambers with 3 judges

TYPES OF PROCEEDING

Actions for failure to fulfil obligations under the Treaties (Commission *v.* Member State)	Actions on grounds of failure to act (against the Council or Commission)	References from national courts for preliminary rulings to clarify the meaning and scope of Community law
Actions by one Member State against another		Claims for damages against the Community

COURT OF FIRST INSTANCE
12 judges

Staff cases
Actions in the field of competition law
Actions under the anti-dumping law
Actions under the ECSC Treaty

SOURCE *The ABC of Community Law*, 3rd edn (Luxembourg: Office for Official Publications of the European Communities, 1991).

of five judges. The chambers take cases in rotation and do not specialise. Cases brought by individuals or firms may be referred to chambers rather than to the full court.

The Single European Act of February 1986 led, in October 1988, to the attachment of a 'Court of First Instance' to the Court of Justice. It has twelve judges who may also act as advocates-general. It hears cases brought by officials of the Community on staffing matters, actions on competition law, actions concerning the anti-dumping laws and cases under the ECSC Treaty. It does not hear actions brought by member states nor deal with questions referred for preliminary rulings. There is an appeal from its decisions to the Court of Justice on points of law.

It is important to realise that, although the Court of Justice is the Community's supreme judicial body and that there is no appeal against its judgments, other national courts at all levels also apply Community laws.

The role of the Court of Justice

In the beginning the court dealt mainly with the problems arising from establishing a customs union. This led, gradually, to common rules on transport, agriculture and an assortment of freedoms such as the right to establish a business anywhere, the right to provide services, and freedom of competition, Increasingly, the work of the court moved into social areas and to the consideration of the freedom of workers, the right to social security and the rights of migrant workers. As with any legal system a number of important cases are quoted as test cases. They have established certain principles which have been accepted as precedents. The American Supreme Court did the same in the first few decades of its existence. In both Europe and America there is a slow evolution over time as cases are brought before the courts.

In principle a court can order an individual, firm or institution to do something it is supposed to do, to stop doing something it should not do, and to do something differently. It can also draw up limitations on the scope of their actions. These various forms of action have precise names:

(a) *Proceedings for failure to fulfil an obligation* There have been over 400 cases under this heading since 1953. Some have been brought by member states against other members because of alleged failure to meet regulations, for example on the free movement of sheep meat or restrictions on fishing. Usually the states comply with the court's ruling by modifying their national laws. Occasionally, they stall until another action is. brought. If the member is desperately keen to continue its policy it may use delaying tactics until the Community rules are changed.

(b) *Proceedings for annulment* These are a way of reviewing the legality of Commission decisions and regulations and of settling conflicts over the respective powers of the various institutions of the Community. There have been very few actions brought by member states against the Council of Ministers. There have, however, been about forty actions brought by them against Commission decisions. These have related to whether national financial help is lawful, to transport, to the free movement of goods and to the settlement of agricultural payments. A few cases have been brought against the European Parliament. It, for its part, once intended to take the Council to the court over a budget dispute but withdrew when the Council gave way. The court has, subsequently, in 1985, had to settle a dispute between the Council and the Parliament.

(c) *Failure to act* These proceedings in the court enable people to punish inactivity which can be damaging. Most of these proceedings have been declared inadmissible, especially those from private individuals and firms. They can only be admissible if the institution in question has previously been called upon to act. In the early 1970s, in a celebrated case, the Parliament brought such an action against the Council of Ministers for failure to act to introduce elections to the Parliament by direct election and universal suffrage, instead of indirect appointment. The court's decision was preempted by the 1974 agreement of the heads of governments to hold direct elections.

(d) *Actions to establish liability* The court has the exclusive jurisdiction to order that the Community pays damages because of its actions or its legislative acts. This is on the principle of non-contractual liability. The Community's contractual liability is dealt with by the individual members' laws and courts.

(e) *Fines* The Union Treaty gave the court the power, from 1993, to impose fines on member states which did not comply with its judgments or which fail to implement Community law. It will be interesting to see how this power is used and the response to its existence. Will member states behave differently?

The Court of Justice acts in the above ways. Thus member states may be brought to observe the law and a greater uniformity of practice is assured. The general long-term effect of the court has been to speed up social and commercial integration.

How do Community law and national law mix?

We tend to hear most about conflicts between Community law and national law because the question of national sovereignty is involved. There is, however, a great area of positive interplay between them where no obvious conflict arises.

The area of interplay is where Community law refers to the members' legal systems in order to complete its own requirements. For example, until the implementation of the Single European Act after 1992, freedom of movement and the right to establish businesses was given only to nationals of the members. It was left to the member states to decide with their own laws who is a national of their state.

Sometimes Community law uses the national law's legal institutions to add to its own rules. This is usual with the enforcement of judgments of the Court of Justice. An article of the Treaty of Rome says that enforcement is to be governed by the rules of civil procedure in the state concerned. In addition, the treaty sometimes refers to the general principles common to the laws of the members.

Despite the wide areas of agreement or interplay referred to, there are conflicts between Community law and member states' laws because the Community law sometimes creates direct rights and obligations for its citizens. These apply directly to member states and may not be consistent with the rule of the national law. In such instances, one of the systems has to give way. There is no written Community law that resolves this problem. Nowhere does it say that Community law takes precedence over national law. Yet it is obvious that it must if the Community is to survive.

The issue of conflict is, in practice, resolved by the Community law having precedence, the basis of which is aimed at ensuring *the ability of the Community to function*. The members have given the Community the legislative powers to function and it would not be able to do so if its legislation were not binding on all its members. The Community could not continue if members could annul its laws at any time that it suited their national convenience to do so. The legal consequence of this is that any provision of national law which conflicts with Community law is invalid.

These conclusions have been established over the years by a series of cases before the Court of Justice. The most important of these was the 1961 case of *Costa* v. *ENEL*. At the end of the summing up the court said 'it follows from all these observations that the law stemming from the Treaty, an independent source of law, could not, because of its special and original nature, be overridden by domestic legal provisions, however framed, without being deprived of its character as Community law and without the legal basis of the Community itself being called into question'.

Later cases related to national constitutional law. The Dutch have removed any potential problem by writing the precedence of Community law into their constitution. Germany and Italy have constitutional courts which used to make an exception to the principle of the supremacy of Community law where it conflicted with their constitutional guarantees. They argued that any dispute should be settled in favour of fundamental rights. They eventually ended their resistance when they came to consider that the Community had protected fundamental rights sufficiently with guarantees. Thus we now have a situation where Community law is predominant even over the individual members' constitutional laws.

The United Kingdom has no separate written constitution and no explicit Bill of Rights, although it does subscribe to the European Convention on Human Rights. It is assumed that United Kingdom citizens have rights unless they are explicitly removed by law. It is clear that many British parliamentarians and commentators have been very surprised at the extent to which Community law has impinged on British law and new legislation. They were, for example, very shocked in 1991 when the European Court ruled that an Act of the United Kingdom Parliament, which intended to prevent Spanish fishermen from registering their boats in the UK in order to take advantage of the UK's fishing quota, was illegal. As the Single European Act is implemented it is clear that their views of national sovereignty need to be revised to take account of the supremacy of Community law. It is interesting that, in late 1991 and early 1992, the United Kingdom government used the fact that it was awaiting European Court rulings on Sunday trading as an excuse to do nothing about large multiple stores that were flouting what everyone had understood to be the law since the late 1950s.

Democracy

In democratic terms the Community is a strange animal. The European Parliament is elected by universal suffrage every five years by proportional representation in every country except Great Britain where the first-past-the-post, or relative majority system, is used. Yet the Parliament is largely a consultative body and has little power of decision, although since the Single European Act was put into force in July 1987 a new cooperation procedure has been adopted whereby the Parliament, Commission and Council of Ministers consult and attempt to draw up a common position. (Changes will be made to this system as the Union Treaty of 1992 comes into effect.) The final decisions are made by the Council of Ministers which is a meeting of the relevant national ministers for a topic such as transport, finance or agriculture. They make decisions that commit their national governments to policies and to the possible changes of legislation needed to implement them. The assumption is, of course, that these ministers are democratically representative of their people, an assumption that is not always easy to sustain.

In some countries, because of the way in which their systems of proportional representation operate, the individual voter, once his vote has been cast, is largely ignored and the government which is formed is the result of a complex set of negotiations and compromises between parties as the seats and ministerial posts are allocated. Thus the ministers who make agreements on behalf of their governments at Community level may be far removed from the original political desires of the electorate. In the case of the United Kingdom the minister may represent a government that has been elected by a minority of the total votes cast or his party may even have a majority in the lower house, the House of Commons, despite having fewer votes than the main rival party. This situation arises because of the allocation of seats without regard to the equality of weighting of votes. There is no concept in the United Kingdom of the fully equal distribution of electorate in each constituency. Once elected a United Kingdom government can use the ancient powers of the royal prerogative to exercise powers of patronage, to make treaties, declare war, introduce delegated legislation with the minimum of parliamentary consultation, massage the flow of information to the public under a cloak of secrecy, and choose a date for an election to suit its own party advantage. It is also able to remove, almost at a stroke, the powers of locally democratically elected bodies subordinate to it. Nor is it subject to the rulings of a constitutional court and it has shown itself willing to rewrite the law if the decisions of its final court of appeal, part of the non-democratic House of Lords, are not in its favour. It is difficult to credit the idea that, if anyone were given the task of setting up a democratic state in the 1990s, they would follow the United Kingdom pattern.

The Council of Ministers does not, of course, operate in a vacuum. The ministers receive advice and guidance from their national civil servants and diplomats and from the European Commission. Much of the work is done through the Council Working Groups, that is, national officials, and through COREPER, the committee of permanent representatives of the member states which is part of the Council.

The Commission is, in theory, the executive body which works on behalf of the Council of Ministers to give it advice, to prepare reports and to implement decisions. It has, however, built up its own authority and has become an important source of ideas and a powerful cohesive force in creating a 'European' attitude. Yet its members are not democratically elected but chosen by national governments. Once in place they have a high degree of independence until their term of office is concluded but they must, by definition, be acceptable to the national government at the outset. The composition and terms of office of the Commission will change from 1 January 1995 as a result of the Maastricht agreement (see page 213).

The committees of the Community are not elected either. The most established, the Economic and Social Committee, with its 189 members representing employers, trade unions and consumers, consists of appointees although some may be nominated as a result of sectional elections. The Council has created a number of other consultative committees, none of which is elected; rather they consist of appointees from various, often conflicting, pressure groups and sectional interests. It is perhaps as well that they can only give advice and not make decisions. It was decided in December 1991, at the Second European Parliament and Regions of the Community Conference, to call for the creation of an elected independent committee to represent European regions and at Maastricht it was agreed that it should be an advisory committee of 189 members nominated by the member states. Some members may nominate members elected by some method so there may be some democratic aspect to it.

The Democratic Deficit

The phrase 'democratic deficit' became fashionable in the late 1980s as the proposals for the reform of the political structures of the Community began to be discussed prior to the Maastricht summit on economic and political union. It has two meanings. The main one is how to maintain democratic participation and control if powers are transferred on any significant scale from national assemblies to Community institutions. The second was an idea favoured by supporters of greater powers for the European Parliament, that is, that it should be given far greater powers in accordance with its democratic basis of election. It was assumed that the new Union Treaty would advance the Community towards stronger centralised institutions and that the democratic aspects would need to be underpinned in order to protect them. Those who wanted a much more powerful and influential European Parliament were disappointed by the Maastricht agreement, especially as they had been encouraged by Chancellor Kohl of Germany's demands for greater authority to be given to it on the basis of its democratic nature. The extension of powers of the Parliament is dealt with below on pages 215–18.

A Conference of the Parliaments

One idea put forward to make up the democratic deficit was the creation of a 'Congress of Parliaments', that is regular meetings between representatives of the European Parliament and of national parliaments. The Union Treaty agreed at Maastricht contained a declaration saying 'the European Parliament and the national parliaments are invited to meet as necessary as a Conference of the Parliaments'. The Conference 'would be consulted on the main features of the European Union'. Sceptics have expressed the view that the proposed Congress was nothing more than a cosmetic exercise, and that it would be yet another talking shop with no powers, but it is much too early to make any judgement on the Conference until more details emerge and some meetings have occurred. In the meantime we can speculate on the initials by which it will be known – COP, perhaps?

The European Parliament

The European Parliament was called the 'Assembly' in the treaties establishing the Community. Until 1979 the members (MEPs) were appointed from their national parliaments. The appointments were, of course, related to party strengths. The original treaties had intended members to be elected but disagreements among the Six prevented this happening until after the accession of the United Kingdom, Denmark and Ireland in 1973. Even so, the first British MEPs were appointed, not elected. In the election of 1979 410 MEPs were elected to the Parliament. This number rose to 518 after the accession of Greece in 1981 and Portugal and Spain in 1986. The elections are held every five years – 1979, 1984, 1989, and the next in June 1994. The number of MEPs per country is based broadly on population but not as exactly as, say, the United States' electoral districts for Congressional elections. The intention of the European Parliament since 1982 has been that the elections should be by a regionally-based system of proportional representation. This was intended to improve the chances of election of all but tiny parties. The member states did not agree and the 1984 election was held with a mixture of systems according to country. They also failed to agree for the 1989 election. The United Kingdom proved a major stumbling block to agreement. Britain's main parties have a vested interest in retaining the archaic first-past-the-post method of election. It enables them to exclude other parties, even those with a significant measure of support. In an act of condescension, however, they graciously permit the people of Northern Ireland to elect three MEPs in a single constituency by the version of proportional representation known as the single transferable vote (STV). The STV is used in Northern Ireland local elections and in Ireland's parliamentary elections. England has 66 MEPs, Scotland eight, Wales four and Northern Ireland three, making a total for the United Kingdom of 81.

In 1989, the Conservatives had 32 and Labour 45 European Parliament seats. The Scottish Nationalist Party had one seat. The three Northern Ireland seats were Official Unionist, Democratic Unionist, and Social Democratic and Labour (see Table 9.1).

The United Kingdom, France, Germany and Italy each have 81 MEPs, despite their population differences. Spain has 60, The Netherlands 25, Belgium, Greece and Portugal 24 each, Denmark 16, Ireland 15 and Luxembourg six. The effects of the British electoral system can be seen by comparing the figures in Table 9.1 of the percentage of votes received and the number of seats won. The Green party with almost 15 per cent of the votes received no seats.

All of the numbers given above may change at the next elections in 1994 because one of the consequences of German unification has been the request for more MEPs for the enlarged country. In October 1991 the European Parliament agreed on an increase of 18 to be allocated to the Länder of the old Democratic Republic of East Germany but the Maastricht negotiations failed to insert it into the new Union Treaty and the matter will be subject to debate in 1992. Without the increase each German MEP will represent one million people as against the Community average of 700 000. There is a strong possibility, however, that there will be an increase in the number of German MEPs in time for the 1994 elections. Some commentators see this as an ominous sign of the united Germany flexing its muscles. Others see it as a perfectly reasonable reflection of the expanded population and a necessary democratic change. The issue does raise the problem though of the long-term size of the European Parliament as other nations join, especially if the new Union expands to the 25 or 30 nations envisaged by some people. An additional problem raised in this context is that of the potential increase in the number of languages and the practical difficulties of dealing with translation.

TABLE 9.1

Results of the June 1989 Elections for the European Parliament

Great Britain

	Votes	%	Seats
Labour	6 153 604	40.12	45
Conservative	5 224 037	34.15	32
Green	2 292 705	14.99	–
SLD	986 292	6.44	–
SNP	406 686	2.65	1
Plaid Cymru	115 062	0.75	–
SDP	75 886	0.49	–
Others	39 971	0.30	–
	15 294 243	100	78

Electorate: 42 590 060

Turnout: 35.91%

Northern Ireland

	First preference	%	Seats
Paisley, Ian (Democratic Unionist)	160 110	29.94	1
Hume, John (Social Dem and Lab)	136 335	25.49	1
Nicholson, Jim (Official Unionist)	118 785	22.21	1
Morrison, Danny (Sinn Fein)	48 914	9.15	–
Alderdice, John (Alliance)	27 905	5.22	–
Kennedy, Lawrence (Nth Down Con)	25 789	4.83	–
Samuel, M. H. (Green)	6 569	1.23	–
Lynch, S. (Workers')	5 590	1.04	–
Langhammer, Mark (Lab Rep in N.I.)	3 540	0.66	–
Caul, B. (Lab 87)	1 274	0.24	–
Total	534 811	100	3

Turnout: 47.7%

Electorate: 1 120 508

Elections in Northern Ireland are conducted under a system of proportional representation, using the single transferable vote in a three-member constituency.

SOURCE *European Parliament News*, July 1989.

FIGURE 9.2
The European Parliament, May 1992

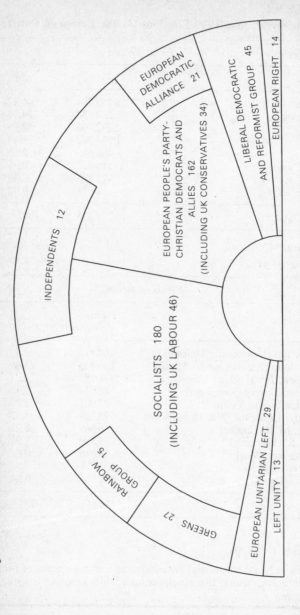

The committees of the Parliament

The number of permanent committees of the European Parliament was raised from eighteen to nineteen in January 1992. They are at the root of its work. Their membership is reasonably representative of the strength of the political groupings within the Parliament and their meetings are frequently attended by Commissioners and officials. Public hearings are held at which specialists and experts give evidence; some of these are, of course, pressure groups. The Parliament debates the committees' reports and may amend their recommendations before they are sent back to the Commission which then presents them to the Council for final decision. On most matters it is legally necessary to obtain the Parliament's opinion before legislation can be made. Most of the committee meetings are held in Brussels but some are held elsewhere, even in member countries.

The committees in 1992 were: Agriculture, Fisheries, and Rural Development; Budgets; Economic, Monetary, Industrial; Energy, Research, Technology; External Economic Relations; Legal, Citizens' Rights; Social, Employment and Working Environment; Regional Policy and Planning; Transport and Tourism; Environment, Public Health and Consumer Affairs; Overseas Development and Cooperation; Budgetary Control; Procedure, Immunities and Credentials; Petitions; Women's Rights; Institutional Affairs; and Youth, Culture, Education, Media, Sport. In 1992 the Foreign Affairs and Security Committee replaced the Political Affairs Committee because of the changes agreed at the discussions on the Union Treaty. The new committee was set up on Civil Liberties and Internal Affairs to cover the new intergovernmental arrangements set up at Maastricht for asylum and immigration. Membership of the committees varies between 25 and 56. There has been some reshuffling of the topics covered over the years but this list gives an insight into the attitude and interests of the European Parliament.

What impact have the MEPs made?

Before the enlargement of the Community after 1972 the European Parliament was a rather innocuous, largely powerless talking-shop. Since then the European Parliament and its MEPs have gained in power and influence. Both the Single European Act of 1987 and the Union Treaty of 1992 enhanced its authority. As a generalisation it is true to say that the United Kingdom MEPs have a more direct relationship with their constituents than most of the other member states' MEPs because of the nature of the regionalised proportional

TABLE 9.2

Composition of the European Parliament, May 1992

	B	Dk	G	Gr	S	F	Irl	I	L	N	P	UK	Total
Soc	8	4	31	9	27	22	1	14	2	8	8	46	180
EPP	7	4	32	10	18	11	4	27	3	10	3	33	162
LDR	4	3	5	–	5	9	2	3	1	4	9	–	45
EUL	–	1	–	1	4	–	1	22	–	–	–	–	29
Greens	3	–	6	–	1	8	–	7	–	2	–	–	27
EDA	–	–	–	1	2	12	6	–	–	–	–	–	21
RBW	1	4	1	–	2	1	1	3	–	–	1	1	15
ER	1	–	3	–	–	10	–	–	–	–	–	–	14
LU	–	–	–	3	–	7	–	–	–	–	3	–	13
Ind	–	–	3	–	1	1	–	5	–	1	–	1	12
Totals	24	16	81	24	60	81	15	81	6	25	24	81	518

KEY TO ABBREVIATIONS

Soc	–	Socialist Group	RBW –	Rainbow Group
EPP	–	Group of European People's Party (Christian Democratic Group)	Ind – B – DK – F –	Non-attached Belgium Denmark France
LDR	–	Liberal Democratic and Reformist Group	G –	Germany
Greens	–	Group of Greens in the European Unitarian Left	I – Irl –	Italy Ireland
EUL	–	Group for the European Unitarian Left	L – N –	Luxembourg Netherlands
EDA	–	Group of the European Democratic Alliance	P – S –	Portugal Spain
ER	–	Technical Group of the European Right	UK –	United Kingdom
LU	–	Left Unity		

SOURCE *European Parliament News*, April 1992.

representation system used in the other countries. The United Kingdom members 'belong' to a constituency although no one pretends that MEPs are well-known, and turnout at the elections is very low. In contrast, the majority of MEPs in the other countries are allocated to a region as a result of the proportionate allocation of seats after the votes are counted. One consequence of this is that distinguished politicians from countries like France ind it easier to become members of the European Parliament and to integrate the work with their other interests, than do their British counterparts.

The British press, rather arrogantly, assumed that the introduction of British MEPs would be like taking the light of the gospel of parliamentary democracy to the benighted heathen. They ignored, of course, the extent to which the United Kingdom Parliament had, in the words of Enoch Powell and Tony Benn, become 'craven' – that is, the feeble rubber stamp to the proposals of the government of the day. Much was made of the introduction of the more extensive use of 'questions' in the European Parliament. This extra use of questions for both written and oral reply by the responsible people has greatly benefited the MEPs in their role as democratic guardians. In 1990 3075 written and 1766 oral questions were put. Each question is inordinately expensive to answer though, because of the translation and printing costs associated with replies. In Britain, Question Time, especially on Tuesday and Thursday when the Prime Minister answers a tiny number of questions, is seen as a forum for the gladiatorial nature of confrontational politics. Its impact and effectiveness is grossly overrated except for rare moments of historical importance. The European question sessions are more constructive, genuinely seek information and clarification and usually have less crudely political motivation. This is mainly because the Parliament is not a bipartisan confrontational assembly but a shifting series of alliances. It is also because the 'audience', the electorate, is not usually informed on a daily basis of the doings of the European Parliament and there is no need to play to the gallery of public opinion.

The Treaty of Union made formal the right to present petitions to the Parliament (774 petitions were received in the 1990–1 parliamentary year), and extended the co-decision-making procedure between the Parliament and the Council of Ministers to give the Parliament a 'negative' power of veto. Both of these changes should extend the opportunities MEPs have to influence events.

One major impact of the advent of the United Kingdom MEPs was the introduction of English as the major language, with French, for communication. English had often been the only common language of MEPs and was in frequent use but its introduction as an official language raised its status, availability and use.

National groups of MEPs from the same party have usually operated as fairly tightly disciplined blocks. They consult together, plan coordinated approaches and decide voting tactics and strategies. They try to maintain constant alliances with like-minded groups from other nations. The Conservative MEPs from the United Kingdom, for example, have been particularly active in reflecting the wishes of the home leadership of the national party in the issues being debated in relation to the single market. As a result, after the 1989 elections, they were almost completely isolated in that the European Democrats in the chamber consisted of 32 United Kingdom Conservatives and two others from Denmark. They tried to make alliances but without success until April 1992 when they joined with the European People's Party. The European Parliament sometimes tends to be dominated by left of centre and centre coalitions with a preference for social democracy and interventionism. The United Kingdom Conservative MEPs have been very active in opposing these principles. Occasionally they have been the only group apart from the European right to vote against measures proposed by the Commission. Sometimes the Parliament is dominated by centre and centre-right groups. Between the elections in 1989 and January 1992 sixteen MEPs changed political groups and the larger groups have been making more of the decisions. The result is that the smaller groupings are increasingly looking for alliances.

It is difficult to separate the effects of the advent of United Kingdom and other new members from those resulting from the introduction of elected representatives and the passing of the Single European Act which extended the European Parliament's power. On the whole most of the changes seem to have stemmed from the fact that members are elected instead of appointed. Elections have given MEPs greater confidence and independence and this has been reflected in the growing willingness of Parliament to confront the Commission and criticise proposals of both it and the Council of Ministers. Parliament has begun to propose an increasing number of ideas for legislation on its own initiative. The Commission has acted on most of these. It is evident that MEPs are increasingly concerned at the failure of the Council of Ministers to agree on measures that have already been approved by Parliament. Indeed, the European Parliament has taken the Council of Ministers to the European Court of Justice for failing to implement a transport policy which the Parliament had approved. This event is of very great long-term importance because it shows that the European Parliament could develop into a highly effective and democratic force. Some of the changes made in the Union Treaty of 1992 reflect this growing strength and it can reasonably be anticipated that, after the review of the Community's institutions in 1996, there will be further increases in the European Parliament's powers and authority.

The European Parliament has the right to reject the Commission's budget and has done so twice in 1979 and 1984. The European Parliament's Budgetary Control Committee is also quite effective. It checks the ways in which money is spent and can ask the Court of Auditors to carry out special enquiries. The court may advise the Parliament to refuse to accept the annual accounts if it is not satisfied.

The impact of the United Kingdom Euro-MPs has, therefore, been significant but it has not been in the nature of the transformation from darkness to light that was originally predicted. Indeed, over the next few years, especially if proportional representation is adopted throughout the Community, more and more people will see the European Parliament as the true centre of effective democracy and the main protection of individual liberties. A national parliament such as the United Kingdom's will appear to have diminished in relevance and importance. This may be less true in some European countries where their electoral system, party systems and parliamentary procedures have been updated. The United Kingdom, with its increasingly unrepresentative Parliament, its archaic structures, its executive-dominated legislature, its unelected second chamber and its lack of explicit protection for the individual's rights, will inevitably suffer in comparison.

Why has Britain's Policy been so Negative?

This question deserves attention both from the point of view of the other eleven members of the Community and from that of the ordinary citizen of the United Kingdom. Both groups must, on occasion, be extremely puzzled by, for example, the way in which the United Kingdom approached the Maastricht negotiations on economic, monetary and political union and emerged with an opt-out clause on monetary union and forced the other eleven into a separate protocol on the Social Chapter. The United Kingdom Prime Minister, Mr Major, used a tennis term to boast that he had 'won – game, set and match'. It was surprising in the circumstances that he did not employ a phrase related to his favourite sport, cricket, and say that he was stopping the others playing because it was his bat and ball, and he wanted to play according to his rules and no one else's.

In a negative way the United Kingdom has assumed a very important role in the Community and has frequently set the political agenda and the pace of change. In many fields such as technological and scientific research programmes, monetary reforms, tax harmonisation and the removal of customs barriers, immigration controls, and above all the Social Charter, the United Kingdom has acted as a sort of drag anchor. It has had the same effect on most environmental proposals such as those to control atmospheric pollution and exhaust emissions, although there have been some signs of a change in attitude since 1989.

It is very difficult to find any area in which the United Kingdom has been in the forefront of constructive change and where it has generated general support from the other members. It is sometimes alleged that Mrs Thatcher and the United Kingdom were in the forefront of the move towards the Single European Act, and even proposed it. This does not bear close examination because the United Kingdom government initially strongly opposed the Delors proposals and those of Commissioner Lord Cockfield. Britain was a late convert to the idea of a single market although, once converted, it pursued the policy with vigour. It has, however, frequently allied itself with one or other of the other leading members in order to frustrate change, even if its motives are very different from those of its fellow objector. This approach, which is seen essentially as one of national self-interest, has sometimes led continental observers to recommend that the United Kingdom leave the Community because its thinking is not 'European'. These observers recognise that other members, particularly France, also act in a narrowly self-interested fashion from time to time but they assert that the United Kingdom persistently acts in this way to the long-term detriment of the Community.

There are many possible reasons for this negative, obstructionist attitude on the part of the United Kingdom. One is an innate sense of Anglo-Saxon superiority which may be completely unjustified but is hard to shift. This may create an attitude of contempt and suspicion for continental methods and solutions. One of the more worrying aspects of this sense of superiority is that it seems to prevent an objective appraisal of the relative successes and failures of initiatives and policies which have originated in other member states. One might have expected, for example, that the undoubted success of the German economic and social policies would have led British policy-makers to emulate them. Perhaps the success of continental urban transport systems or of, say, French regional planning, deserves more attention. The British have traditionally boasted of their pragmatic or empirical approach and scorned the supposed methods of philo-sophic, intellectual, rational argument from first principles adopted by continentals. But pragmatism may quickly dissolve into a confused and tangled muddle with conflicting and non-cohesive policies. The emphasis on *ad hoc* solutions to problems is inherent in the British system of administration. It has produced ineffective and overlapping bureaucracy. The structure of British government creates great problems of liaison and consultation between depart-ments, particularly in the transport and environmental areas. Delays inevitably accompany this process.

Another cause of the United Kingdom's rather negative approach to many European proposals has been the baleful influence of pressure groups. Until 1988, say, or 1985 depending on how you interpret the evidence, the National Farmers' Union had a powerful influence on British policy in the context of the CAP. The same can be argued about all the farming lobbies in Europe, but the British lobby gave the impression of being a puppeteer pulling the strings with the Minister of Agriculture as the puppet. Similarly, the United Kingdom vehicle manufacturers seem to have exerted enormous influence on ministers in persuading them to go for a low level of targets for the control of vehicle exhaust emissions. The power generators and those who put large volumes of pollutants into the atmosphere also helped to set low targets and postponed dates for the targets that were agreed. The water supply industry dragged its feet over cleaning up water and beaches, although it can be argued that this was because the government, prior to privatisation, would not permit it to invest sufficiently in improvements. The United

Kingdom government has also proved reluctant to join the other Community members and the European Parliament in banning tobacco advertising, despite the overwhelming case on health grounds and the revelation of the serious risks of 'passive' smoking. In each case the British consumer will suffer in the long run through higher prices and has suffered in the short run from inferior products and pollution. In addition, the United Kingdom has incurred much displeasure among its more forward-looking partners in the Community.

Another probable cause of the United Kingdom's negative approach to many Community programmes is the fact that it, more than any other member, has extensive international, extra-European, political and economic links. There is still an extensive trading and commercial link with the Commonwealth. There has also been a heavier commitment to the North Atlantic alliance and a deeper involvement in the Far East and central and southern Africa. The United Kingdom has also been more important, relatively, as the site for foreign investment, particularly North American, Japanese and Middle Eastern, although this appears to be changing in the 1990s. Until the entry of Spain and Portugal whose languages are used in South and Central America, the United Kingdom was unrivalled in the influence it exerted through its linguistic links. The United Kingdom remains important because of the use of English as the major language of commerce, science and literature although recent evidence indicates that in Central European areas German has become more popular as a second language than English.

It may be that Britain's tendency to obstructionist policies is a temporary phenomenon which will pass with the eventual demise of the doctrine called 'Thatcherism', which has survived her fall from office. On the whole the free-market, enterprise culture emphasis of Thatcherite economics is incompatible with the long-term prevailing tenor of the Community. This accepts and recommends liberalisation of individuals, institutions and trade within a positive interventionist framework of controls. Such an approach has generally been highly successful. It developed, of course, to counteract exactly those evils of the free market which the proponents of Thatcherism have conveniently forgotten existed. The mature, coalition-type, consensus-seeking governments of Europe have learned the great lesson of human society that cooperation achieves more in the long run than aggression, conflict and confrontation. It is highly unlikely that the efficient, effective and popular social democratic governments of the majority of European states will be supplanted by *laissez-faire*, free-marketeer supporters. Indeed the upsurge of 'green' or environmentalist parties demonstrates the opposite trend, though a warning note must be sounded about the resurgence of neofascist or nationalist parties of the right. But even they are rarely supporters of *laissez-faire*. Indeed they often advocate wholesale state intervention.

The Commission, Guardian of the Treaties

The Commission is the executive of the Community and is, supposedly, independent of the national governments. It has the role of guardian of the treaties which form the Community. It answers to the European Parliament for its initiation and execution of policy. The Commission has seventeen members (until 1995), two each from the United Kingdom, France, Italy, Germany and Spain and one each from the others. The President chosen in 1985, Jacques Delors, proved to be particularly dynamic in fostering the single market, the Social Charter and the Union Treaty. The members of the Commission are appointed for four years by national governments and then distribute their responsibilities among themselves. In the United Kingdom, the government nominates one and the opposition the other. In practice the opposition's nominee needs to be acceptable to the Prime Minister. Commissioners, once appointed, are intended to be completely independent of their national governments. This makes it essential from a government's point of view that the people chosen have attitudes which will not lead to a sacrifice of national self-interest. The Commission has become a vital power-base in Europe and its President has an important relationship to the heads of government of Community members.

A new group of Commissioners began work in January 1989 and is due for replacement in 1993. Under the 1992 Union Treaty, however, the Commissioners will, from 1 January 1995, have a five-year term to bring them into line with the Parliament's term, and the Commission as a whole will be subject to a vote of confidence of the European Parliament. The Parliament will also be consulted over the appointment of President of the Commission. The number of Commissioners may be reduced to twelve in 1995, depending on the outcome of discussions in 1992.

The Council of Ministers

The Council of Ministers sometimes comprises the twelve finance ministers of the members, or the twelve agriculture ministers, or the twelve transport ministers, and so on, plus Commission representatives, so it is democratic at second remove. The Presidency of the Council changes every six months. In the second half of 1992 it will be the United Kingdom's turn. These meetings lay down the Community policy and the important decisions must be unanimous although many may be by a qualified majority of 54 votes out of a total of 74. The topics subject to the qualified majority vote (QMV) are laid down in the Single European Act, which applies QMV to proposals to implement the single market, and the Union Treaty which extended QMV to a limited number of new areas. These are: some aspects of environmental policy, development aid, public health policies, consumer protection, trans-European networks, individual research programmes, certain aspects of transport and competition policy, some social policy, and implementation of the Social Fund. Unanimity still applies to taxation and policies with financial implications. It also applies to most decisions on social policy, transport policy, citizenship, the review of the research, social, and regional funds, environment programmes and visa policy.

The ministers are at the Council to act as spokesmen but the real work is done by their civil servants. The meetings have had a reputation for brinkmanship and making decisions only at the very last possible moment. These gatherings usually receive very slender treatment in the press but are frequently of major, long-term importance. The Council has a committee to service it called COREPER or the Committee of Permanent Representatives. These are the ambassadors of the members to the Community and their advisers.

In addition, at least twice a year, there is a meeting of the European Council which is attended by the heads of government; foreign ministers also attend to give background advice. The President of the Commission is another participant. These so-called summits have sometimes had enormous influence in shifting the path of the Community towards new objectives The system of each member having a six-month stint acting as President of the Council of Ministers leads to beneficial shifts of emphasis. Some periods are highly productive in new ideas whereas others largely consolidate past efforts. The meetings are a welcome media event for the national leaders who can be seen acting as their nation's champions, in company with their equals or more powerful neighbours. Such division as occurs is played down by the public relations machine and each leader's point of view is presented in its best light for home consumption. If the divisions have been deep and real the final communiqué will be rather bland and non-committal. It may be couched in what is often called 'eurospeak' which is a mixture of fine-sounding phrases capable of several interpretations and technical jargon which gives new terminology to ideas and policies. Examples include 'extensification', 'harmonisation', 'set aside', and a whole range of initials and acronyms. Many of the words are already in the new edition of the Oxford English Dictionary. There are also dictionaries of Eurojargon available. Some of the 'eurospeak' words are simply French words for which there is no straightforward translation, some are acronyms and others are invented. No one has taken much notice of the desire of the Esperanto Society to have esperanto made an official language of the Community!

How will the Union Treaty of 1992 affect Democracy?

The answer to this question will lie in the ways in which the European Parliament uses the small extension of powers granted to it. Those who hoped for a great extension of the Parliament's power as a result of the intergovernmental conference and treaty have been disappointed. However, the treaty provisions may, if used carefully, raise the status and authority of the Parliament so that, at the revision conference in 1996, its powers are extended further. In this discussion we should remember that the European Parliament does not, from its own authority, legislate. Under the existing system, pre-Maastricht, the Commission proposes and executes, the Council of Ministers decides, and the Parliament is consulted. The legislative power is, therefore, in the hands of the Council, a body of people representing each government but not the electorate directly. In practice a piece of legislation can be adopted without the approval of either the European Parliament or the national legislatures.

The Negative Assent Procedure

The hope of those interested in increasing the democratic authority of the elected European Parliament was that the Parliament would be given at least joint decision-making power with the Council of Ministers. This desire was embodied in a resolution of the European Parliament in November 1990. Instead the Maastricht agreement introduced a *negative* co-decision-making procedure. It is also called the 'negative assent procedure'. It will replace the present system whereby Parliament's amendments at a second reading of legislation can only stand if the Council of Ministers is divided. The new procedure establishes the convening of a conciliation committee comprising equal representation from each institution if the two sides disagree. As a last resort it allows the Parliament the right to reject the legislation if it is still not satisfied. Parliament can only reject the legislation by an absolute majority of its 518 members, so there would need to be support from more than one major political group.

The new power of co-decision-making will apply to the following areas where the Council of Ministers reaches a decision by use of the qualified majority vote, that is, rules about the internal market, the free movement of workers, general environment programmes, and the so-called right of establishment which includes the recognition of qualifications and the treatment accorded to foreign nationals. It will extend to certain new areas such as education and training, trans-European networks, action on health and consumer protection. In addition the procedure will apply to a few areas where the Council must reach unanimous agreement, that is, the framework programmes for research, and the cultural and educational cooperation programmes.

The negative assent procedure is viewed with suspicion by some MEPs because it is, in effect, loaded in favour of the Council in that it challenges the Parliament to exercise its veto, something it will be very reluctant to do. Throughout the treaty the power is referred to as 'the procedure laid down in Article 189b' as a sop to the United Kingdom government which would prefer not to broadcast the implications to its national sovereignty of this new power of co-decision of the European Parliament.

The Assent Procedure

The Single European Act gave the Parliament the right to approve by an absolute majority any enlargement of the Community and any association agreement linking other countries with the Community. This power of assent has been considerably extended by the Union Treaty. The use of the approval may be very important in the development of the Parliament's role in the Community and in the growth of democratic pressures. The extension of application is to all international agreements that require the establishment of institutions, or have financial implications, or need legislation under the co-decision procedure, and to a group of other points. These latter are the proposed uniform electoral system for the Community, citizenship, especially rights of residence, the reform of the structural funds (agricultural, regional and social), and the role of the proposed European Central Bank. Potentially these areas of approval give the Parliament strong influence, particularly the requirement for assent to budgetary aspects of foreign agreements. In this context the Parliament has already, before the treaty, delayed payments to Israel and Turkey so it may be prepared to take a stronger line in foreign policy than the leaders who agreed the final treaty intended.

Other Maastricht Changes

The European Parliament failed to obtain the long-desired right to initiate legislation but it was formally awarded the right to do what it has often done in the past, that is, to ask the Commission to produce a legislative proposal. There may not prove to be much practical difference if the right is used carefully.

Another provision of the treaty gives formal recognition to the right of the Parliament to set up temporary committees of enquiry on subjects that are not already *sub judice* but the exact terms of reference of such committees will be subject to agreement between the various institutions of the Community. The Parliament has already had such committees on drugs and racism.

The Parliament was given greater control, beyond the original power of rejection, over the budget . It will now be able to question the Commission on the management of the budget and will be able to insist on being given information that is at present withheld.

The Union Treaty also proposes the establishment of a Parliamentary Ombudsman. Any citizen of the Community will be able to complain about 'maladministration in the activities of the Community's institutions'. This meets a long felt need among many MEPs.

We shall probably see, over the next ten years, the gradual flowering of the European Parliament as the true seat of European democracy, but long term developments depend upon the accession of new members and the manner in which they are catered for and on the extent of the growth in importance of the regional governments of the Community. Subsidiarity may be an ugly word but it is a very important concept if democracy is to flourish at the lowest possible levels in the Community. Assuming that the problem of Denmark's rejection of the Maastricht Treaty in its referendum is resolved, the Danish people's protest may lead to an acceleration of the democratisation of the Community's institutions. It is possible that the very long-term political future of the Community will see a growth of the authority of regional assemblies and a relative decline in the role of national legislatures.

The Future and the Single Market 10

What Alternative Policies for Development Are There?

Some see the future of the Community as an expanding free trade area with the emphasis on free markets, the mobility of factors of production, labour, capital and enterprise, and a legal framework that regulates commerce and trade with the minimum of hindrance. They stress the 'market of 345 million people', economies of scale, the position to influence international affairs and the maintenance of distinctive national customs and culture. They support the policies put forward in the Single European Act because they see the completion of the internal market as realising their hopes. They tend to emphasise the principle of subsidiarity.

Others see a European Community of the future as one without trade barriers, without hindrance to the mobility of factors, with the economies of scale but with a legal framework that encourages the harmonisation of standards and has a major social dimension. They envisage a more interventionist approach, a more positive direction through regulation, expenditure and taxation to achieve social goals such as lower unemployment or decreased poverty. They see the Community as essentially an economic union which has a major social role. They are also in favour of the principle of subsidiarity but put greater emphasis on the Community making decisions on both framework policies and detailed applications.

There are others who go further and look forward to a deeper and more far-reaching political union. They see the economic harmonisation leading inexorably towards some more concrete political union such as a federal state of Europe. This concept has already been discussed. Their expectation is that initially there will be greater economic and social cohesion bringing with it the ECU as a single European currency for those members who meet the convergence criteria, followed at a later date by the other members. It is unlikely that the United Kingdom, if it meets the criteria, will be able to resist the economic pressures to adopt the single currency, despite its Union Treaty protocol permitting it to make up its own mind over Stage 3 of monetary union. This decision to adopt a single currency may be as early as 1996, and it is a certainty that, assuming the treaty is adhered to, some members will adopt it in 1999. At the same time, the process begun in 1990 in starting Stage 1 of monetary union will bring progress towards the establishment of a European Monetary Institute and then a European Central Bank to administer the common monetary policy and to regulate the foreign exchange value of the ECU. They think that even if initially some taxes are not harmonised the long-run pressures will be towards harmonisation. If, for example, France and Germany maintain different VAT rates there will be a tendency to cross-border trade which will force governments into equalising rates. This principle would, they allege, apply in many areas of economic activity if differences are maintained.

A Community Foreign Policy?

These supporters of deeper political union were probably somewhat disappointed by the Maastricht agreement on the development of a common Community policy for defence and foreign affairs (see below) but the treaty may provide unexpected scope for change in that it is how the members act that matters, not the wording of generalised statements of intent. The optimists in this field have been encouraged by the development of united Community foreign policy initiatives in relation to Third World issues, to Namibia and southern Africa, to Iran and the Salman Rushdie affair, and to united action against terrorism. These developments took place as a result of the European Political Cooperation (EPC) policy adopted after 1986. The Community is increasingly seeking to put a collective voice in the United Nations and the International Monetary Fund. There are different interpretations of the role of the Community in the Gulf crisis of 1990–1. Some see it as revealing the deep divisions between the members and call the episode a shambles that augurs very badly for any attempt to create a Community foreign policy. Others see it as part of the learning process and an indication that proper structures are required for common policy to be formulated. Much of the criticism originated in Britain where there seemed to be little comprehension that countries such as Germany were bound by constitutional requirements not to become involved in military operations outside the NATO area. It may not be altogether a good thing that Germany may amend its constitution to allow its troops to serve outside the NATO area, probably for the United Nations. The Japanese also, for good reason, have a constitution which restricts them to 'self-defence' forces (which are very large), and they too did not send military forces to the Gulf.

The Community had a better experience in dealing with the Baltic states as they broke away from the Soviet Union, largely because the historical background was one of forced annexation by Stalin of states established at the Peace of Versailles. The Community managed a high degree of agreement over relations with the crumbling structures of the Soviet Union as it dissolved before 1991. There was less unanimity during the period of the attempted coup against Mr Gorbachev in 1991, but unity was regained as the new Commonwealth of Independent States was created. If it survives, which is by no means certain, it is likely that once again Community foreign policy will be dictated by Germany which is closest to the problem geographically and has most to fear from a flood of economic refugees. Indeed Germany has been most active in supplying economic aid and has paid huge sums to pay for the resettlement of Soviet troops from off the territory of the old East Germany. Between September 1990 and January 1992 Germany provided 57 per cent of world aid to the former Soviet Union, the USA provided 6 per cent, and the United Kingdom 0.2 per cent. The German provision was DM60 billion, or £21.5 billion.

The Yugoslavia crisis of 1991–2, however, revealed significant differences of opinion, largely on timing of recognition of the independent status of Croatia, between the members of the Community. The episode will probably be seen by historians as marking a watershed in the postwar development of Germany, in terms of it reasserting its traditional role as *the* great power of Europe. Its productive capacity, wealth, and dominance in the ERM and monetary matters, and its enlarged population and area after reunification in 1990 could not be gainsaid. It pushed the other members into fixing a final date for collective recognition in January 1992 but acted before that date to give its own recognition to Croatia. This conflict was occurring at the same time as the negotiations at the Maastricht summit in December 1991.

The Union Treaty and Foreign Policy

Foreign policy and defence are referred to as the 'second pillar' of the Community, and the Council decided that they would be dealt with outside the scope of the existing treaties by intergovernmental cooperation. The Commission and Parliament will receive reports on what is decided and the Commission will have the task of maintaining consistency between different areas of policy. Its role may become very important over time but the treaty does not appear to stress its functions. The wording of the Union Treaty will show what was decided, but as already stated, it is what actually happens in the future as a consequence of the high-sounding phrases that matters. The real, permanent changes may occur after the situation is reviewed in 1996.

> The Union and its Member States shall define and implement a common foreign and security policy. [The objectives of these shall be:]
>
> To safeguard the common values, fundamental interests and independence of the European Union;
> To strengthen the security of the Community and its Member States in all ways;
> To preserve peace and strengthen international security;
> To promote international cooperation;
> To develop and consolidate democracy and the rule of law, and respect for human rights and fundamental freedoms.

The intention of the treaty is that there will be cooperation between governments who will gradually implement joint action between them. To quote the treaty again, 'Member states shall inform and consult one another within the Council on any matter of foreign and security policy of general interest in order to ensure that their combined influence is exerted as effectively as possible by means of concerted and convergent action.' This leaves plenty of scope for argument about what is of 'general interest' but the treaty continues, 'Whenever it is deemed necessary, the Council shall define a common position. Member States shall ensure that their national policies conform to the common positions.' It goes on to require the members to coordinate their actions at international bodies such as the United Nations and at international conferences, and to uphold common positions if not all members attend.

The Council of Ministers will decide on joint action by unanimity and will lay down the details of timings, procedures and implementation. In this process it will also define which areas in the joint action will be subject to a qualified majority decision. The Presidency of the Council will be responsible, during its six-month term of office, for representing the Union in matters coming within the common foreign and security policy. The Commission 'shall be fully associated in these tasks'. The treaty lays down a procedure for emergency meetings in periods of crisis but policy will usually be made at Council of Ministers meetings, that is by foreign ministers, after the heads of government have defined the principles and general guide-lines for the common foreign and security policy. The expectation is that eventually there will be Community, or European Union, embassies and consulates in some smaller countries. The multiplication of states within the Commonwealth of Independent States demonstrates the common sense of this, although it may go against the grain for diplomats who may see their career opportunities reduced if their national embassies decline in number.

A Community Defence Force?

There has been a growing interest, or rebirth of interest, in the idea of a collective European defence force and its possible replacement of NATO. France and Germany have already operated a joint battalion of troops as an experiment and, in May 1992, have agreed to create a joint army corps of up to 40 000 men. Before the Maastricht summit there was considerable pressure to restructure the defence of Western Europe either under a Community organisation or by turning the Western European Union into a stronger body. There was, however, very powerful opposition to this from the United Kingdom which wished to see NATO retained as the heart of European defence, and there has even been talk of Russia joining NATO. The main attraction of NATO from the British point of view is that the United States bears a high proportion of its financial and manpower costs, and the United Kingdom wants to keep its 'special relationship' with the United States. It received some support from Italy for its line on NATO. The USA has withdrawn large nuclear and conventional forces from Europe and will continue to do so through the early 1990s. Some American experts are wondering why the United States wishes to maintain forces in Europe at all, and there is little doubt that, if they were not there already, no American president would, in the face of the isolationism endemic in the USA, dare to suggest sending them. This argument is reinforced by the realisation that the USA spends about $36 billion a year on European defence. Economic and political logic will dictate that they will eventually be entirely removed, although there may be a rapid response force retained as a gesture. The Maastricht agreement came down in favour of developing the Western European Union (WEU).

The treaty says that the WEU will be developed as the defence component of the Union and as the method of strengthening the European pillar of the Atlantic Alliance. Its decisions 'shall not affect the obligations of certain member states under the NATO Treaty and shall be compatible with the common security and defence policy established within that framework'. Greece will be invited to join the WEU and, as a balance, Turkey, which is a member of NATO and was very cooperative during the Gulf crisis in allowing its bases to be used, is to be offered full participation but not formal membership. Of the other members Ireland and Denmark do not belong to the WEU.

In the foreign and security fields the European Parliament will be consulted on its main aspects and basic choices and kept informed. The European Court will have no powers in this context. The Commission will have the role of making sure that the policies do not conflict with the external economic policies of the Union. The Maastricht agreement contains a declaration that a series of other items may be subject to joint action. Some of these will become of great significance now that the old Soviet state, after its break-up, has shed its control over much of its arsenals. They include arms control, non-proliferation matters, the export of military technology to other countries, cooperation in the technological fields of armaments, peace-keeping functions for the United Nations, humanitarian ventures, and work under the Conference on Security and Cooperation in Europe (CSCE). Relations with the United States and the CIS are included here as well. The above points need to be seen against the changing political climate in Central and Eastern Europe. Another factor is the desire of the United States to reduce its colossal balance-of-payments deficit and to cut the costs of its NATO commitment.

The Single European Act

In 1985, the heads of government asked the Commission to put forward proposals to achieve a fully unified internal market by the end of 1992. The Commission produced a White Paper in June 1985 which set out a programme and timetable for action. The heads of government accepted the proposals at their meeting in Luxembourg in December 1985. The Single European Act incorporating the decisions was signed in February 1986 and came into force on 1 July 1987. It had taken thirty years from the Treaty of Rome to reach the decision to complete a genuine, unified market.

The aims of the Single European Act

At its simplest the aims are to do what the Treaty of Rome originally intended. That treaty begins: 'Determined to lay the foundations of an ever closer union among the peoples of Europe. Resolved to ensure the economic and social progress of their countries by common action to eliminate the barriers which divide Europe.' In practice many of the barriers remained. They were physical, technical and fiscal in nature. Some had simply never been removed; others had been created or strengthened to protect national or sectional self-interest. Looked at closely the Community was rarely a single, unified market. More often it remained a series of separate, national markets.

As a result the main aim has been to remove the remaining obstacles to the free movement of people, goods and services. These consisted of a great variety of different national technical specifications, health and safety regulations, quality controls and environmental standards. Added to these was a formidable array of legislative differences relating to companies, financial markets, banking, direct and indirect taxes. It has been possible to get a good idea of the extent of these obstacles from the Department of Trade and Industry's information package called 'The Single Market – the Facts'. This is regularly updated and is distributed free to all interested businesses and persons. A very detailed analysis of the costs of not having a unified market is contained in *The European Challenge, 1992: The Benefits of a Single Market* by Paolo Cecchini (published by Wildwood House for the European Commission). His research revealed the colossal cost of what is now called 'non-Europe'.

What were the Costs of a 'Non-Europe'?

The cost of not having a genuine unified market could be measured in terms of the inefficient use of resources, leading to extra costs being imposed on the taxpayer and consumer. These costs could be reduced if the market were improved.

The research had to make some assumptions which could, no doubt, be challenged in some respects. Its main conclusion was that the total economic gain from the completion of the internal market would be the equivalent of about 5 per cent of the Community's gross domestic product – about 200 billion ECU at 1988 prices. This figure included savings from the removal of barriers to intra-Community trade (border formalities and delays), together with the benefits from the removal of obstacles to entry to different national markets, and from an end to restrictions on competition.

Another indication of the research was that the medium-term effect of creating a single internal market would be the lowering of consumer prices by about 6 per cent. At the same time output, employment and living standards would rise. The number of new jobs created would be between 2 and 5 million depending on what macroeconomic policies were adopted. The savings from increased economies of scale for manufacturing industries were estimated at 2 per cent of the GDP of the Community. Some sectors might gain cost reductions of only 1 per cent but others might gain 7 per cent.

These figures of cost reductions and net potential gains were very impressive. However, there will be other less quantifiable gains arising from greater freedom to move about Europe for work or leisure and a greater competitive capacity in international markets compared with Japan and the USA.

What Physical Barriers Needed to be Removed?

The physical barriers concerned were mainly immigration controls and customs. When the single market is completed there will still be immigration controls on people from outside the Community. The earlier, pre-single market frontier controls on Community citizens were aimed at checking passports or identity cards to prevent illegal immigration and to check that taxation has been paid. From 1967 the barriers at internal frontiers ceased to be customs posts and the phrase was not used after January 1988 on internal borders. There was a variety of different levels of checking at these internal frontiers depending on whether the mode of transport was road, rail or air. At one extreme there might be no regular check; at the other there might be a full computerised record made of entry. The intention has been to remove all controls at the internal frontiers of the Community by the end of 1992 by means of a gradual relaxation. It has been necessary to modify the VAT recording system in order to make this possible and at the start of 1992 there were still some details to be agreed. The full harmonisation of VAT levels and regulations would make this easier but decisions have been taken which will postpone this beyond the start of 1993.

The United Kingdom expressed great concern about the removal of these controls because it sees them as essential to check the movement of criminals, drug traffickers and terrorists. Ireland and Denmark agreed. The other members disagreed and argued that the redundant internal border officials could be shifted to the external frontiers to make the outer perimeter more effective. They would also use frequent spot checks on internal borders. The Maastricht agreement provides for visa policy and police cooperation to be dealt with by intergovernmental arrangements. In contrast to the United Kingdom's reluctance to end border controls, five of the other members were anxious to end them in 1990 rather than wait for 1992. In March 1989 France, West Germany, Belgium, The Netherlands and Luxembourg produced a draft plan to introduce a border-free zone. They were joined by Italy and in June 1990 signed what is called the Schengen Group proposal. It is due to come into force in January 1993 but many border controls have already been suspended. Once free borders are introduced inside the zone they will create a stricter 'fence' around them to control immigration of non-Community nationals. Foreigners (non-EC nationals) will require only one visa to travel in all six countries. The draft agreement provided for special short-term border checks if national security or public order were at stake. This Schengen Group proposal became the basis of the agreement reached at Maastricht. The actual operation of the scheme in its initial experimental stage proved successful and popular but led to the early adoption of proposals for a shared police computer and centralised information network. The Maastricht summit agreed to set up a 'Europol' to act as a Community-wide police information-sharing organisation, akin to Interpol. There has been criticism of this decision from Interpol because of the duplication involved. There may be a Community police force one day far into the future, at a lower level than Europol.

Another main physical control concerned the movement of goods. These presented considerable and expensive delays, especially to commercial vehicles. The checks at borders were for a variety of purposes, to collect taxes, obtain statistics, control plant and animal diseases, enforce trade quotas, reject banned goods, and to license some imports and exports. Major progress has quickly been made in removing some of these requirements. Since January 1988 there has been a Single Administrative Document (SAD) for vehicles transporting goods across internal frontiers. This replaced about seventy separate forms. The SAD itself will be abolished in January 1993, an event that has made agreement on VAT bureaucracy essential. Many duplicate checks were also eliminated and other inessential checks will have gone by the end of 1992. These included some which dated from the national quotas on steel production which were abolished in 1988. Other obstacles, such as agricultural and health controls, will be eliminated by harmonising policies so that there are no significant differences between national standards.

Another important physical obstacle to be removed is the quota system on the number of journeys that foreign, or sometimes even national, hauliers can make. These quotas have been gradually relaxed by the simple device of expanding them and they will then be abolished from January 1993. The removal of quotas will allow hauliers to operate freely throughout the Community and remove the need for frontier checks. This has created the need for a new, common, set of safety standards for vehicles and consistency in their application and enforcement and has led, among other things, to the compulsory application of speed limiters to heavy goods vehicles and to some passenger vehicles.

What Technical Barriers Needed to be Removed?

It was realised that even if all frontier barriers were removed there would still be a great hindrance to free trade because of the enormous variety of technical standards applied by each member state. Many of these differences related to basic factors such as electrical voltages, wiring regulations, plumbing regulations and safety rules. Some related to differing technical standards such as the three main colour television systems or the two video standards, VHS and Betamax (which is discontinued). A manufacturer of washing machines, for example, might need to produce up to thirty slightly different versions of one model in order to satisfy all international markets. Most of the variations would relate to regulations about electrical wiring. The majority of manufacturers face similar problems.

Although some of these technical varieties were genuine and arose from historical developments, others were artificial and were introduced as a form of trade protection. The Germans, for example, had, to their great benefit, maintained the quality of their beer by keeping out foreign beers on the grounds that they contravened German food purity laws. Unfortunately for the German beer drinkers they have now been forced to accept other Community members' beers containing carbon dioxide and other 'additives'.

All these differing technical standards imposed considerable costs on producers. They reduced the available economies of scale and added significantly to research and development costs. Another effect was to hinder the development of Community-wide companies as it was easier for them to work within their own national boundaries.

Will Harmonisation Remove Technical Barriers?

The Community's early attempts at technical harmonisation may have done more harm than good in the attempt to impose elaborate and ambitious agreed standards. The idea was that everything in the Community should be uniform – Eurosausages, Europotatoes, and so on. This approach was largely ineffective although it did achieve improvements such as tachographs in the cabs of commercial vehicles. Much more progress was made through the European Court of Justice. The most important single decision was made in 1979 in the *Cassis de Dijon* case which applied to the sale in Germany of cassis produced in France. The court ruled that there was a basic right of free movement of goods and that, in principle, goods legally manufactured in one member country could be sold in another. Thereafter, competing products from other members could not be precluded simply because they were slightly different but only to protect consumer interests if the ban conformed to Community law.

Progress in removing technical barriers towards 1992 required another approach towards harmonisation. This involved Community legislation which only laid down mandatory requirements as general levels or standards of protection. The fixing of the details of their application is being left to European standardisation bodies. In addition there will be some national rules which do not concern these requirements. Community legislation or harmonisation will not apply to them but they will be automatically subject to national mutual recognition which will be enforceable by the European Court of Justice. Such a system will prevent unnecessary harmonisation and will save a great deal of wrangling over detailed technical specifications. Some practical problems arise when environmental matters are concerned. The United Kingdom, for example, has insisted in 1992 on keeping the right to produce its less efficient and atmospherically more harmful domestic heating boilers because they are cheaper to make than the type usually used on the continent, although it has given up the future right to export them to the rest of the Community.

There are, inevitably, some exceptions to this freer approach, mainly in high-technology areas applicable to new developments and where operating standards must be the same, for example in telecommunications. Another major area is broadcasting, especially with satellites. After a long and very bitter debate, and determined lobbying from all around the world, the Community decided in late 1991 to adopt a single standard called D2-MAC for all satellite broadcasts as an intermediate step towards a full high-definition television standard called HD-MAC which will help to create a

Europe-wide audiovisual market. It may keep the Japanese at bay for a little longer. A set of common legal as well as technical standards is necessary and the financial gains from harmonisation in this sphere are enormous. The process of technical harmonisation partly explains the keenness of Japanese firms to establish themselves in the United Kingdom and, increasingly, in Germany.

The harmonisation process has already begun to take effect. Gradually there will be a noticeable impact on people's lives. New television sets already have 'euroconnection' ports on them. Computers and their printers also have standardised connectors, plugs and sockets. Vehicle lights and exhaust emission control systems meet the same European standards, and so on. Nevertheless national diversity will remain. For example, the British 13 amp square pin plug and ring main system, and the domestic central heating boiler referred to above, will remain for the foreseeable future.

Will We Have Harmonised 'Eurofood'?

People have been afraid that local, regional or national foods will be squeezed out by food produced to harmonised European standards. This will not happen because members will be able to keep their own regulations on matters relating to health and safety. They will have to allow other members' products into their country provided that they match the country of origin's standards. The Community simply asks for legislation guaranteeing that a food is fit to be eaten and that the labelling will give the purchaser full details of its contents. Once this is so the food can be sold anywhere in the Community. New labelling practices were introduced at the start of 1991.

Other Freedoms

The intention is to remove all physical restrictions on the movement of people within the Community. The main constraints were on the ability to study or work in other Community countries chiefly because of the lack of standards for educational qualifications, which were not always mutually recognised. This problem will be removed as the Commission's proposal for the mutual recognition of higher education diplomas is adopted. From 1 January 1992 the student who has certain basic qualifications will be able to go freely anywhere in the Community to study. Students will receive a special residence permit, renewable annually provided they are enrolled on educational courses for vocational training purposes as defined by the regulations and that they can support themselves financially during the course.

There is an associated problem of the non-acceptability of vocational qualifications. The line of action being adopted by the Commission is to produce a 'vocational training card', the possession of which will mean that the owner has reached a certain generally accepted training standard and can seek work anywhere in the Community. It will have a major impact on training schemes and on labour mobility.

A similar problem of non-recognition of qualifications existed for many years in respect of professional people and the self-employed in general. The old approach was to work laboriously towards directives. Much progress was made by this method in the health sector with a harmonised basic training for doctors, dentists, midwives and veterinary surgeons. This, with other regulations, gave them a 'right of establishment' and they could practise in all member states.

The use of directives proved to be very cumbersome. It took seventeen years, for example, to agree directives to enable architects to practise anywhere they liked in the Community. In the run-up to 1992 a new approach was adopted by applying the 'Cassis de Dijon' principle again, whereby if a person is qualified to practise a vocation in one country of the Community then that person should, in principle, be able to practise it in another. The Community has therefore adopted since January 1991 the idea of a single system of mutual recognition which applies to higher educational qualifications, leading to an entitlement to practise a vocation or profession. There may sometimes be a test of language comprehension in the area of expertise to be practised. However, it is very hard to predict the extent to which these changes will promote the movement of professional people but there seems to be a growing tendency for architects to practise outside their own countries. This is, to some extent, a return to the days preceding official qualifications when architects practised wherever their clients wanted them.

Some of the proposals to free the movement of workers came under the Social Chapter and the Commission said, in late 1991, that it was disappointed at the rate at which the Council of Ministers had reached decisions on its recommendations. This slow rate of adoption was one reason for the eleven opting out with their own Social Chapter at Maastricht. They may make much faster progress without the United Kingdom having the ability to veto their schemes.

Pensioners and those of independent means can, from 1 January 1992, receive a residence permit from a host country's authorities valid for five years and renewable. They will need to produce proof of their ability to maintain themselves so that they do not become a burden on the host country's social security system. This change may instigate an even greater flight to the sunnier south of the Community over the next few years.

What will be the Effects of the Single Market on the Location of Industry and Commerce?

The answer to this question is a mixture of speculation and extrapolation from past trends. Even these speculative answers depend on what happens as a result of the unification of Germany. If past trends continue there will be a continued concentration of commerce, industry and wealth creation in the central Northern European area of the Ruhr, the Benelux countries, the Ile de France and southern England. This so-called 'power house' of the Community contains the main centres of government and administration, both national and Community. These naturally generate a large service sector and extensive tertiary employment. The transport and communications networks are geared to exploiting the concentration of population, wealth and employment. An additional area of above average growth is likely to be the so-called 'southern arc' from northern Italy, through southern France to Spain which is proving increasingly attractive, for climatic reasons, to industry. Over a longer period of time it can be assumed that market forces will ensure some geographical expansion of these areas. Labour and land will become relatively more expensive than on the peripheries. This should create a deterrent effect, pushing new firms and the expansion of existing firms to other areas.

Three other major factors will help to counterbalance the tendency to concentration in Northern Europe. The first is the European Regional Development Fund (ERDF) which, depending on how it is administered, should put more funds into the disadvantaged, peripheral regions such as parts of Spain, Ireland, Portugal, Greece, southern Italy, Wales and Scotland (see the map on page 167). Linked to this are the Integrated Mediterranean Programmes. The ERDF has risen from £5 billion in 1987 to £9 billion in 1992. The plan has doubled the share of these 'deprived' areas and they receive between 60 and 70 per cent of the fund. Portugal receives even more assistance from a special five-year industrial modernisation scheme.

The second factor is the size and application of the Cohesion Fund agreed to at the Maastricht summit as a means of helping Spain, Portugal, Greece and Ireland counter the possible harmful effects of the transition to the single market and the movement towards monetary union. This fund should be set up by the end of 1993 to support environmental and infrastructure projects in member states with a per capita GNP of less than 90 per cent of the Community average. Argument has already begun on who is going to contribute to the fund and on what basis, so its effect is unpredictable.

The third factor that may offset the centralising tendency will be the development of a Community policy on networks, that is telecommunications, pipelines, transport and electricity grids. One practical example of this is the financial aid to be given in 1992 to a gas pipeline connecting an east-coast Scottish processing plant with the west coast and then across the sea to near Dublin. The transport improvement programmes, especially the railway modernisation and renovation schemes will create a Europe-wide network of high-speed railways for passengers and freight. Experience in France suggests that this will help to revitalise those areas touched by the new and improved routes. Germany is busy changing the orientation of its rail network from the present east–west to north–south. The old network was designed with military considerations in mind so that troops could be easily switched between eastern and western borders. The new orientation is helping to generate economic growth on a more even basis in Germany. Improvements in transport infrastructure are vital to the swift integration of the East German economy into the Community. They are also an essential part of the creation of the EEA, as is demonstrated by the Austrian and Swiss plans to drive three more rail tunnels through the Alps to cope with increased freight.

The great worry for the United Kingdom in this context is that its government has never shown any understanding of the potential of modern railways. Since 1979 it has concentrated on reducing public expenditure on public transport, including the railways, and has insisted that private funds be used for new developments such as the Channel Tunnel or that the money comes from British Rail's own resources. These are inadequate. European governments heavily subsidise their railways and are increasing their commitment. At the same time, the United Kingdom government has been cutting its allocation for railway subsidies. There is a serious risk that this blinkered approach, which has only been slightly modified since 1990, will leave the peripheral regions of the United Kingdom cut off from the benefits of the continental railway system. These benefits will stop at the London terminals of the Channel Tunnel link and not continue for some years to the North, West or South-West. Some work has begun on northern freight terminals but it is fair comment that lack of government vision and drive have led to serious delays in the essential programmes. Track and rolling-stock modifications are needed to operate continental standard trains on British lines. Cheap, fast and efficient rail links are essential if the United Kingdom's outlying regions are to compete in Europe. A general issue arises here, in that it is surely perverse to accept state responsibility for the trunk road network but not for the railway system.

There is a fourth element which will affect the location of industry, that is, the price of labour. The labour force in some areas of Europe may be regarded as cheap in comparison with others, including Japan or the United States. If the problems of training can be overcome then this makes them attractive for 'screwdriver' plants which assemble and package products that are designed and researched elsewhere. This has already happened on a significant scale in the United Kingdom with the influx of Japanese assembly plants and in Ireland, Spain and Portugal with multinationals. They train the workers very effectively for their limited tasks and, using the latest high-productivity technology, produce at low comparative cost. They do not, however, bring sufficient research and development and design employment with them. These plants, therefore, remain as classic expendable branch factories, easily contracted, expanded, or closed as market whim dictates. If the overall level of costs and wages rise in the 'host country', this type of plant can easily be moved or set up in lower-cost countries within the Community. The pessimistic conclusion here is that cheap labour may be only a temporary attraction.

In the long run location is supposed to depend upon the overall comparative costs of an area compared with others. In theory, areas are competing with each other for the location of firms, offering them a variety of natural and acquired advantages. Also, in theory, the industries are competing with one another for the factors of production in an area. The most profitable industry can buy more of the factors it needs. In so far as this applies in practice each country must ensure that it has a well-educated, trained, skilled and adaptable labour force and minimum costs of transport and distribution. There are many imperfections in the markets for factors and the location of industry is affected by many influences not covered by the simple theory. The Commission, for example, needs to be a very effective watchdog preventing governments giving hidden subsidies to incoming investment, or to its own industry.

What are the Gains from Membership?

The economist often talks about 'opportunity cost'. This is the cost, in financial terms, of the next best alternative foregone if a particular course of action is chosen. If a country chooses to spend £9 billion on a missile system there is an opportunity cost involved of the other things that could have been bought with the money – roads, schools, hospitals, aircraft or pay rises for government employees.

In the case of membership of the European Community it is very hard to measure the opportunity cost of membership. Nobody can tell accurately what would have happened to an economy if the country had not joined. Some might argue that its future would have been rosier and that like Norway, for example, their country would have done very well outside the Community. They might point to an accumulated net contribution to the Community over the years, especially in the case of Germany, although the exact figure is hard to quantify. They may see that as money wasted. They may also see the Common Agricultural Policy as an unnecessary expense that has placed a considerable extra burden on every household every year. Some place this figure as high as an extra £500 per household per year in the United Kingdom, for example, in the 1980s.

Against this net outflow, which is not accurately quantifiable, must be set the gains from the Regional and Social Funds. These sums have mainly benefited the areas of high unemployment but not exclusively so. Some governments have used these inflows to cut their own taxation revenues allocated to regional assistance. In 1991–2, for example, the European Commission suspended payments to the United Kingdom from the Regional Fund because it was failing to spend the money in the coal mining areas to which it had been allocated. But what is hardest to measure is the gain from trade arising from the large common market. Although this will not be a true 'single' market until after 1992, the gains from specialisation, economies of scale and the incentives to greater competitive efficiency have been very large. The gains to the commercial and financial sectors have also been extensive. There have, however, been casualties and many firms and individuals have suffered materially from the greater competitiveness of some European firms. The peripheries have sometimes been hardest hit and there is a tendency for the central wealth-generating 'power house' of the Community to lie in the Ile de France, the Benelux countries and north-western Germany with an overlap into southern England. Economic geographers pay a great deal of attention to monitoring the growth of this region. A new analysis in 1991 found evidence of what has come to be called a 'hot banana', that is a banana-shaped area of higher than average development sweeping from the borders of Spain across to Germany.

There is a major gain to all members in terms of the mutual help given to less favoured regions and the assistance given to cushion declining industries. This redistributive aspect is not welcomed by all especially when the needs of Portugal, Greece and East Germany are taken into account. There is also a major gain to all in the fields of scientific and technological research cooperation and education. Although these programmes do not compare in scale with Japanese and American expenditures they are beginning to make inroads into the research backlog and permit competition in selected areas.

On balance, therefore, an individual country may or may not be out of pocket financially as a result of membership. Those who are out of pocket may regard the cost as an acceptable price to pay for political stability and the absence of conflict. There is no doubt, however, that the members are stronger both economically and politically within the Community than if they had remained outside. Each member has some particular cause to be thankful for in its membership. The people of the United Kingdom, for example, have been increasingly looking to Europe and its Court of Justice for protection of basic rights and freedoms. The idea that some people in the United Kingdom have of leaving the Community is unrealistic nonsense based on a romanticised view of British history and an over-optimistic assessment of the future. There might be a sort of half-way house as an associate member but that will be less viable after the 1992 single market becomes fully effective and virtually impossible after monetary union takes place.

Europe 2000

One of the admirable qualities of the Community is its forward thinking. 'Europe 2000: Outlook for the Development of the Community's Territory' is an example which applies to the subject of regional development and liaison between regional authorities. We shall hear a great deal more about it over the next decade. Europe 2000 is an initiative launched in 1991 to examine on a Europe-wide view, not solely a Community view, the more coherent use of land as the effects of the single market physically reshape the Community by creating new zones of wealth and population.

The basic premise of the initiative is that the regions must develop harmoniously with equal access to a communications and public service infrastructure. This arises from the recognition that the single market forces the Community to address the problem of regional disparities more energetically. The strategy behind Europe 2000 is to encourage regional and local planners to liaise on development projects that are inherently cross-border. This will be helped by the inclusion of Community networks for transport and telecommunications in the Union Treaty reforms. It is intended to apply the principle of subsidiarity to the initiative as far as possible to involve local people and not to impose a blueprint from above.

The initiative will involve the complex intertwining of a large number of important influences such as energy, transport, telecommunications, water and waste management, pollution, demography, and the special problems of the coastal areas and islands. The aim is to coordinate the work with regions inside the boundaries of states neighbouring the Community. That is why the project is called 'Europe 2000' and not 'Community 2000'. In the same spirit as the initiative are the 'Cooperation Networks' that were set up in 1991 to enhance cooperation between cities and regions of the Community. The scheme was begun experimentally in 1990 and is a sophisticated, and reasonably well-funded, version of town twinning, with an emphasis on linking strong and weak as partners. It is financed under what is called a RECITE programme, under the Regional Development Fund, or 'Regions and Cities for Europe'. A version of it called ECOS is a project to link cities and regions, especially in the less favoured regions of the Community, with counterparts in Central and Eastern Europe. An example of such a network is one formed by the following: Strasbourg (France), Charleroi (Belgium), Coimbra (Portugal), Piraeus (Greece), Malaga (Spain) and Stuttgart (Germany).

Conclusion

The European Community has changed significantly since its inception in the 1950s. Its change of name from the European Economic Community (EEC) or the Common Market to European Community is, in itself, of note. The latest change to the word Union also marks a shift in underlying attitude. The word Community involves an acceptance of a social as well as an economic dimension. It implies a working together towards common objectives rather than competition. The word Union implies cooperation on a wider range of policies and a deeper constitutional relationship. The maturing of the European Parliament and the introduction of qualified majority voting in the Council of Ministers on a range of issues has ensured more democratic participation and more effective decision-making. The pace of change appears to be quickening. If the intentions of the Single European Act are realised, the Community will, within the European Economic Area, become the world's largest and richest trading and political grouping. This could be achieved whilst maintaining very much the same degree of national diversity as exists at the moment. There is bound to be some trend towards greater uniformity because that is one of the effects of better communications, modern technology and economies of scale. Diversity tends to flourish in isolation. Uniformity tends to be part·of the price of knowledge and communication. The hope is that a large degree of this uniformity is based on the adoption of the best standards and practice and not of the second-rate.

There are alternative visions of the future. These have been expressed by M. Rocard, the former French Prime Minister. He said, in April 1989, that two conceptions of Europe confronted each other. The first was Mrs Thatcher's 'Europe of the jungle, a house open to the four winds, a plane without a pilot'. The second was a vision of a Europe of free exchange and economic competition, but with ground rules.

The lesson of history is that human society needs ground rules although these may require to be altered over time. Europe is passing out of the phase of the dominance of the nation state and entering the era of cooperative decision-making. The modern European experience in consensus and coalition politics within their own nation states will enable the transition to be accomplished more easily. If 'the Europe of regions' as described above comes about, it could help to overcome one of the most persistent problems of the modern national state, that is, how to combine the strength derived from size and unity with the desires of minorities for self-determination. Nations will be able to obtain strength from membership of the European Union. Minorities will be able to retain their individuality by being a separate region within a member state of the Union. Such a development may solve some of the numerous minority problems of the Community, from the more violent conflicts of the Basque country and Northern Ireland, to the less troublesome but persistent calls of northern Italian and Walloon separatists, to the gentler nationalist aspirations of Wales, Scotland, Cornwall and Brittany. Some argue that European Union will nurture self-determination and consequently encourage a return to extreme nationalism but the descent into tribalism which seems to be characterising the break-up of the Soviet empire in Central and Eastern Europe, and in the Balkans, must be avoided at all costs. The European Union holds the potential key to the problem. We shall know that the world has advanced when a permanent European Union seat is held in the Security Council of the United Nations in place of the separate French and United Kingdom seats, with perhaps Japan in place as well.

Postscript

The Exchange Rate Mechanism under Pressure

In August and September 1992 a tidal wave of speculative transfer of currencies forced the United Kingdom and Italy, on 16 and 17 September, to withdraw the pound sterling and the lira from the ERM, and threatened the very existence of the mechanism itself. The financial turmoil took place against a background of uncertainty about the ratification of the Maastricht Treaty on European Union, especially in respect of the French referendum of 20 September. The events in the currency markets sent shock waves through the political world. The media reacted by giving more emphasis than usual to those who predicted the total collapse of the ERM and the demise of the Maastricht agreement. It was, for the United Kingdom Government, a traumatic period because it was forced to abandon the central plank of its economic policy, that is the achievement of low inflation by the discipline of the ERM. In what was inevitably called a 'U-turn', it returned to a floating, devalued, pound, to the prospect of higher inflation and to a short-term deterioration of the balance of payments. The only political rewards lay in the ability to cut interest rates, up to a point, and the encouragement of the belief that it could now resume an independent economic policy. On the foreign policy front the United Kingdom Government was in a deep dilemma or, as some alleged, a political vacuum. Although the Prime Minister, Mr Major, had immodestly accepted the Maastricht agreement as a personal triumph, he rapidly suspended the Committee Stage of the Bill which would have put its provisions into United Kingdom law when the Danish referendum narrowly rejected the Treaty in June 1992. Although the French referendum endorsed the treaty on 20

September he still insisted on waiting until the Danish government had stated its policy before he would proceed with ratification. In short, he doubted his capacity to carry the Bill against the powerful and growing 'Eurosceptic' wing of his own party and needed time to put pressure on his backbenchers to vote with him.

Why was Sterling Forced Out of the ERM?

When German reunification took place the Federal Government under Chancellor Kohl took the decision, against the advice of the Bundesbank, to adopt an exchange rate of one Deutschmark for one East German Mark. It also decided to finance the immense cost of reunification not from increased taxation but from reserves and borrowing. These decisions were taken for sensible political reasons but had an inflationary effect. The Bundesbank responded dutifully by tightening its monetary policy and raising its interest rates. On 16 July 1992 it raised its discount rate by three quarters of one per cent to 8.75 per cent, a sixty-year high. The Lombard rate remained at 9.75 per cent. At the same time, the United States was following a low interest rate policy in a desperate attempt to pull its economy out of recession in the run up to the November Presidential election.

The conjunction of high (10 per cent) interest rates in Germany and Europe, and low (3 per cent) rates in the United States stimulated the transfer of capital from US dollar holdings into other currencies, especially the Deutschmark and the Dutch guilder, which was closely tied to it. The yen was also favoured after the Japanese government injected money into its flagging economy. Other European countries were forced to raise their interest rates in line with Germany in order to minimise outflows of capital. Some countries such as Sweden, Finland and Norway which had aligned their currencies with the ECU, and thereby to the Deutschmark, were also forced to raise interest rates. The volume of money that is available for movement in international currency markets is immense and has been growing since the progressive abolition of controls on capital movements after 1979. In September 1992 a spokesman for the United States Treasury estimated the figure passing through the foreign exchange markets at $1000 billion *daily*. Of this, about 7 to

10 per cent relates to trade transactions in visibles, invisibles and capital movements for investment in real assets. The rest is 'hot' money seeking to maximise interest rate yields and short-term capital gains in so far as that is commensurate with security. In contrast, he estimated that the six leading countries' reserves available for intervention in currency markets totalled only $250 billion.

The United Kingdom entered the ERM at a central rate of £1 = DM 2.95, a level regarded as too high by many economists. Its permitted floor in the 6 per cent wide band of divergence was DM 2.7780. By mid-August 1992 it had fallen to the psychologically important low of DM 2.80 mainly because the United Kingdom had not raised interest rates to follow the latest German rise. This was because of the basic underlying weakness of the United Kingdom economy signified by a failure to recover from the recession after the April General Election. The balance of payments was deteriorating rapidly despite the recession, a time when it should have improved. A rise in domestic interest rates would have been politically damaging. The Government comforted itself with the lower inflation rates being achieved and by the strength of sterling against the dollar. The rate reached £1 = $1.99 in late August on the same day it fell to DM 2.79. The British public was assured that it was the dollar that had problems not the pound.

In the last week of August the currency markets became very active as French opinion polls began to predict a 'No' vote. Some intervention buying occurred to help the pound and pressure was put on Germany to cut its interest rates. The United Kingdom borrowed ECU 10 billion to support the pound by an intricate method that received admiration from the money markets until it dawned on them that, despite its cleverness, it was not really different from the much maligned loan from the IMF in 1978. After four days of relative calm the Finnish markka was devalued and floated after breaking its link to the Deutschmark. Sweden and Norway raised some interest rates to very high levels. The pound fell to near its floor on 9 September but the Prime Minister ruled out devaluation or realignment as 'a soft option' and said that the United Kingdom would keep the DM 2.95 central rate even if other countries in the ERM realigned. On 13 September Germany persuaded Italy to realign the lira downwards with an effective devaluation of 7 per cent. Germany had spent about DM 24 billion supporting the lira under the ERM system. In return it promised that the Bundesbank would cut interest rates. The United Kingdom, in a fateful decision, decided not to take the opportunity of realigning the pound.

The promised cut in the German Lombard rate was a disappointing 0.25 per cent. The Bundesbank was asserting its independence and regarded a greater change as unjustifiable in terms of German needs. The markets reacted very strongly. The lira could not maintain its new parity and sterling fell to its floor. The United Kingdom Chancellor, Norman Lamont, tried, very belatedly, to raise interest rates to stem the speculative flows. Minimum Lending Rate was reinstated to raise rates by 2 per cent on the morning of 16 September, and when that had no effect by a further 3 per cent in the afternoon. The 15 per cent rate had no effect and the pound was suspended from the ERM. The 3 per cent rise was immediately removed, followed next day by the removal of the 2 per cent increase. Rates returned to 10 per cent. The currency dealers rejoiced at their profits, which were estimated at £900 million over the week.

The lira also left the ERM and Spain devalued the peseta by 5 per cent. Italy said it would rejoin the ERM within a few days but later changed that to 'at the first opportunity'. The United Kingdom's Prime Minister said, at first, that sterling 'would resume membership of the ERM as soon as circumstances allow'. He later told Parliament that he had a list of conditions that must be met before sterling rejoined. Sceptics suspect that these are not achievable. In the meantime the United Kingdom cut its interest rates by 1 per cent to 9 per cent in order to stimulate the domestic economy. The pound rapidly fell to £1 = DM 2.50, with the expectation that it might fall further. The dollar strengthened as funds flowed back. The devaluation of sterling, which is likely to stabilise between 10 and 20 per cent against the Deutschmark, will be inflationary over the next few years but should have a beneficial effect on employment.

The currency speculators, fresh from their triumph, switched their attention to the French franc, but determined Franco–German resistance in the form of intervention buying drove them off until after the French referendum. They returned but were again repulsed but, of course, they may return to the fray. Ireland, Spain and Portugal, which all suffered from speculative attention, imposed controls on capital movements. Their success may encourage the revamping of the ERM to include controls on capital movements. Some experts say that the new electronic markets make this impossible but others argue that it might make the flows easier to restrict or penalise.

Consequences of the ERM Changes

The first results were bitter recriminations between Germany and the United Kingdom and a desperate search for scapegoats. Some British politicians and some of the media blamed the Germans, and the Bundesbank in particular, for pursuing too narrow a national interest and for failing to support sterling sufficiently. Most European commentators put the blame solely on the underlying weakness of the United Kingdom economy and the unrealistic level of DM 2.95 as the central rate. The failure of the United Kingdom to realign was also criticised, as was the belated use of higher interest rates and intervention buying. Italian problems were blamed on the failure of unstable governments to act decisively to cut their budget deficit. Whereas the Italians were happy about the degree of support from Germany, the United Kingdom government was very unhappy about alleged statements from Bundesbank personnel that undermined the pound at crucial moments.

In the United Kingdom the Eurosceptics celebrated the end of the ERM, probably prematurely. In contrast, Germany, France, the Benelux countries and Denmark began to move more closely together to form an 'inner core'. It was reported, and later officially denied, that Germany and France were preparing a permanently fixed exchange rate between the mark and the franc as part of an accelerated movement towards monetary union to be achieved even if the Maastricht Treaty was not ratified. The prospect of a two-speed or multi-speed Community is therefore strengthening. Germany, France, the Benelux countries and possibly Denmark (despite its rejection of the Maastricht Treaty) would form the fast group to monetary union. Italy, which is keen to rejoin the ERM, Ireland, Spain and Portugal might form a secondary grouping with their currencies linked to the Franco–German core currency. Greece and the Scandinavian countries might join this group. The United Kingdom would continue to float sterling against the European currencies as well as against the dollar and the yen, although that would have very serious disadvantages in the European single market. Some optimists think that the United Kingdom position would be the real 'fast lane' to economic resurrection even if it does not lead to monetary union.

It is likely that the details of the ERM will be refined so that new entrants (or re-entrants) have their central rates fixed for them by the existing members and not at their own whim, as was the case with the United Kingdom in 1990. There may also be a restitution of some of the controls on movements of currency that are not associated with trade or physical investment.

The Ratification of the Treaty on Union

In order for it to become legally established the Treaty on Union must be ratified by the appropriate legislative method of all twelve members. Article R of the Treaty specifies that the Treaty will come into force on 1 January 1993, or 'one month after ratification by the last country'. The intention was for all members to ratify ready for 1 January 1993, but this began to look increasingly unlikely because Denmark, whose referendum rejected the Treaty in early June 1992, was not to conduct another referendum until early 1993 or even later. Much depends on the terms of a White Paper which the Danish Government proposes to issue. Although opinion polls show that anti-Maastricht feeling has strengthened in Denmark since the referendum, the main opposition groupings appear to have split. The anti-treaty movement has become dominated by extreme right-wing nationalists and by extremists of the left. The centre grouping, the Danish People's Socialist Party and the Danish Labour Party have been pro-Community but against the Maastricht Treaty. They have begun to agree a set of conditions under which they would support a 'Yes' vote at a future referendum. Most of these, on monetary union, defence, social and environmental standards, can be met without amendment to the Treaty. The other main requirement, greater democracy in decision-making in the Community, may be achievable by spelling out what exactly is meant by 'subsidiarity' and by defining and extending the role of the national legislatures and the European Parliament.

The Irish referendum in mid-June 1992 gave a resounding 'Yes' to the Treaty. Greece and Luxembourg ratified it in July. Belgium, Portugal and Spain had achieved partial ratification by September 1992 and no further problems were expected. Italy and The Netherlands were expected to ratify with very large majorities in their legislatures.

When President Mitterrand of France decided, in June 1992, to call a referendum to approve the changes in the constitution required to implement the Treaty on Union he was confident of a large majority 'Yes' vote because public opinion polls indicated a 70 per cent majority in favour. This majority was whittled away until, in August and September, it looked as if a 'No' vote would result. As in almost all referendums the single issue in question became obscured, in this case in a welter of nationalistic, anti-government, anti-agricultural reform, sentiment. In a 70 per cent turn out 51.05 per cent voted 'Yes' and 48.95 per cent voted 'No'. There were major regional differences in response and some observers think that French political alignments have changed for ever. The 'Yes' was achieved from support in most big cities, except in the South, from the regions bordering frontiers, and from Brittany. The pro-Treaty lobby heralded it as a magnificent victory on the grounds that a single vote majority was sufficient. The opponents of the Treaty said the narrow majority rendered the Maastricht agreement dead.

The United Kingdom's policy on the Treaty on Union has been bewildering to the observer. Perhaps one day, when the archives are opened, some rationale will be discovered. The United Kingdom ministers who negotiated the Treaty broadcast it as a triumph for British diplomacy and for the Prime Minister in particular. The Treaty itself is ratified under the Royal Prerogative powers but a short Bill was presented to Parliament to implement the legal changes arising from it. This passed a second reading in the House of Commons with a good majority despite the grumbles of 'Eurosceptics'. However, when the Danish 'No' vote was announced in June the United Kingdom Government withdrew, or postponed, the scheduled Committee Stage of the Bill. In July 1992 the United Kingdom assumed the role of President of the Community for six months. It was expected to give a lead to the eleven in continuing ratification, as they had agreed. Parliament, however, went into an exceptionally early and long recess, and the United Kingdom began to await the result of the French referendum, thus helping to create the atmosphere of uncertainty that assisted the currency speculators. When the French referendum produced its narrow 'Yes' vote the United Kingdom Government found another reason to delay the Bill: that is, it wanted to await clarification of the Danish position. This attitude provoked some fury in German Government and Community circles and helped to reinforce the view that the United Kingdom was half-hearted about the Union Treaty and was using the Presidency of the Community for its own national ends to delay progress.

In Germany all the major political parties support ratification of the Treaty and the process should be completed in the Autumn of 1992. The far right, which is growing in strength on a tide of anti-immigrant prejudice, is opposed to the Treaty. The German public has shown increasing uncertainty about the monetary aspects of the agreement, especially the future of the Deutschmark, and a campaign developed for a referendum on the Treaty. The German Government may try to obtain modifications of the timetable and conditions of monetary union once the Treaty is fully ratified. Some argue for an even faster movement to a single currency and monetary union.

In one sense the turmoil of the second half of 1992 has turned the Community a full circle, back to its original inspiration. The Franco–German axis has been renewed and reinvigorated, particularly in monetary matters, and is being expanded in defence cooperation. The Benelux countries too are bound more closely. The United Kingdom is back on the sidelines, perhaps temporarily, with its recent economic policies derailed and its foreign policy confused.

October 1992

Index